# *Fuzzy Monsters*

*Also by Chris Horrie*

Disaster!
the Rise and Fall of News on Sunday

Stick It Up Your Punter!
the Rise and Fall of the Sun

Sick as a Parrot:
the Inside Story of the Spurs Fiasco

# Fuzzy Monsters

## *Fear and Loathing at the BBC*

CHRIS HORRIE
and
STEVE CLARKE

HEINEMANN : LONDON

First published in Great Britain 1994
by William Heinemann Ltd
An imprint of Reed Consumer Books Ltd
Michelin House, 81 Fulham Road, London SW3 6RB
and Auckland, Melbourne, Singapore and Toronto

Copyright © Chris Horrie and Steve Clarke
The authors have asserted their moral rights

A CIP catalogue record for this title
is available at the British Library
ISBN 0 434 00002 7

Typeset by CentraCet Limited, Cambridge
Printed and bound in Great Britain
by Clays Ltd, St Ives plc

*For Lotte and Clare*

# Contents

viii **Contents**

# Acknowledgements

During our research for this book we sought to interview the three men who have held the job of Director General of the BBC since 1982. The first, Alasdair Milne (1982–1987), spoke to us at some length, adding some valuable insights to those provided in his own book: *DG: The Memoirs of a British Broadcaster*.

The second, Sir Michael Checkland (1987–1992), said he was not prepared to talk to us or anyone else about his time in the job which, evidently, was very unhappy towards the end. Sir Michael had, at least, subjected himself to an open and competitive interview process when he applied for the job. For this reason we were able to find out quite a lot about his work and ambitions for the Corporation. Several of the people who worked with Sir Michael on the BBC's Board of Management felt able to talk to us, though some did not want to be identified.

The third and, at the time of writing, current Director General, John Birt, at first expressed an interest in granting us an interview, but declined after seeing the list of questions we wanted to ask him.

As the book was being written the veteran BBC reporter Mark Tully finally went on the record to confirm in public what dozens of people in the BBC at all levels had told us throughout the spring of 1993: that there was a 'climate of fear' at the BBC; that people thought the Corporation was in a state of crisis, but felt they could not speak out.

Earlier, Michael Grade of Channel Four had told us a similar story. After being approached by a lot of friends at the Corporation he had described the BBC as 'a secretive and forbidding place to work'. It was 'an airtight fortress from which no stray opinion is permitted to escape,' he said, where statements had to be 'cleared with the BBC's own thought police. The silence is eerie, ominous.'

John Birt and the BBC's chairman, Marmaduke Hussey, had dismissed all this as 'black propaganda' and 'wild fantasy'. Marmaduke Hussey's only answer, given in an exclusive interview to the *Sunday Times*, was that he had personally spoken to people in the BBC canteen and had been told, essentially, that things had never been better. But Grade was able to point to a foot-high pile of letters from BBC people, which he declined to show on proper grounds of confidentiality, confirming that what he had said was entirely true.

In the circumstances it was remarkable that so many current and former BBC employees, about a hundred at all levels, were prepared to speak to us. Understandably most of them insisted that their contribution had to remain unacknowledged; for the time being at least. However, some were happy to be attributable and provided us with invaluable insights and information. We are therefore able to thank Keith Anderson, James Arnold-Baker, Michael Bunce, Stephen Claypole, Keith Clement, Bill Cotton Jnr, Glen Del Medico, Nick Elliott, Sir Paul Fox, Michael Grade, Vincent Hanna, Ian Hargreaves, Ashley Hill, James Hogan, Peter Ibbotson, Howell James, Peter Jay, Ian Kennedy, Peter Menneer, Alasdair Milne, Peter Pagnamenta, Ian Phillips, Jonathan Powell, Alan Protheroe, Glynne Price, Colin Shaw, Samir Shah, John Slater, Ros Sloboda, Cliff Taylor, John Tusa, Brian Wenham and Paul Woolwich. We spoke to many of the BBC's programme-makers, especially in the area of current affairs, but most have decided as a matter of policy not to be identified.

Others connected with the story of the BBC who were

prepared to be interviewed, sometimes at length, and to be attributed included: Chris Blackhurst, the reporter who broke the story of John Birt's tax avoidance in the *Independent on Sunday*; Greg Dyke of LWT; Alastair Hetherington, a member of the Peacock Committee on the future of broadcasting; Chris Hopson, David Mellor's assistant at the Heritage Department; Sir Bernard Ingham, Prime Minister Margaret Thatcher's press secretary; Charles Jonscher, who provided a detailed study of the television market for the Peacock Committee (and kindly made this information available to us); Andrew Neil, editor of the *Sunday Times*; and Professor Alan Peacock himself.

As ever, our fellow writers about the media were generous with their time and contacts. Many helped us, but we would particularly like to thank Alex Sutherland, formerly of the *Sunday Times*, Jane Thynne of the *Daily Telegraph* and Ray Snoddy of the *Financial Times*. Other people who assisted us directly in one way or another include Roy Ackerman, John Dugdale, William Phillips and several members of the staff and student body of the School of Media at the London College of Printing.

The BBC's press officers were helpful, professional and friendly. We are grateful to Richard Peel for arranging an interview with Samir Shah. Devon Brookes kindly gave us access to many back issues of the BBC's house magazine *Ariel*. We are also grateful to the Royal Television Society, the press officers at LWT and Channel Four, and the Library of the Independent Television Commission. Jackie Riley of the Glasgow University Media Unit helped with information about alleged bias in television.

Much of the fundamental work underlying the book was done by our researchers Martin Nathan and Max Daly, who also contributed many ideas and assisted in writing the final draft. Officially they are credited as researchers, but in reality their contribution was far greater than that. The book would not have been produced on time without their hard work. We would also like to thank our agent Mark Lucas and editor Sarah Hannigan for their encouragement and useful insights.

Final thanks go to Clare and Kim for their patience and support.

# *Preface*

This book does not pretend to be the definitive history of the BBC in recent years. For that readers must turn to the Corporation's own semi-official account of itself, published in 1992 as *The BBC: Seventy Years of Broadcasting*.

Our story concentrates on the period after Mrs Thatcher's landslide election victory in 1983 and, especially, on the time after the surprise arrival of Marmaduke 'Duke' Hussey as BBC Chairman in 1986. These were years when the government sought to bring about a free market transformation in British society. It was obvious enough that the BBC, for many the very essence of the 'Old Britain' Mrs Thatcher loathed, would be caught up in the dramas that resulted. The BBC was high on the Conservatives' agenda for most of this period, and Mrs Thatcher's cabinets commissioned endless studies, held seminars and debated think tank proposals aimed at 'marketising' the BBC. Most of these came infuriatingly unstuck for the simple reason that the market could not provide an alternative people wanted to buy.

It was not for the lack of trying. Since the 1970s Rupert Murdoch, an important character in our story, had tried and failed to establish the same sort of ascendancy in British television that he already enjoyed in newspapers. As one of the great heroes of the enterprise culture, and a keen supporter of Mrs Thatcher, the Americanised owner of the *Sun* and *The Times* was sure to benefit from government policy aimed at ushering in a new age of 'multichannel television'.

But Murdoch's Sky dishes were harder to sell so long as ITV and the BBC could afford to screen the best, and most expensive, popular programmes, films and sport.

Against this background, and with the support of an incessant press campaign, the BBC was cast as being in the grip of an unrepresentative, left-wing elite determined to thwart free market choice and addicted to a licence fee described by Mrs Thatcher as a 'poll tax backed by criminal sanctions'. The truth was much more complicated than this. In some ways the BBC of the 1980s did show some signs of cosy complacency. But the idea that the BBC was ignoring the real world of new technology and market competition was a gross exaggeration. The BBC had always changed, even if the process was slow.

Naturally, much of our story concerns the rise and rise of John Birt, as Director General of the BBC. Birt, who describes himself to BBC colleagues as a man from 'another world', was never subjected to a competitive interview for the job. Despite this he has set out to 'revolutionise' almost every aspect of the Corporation, in a way that Mrs Thatcher failed to do.

Birt's first job was to 'clean up' BBC news and current affairs after intense, and often unfair, claims that it had been wildly biased and 'out of control' for years. This involved introducing 'Birtism', a set of idiosyncratic theories about television journalism Birt had been working on since the 1970s. Although it has been one of the most hotly debated subjects in television for a decade, the exact nature of 'Birtism' still remains a mystery to most people. Critics say Birtism boils down to old-fashioned elitism, tinged with political cowardice, and implies that the BBC will retreat from the mass market. One persistent fear is that John Birt plans to turn the BBC into a 'publisher-broadcaster' like Channel Four, abandoning its role as the leading British programme maker. Others explain 'Birtism' as an endlessly flexible doctrine that amounts to whatever will further the career of John Birt.

Michael Grade was an early victim of Birt's determination to reach the top. They had worked together as the best of friends in ITV. But at the BBC they became rivals. Grade eventually denounced his former friend for introducing 'pseudo-Leninist' management methods that had set the BBC on 'a path of terminal decline'. Birt and Hussey, he said, had set loose an 'army of accountants' who were carrying out a revolution with 'brutal zeal'.

Michael Checkland, the man who Birt eventually replaced as Director General, tended to get caught in the middle of arguments like this. To the bitter disappointment of many, he loyally supported the changes Hussey demanded. Outmanoeuvred in the BBC's ruthless internal power politics, Checkland ended up denouncing Hussey and the BBC's ruling Governors as being too old and out of touch: the sort of people who might think FM stood for Fuzzy Monsters.

But for some, the modernised elitism of 'Birtism' was better summed up by the approach of Peter Jay, the media economics guru installed as one of the BBC's most important journalists. Jay had worked with John Birt at London Weekend Television in the 1970s, where he had been, in many ways, Birt's intellectual mentor. According to legend Jay once told a baffled *Times* sub-editor, who could not understand a word of one of his articles: 'I write for three people in this country; and you are not one of them.' It was a nice phrase.

At the last count there were 56,467,000 people in the UK. This book is written for 56,466,999 people in this country. And Peter Jay is not one of them.

Chris Horrie and Steve Clarke
London, November 1993

# PART ONE

# 1

## *One of Us*

Margaret Thatcher never liked television; and television did not like her. And before the 1979 election brought her to power she was up against avuncular 'Farmer' Jim Callaghan, the Labour Party leader regarded by television professionals as a master of the vital political art of the vacuously reassuring television interview.

Mrs Thatcher's image consultants, Gordon Reece and Tim Bell, organised a complete make-over to soften her television image. Her wardrobe of provincial frumpery was thrown away and replaced by smart blue business suits. The traditional Tory colour was a great stroke of luck. Blue looked great on TV: calming and redolent of open skies and nice weather. Even the shade could be manipulated to good effect with sky blue for cheerful, good news days; navy for the heavy stuff. Her hairstyle was toned down to vaguely resemble the more statesmanlike Indira Gandhi.

Reece and Bell were following the example of the United States, where politics had become largely a matter of projecting the right image. Political 'themeing' had become a cottage industry in Washington DC and the process had reached its natural conclusion with the election of a fully trained actor, Ronald Reagan, as President.

Mrs Thatcher was a devoted fan. Following Reagan's lead, she engaged a National Theatre voice coach, knocking the harsh, lower middle-class edges from her vowels. She diligently practised humming exercises designed to lower the pitch to a frequency of 46 Hertz: halfway between the average male and female pitch and the technical optimum for microphones.

The Prime Minister had also taken to Reagan's 'sincerity machine': a system of mirrors invented to allow The Great Communicator to read his lines without looking at a script. The machine was perfect for Mrs Thatcher. Her forte was grand, sweeping rhetoric at party conferences, supplied by her team of scriptwriters. After triumphs like 'The Lady's Not For Turning' she became a complete master of the game of tossing sound bites and ready-made headlines to the media.

But the grand phrases and hectoring style sounded silly in the more cramped arena of the TV studio, where interviewers had the chance to ask what she meant, exactly. Her advisers had done what they could to keep interviewers at arm's length, insisting whenever possible that interviews took place in Downing Street. At Number Ten the spacious, regal background she needed could be combined with a homely setting, complete with bowls of flowers, comfy chairs and cups of tea. The setting provided an important psychological advantage. Interviewers would look as if they were being rude to a considerate lady hostess in the privacy of her own living room if they asked too many tough questions.

Studio encounters could not be avoided altogether. In the last fortnight of the 1983 election campaign, Mrs Thatcher agreed to appear on a live BBC Television phone-in to be broadcast as part of *Nationwide*, the magazine programme that followed the early evening news. Phone-ins are a nerve-wracking experience for all politicians, and completely alien to Thatcher's way of operating. The fact that *Nationwide* was broadcast from Lime Grove, BBC Television's current affairs centre near Shepherd's Bush, West London, was especially worrying. Lime Grove's very existence was a symbol of everything that was wrong with British television and, in some ways, the country itself. Since the 1940s, when the BBC bought the original studio complex from J. Arthur Rank, Lime Grove had mushroomed into a huge current affairs empire loosely based around *Panorama* and jammed into a dilapidated row of sheds and knocked-together houses. In contrast to the sleek, purpose-built status-symbol office blocks occupied by commercial television companies like LWT, Lime Grove was a chaotic, dingy rabbit warren with scruffy décor and exposed pipes everywhere.

The Lime Grove canteen was vile and was soon to be shut down after a *Newsnight* producer looked up to find a stream of maggots dropping from the ceiling into his *boeuf en croûte*. People working there were constantly ill, and conditions were horrible: draughty, damp and permeated with a constant chemical stench that reminded people of embalming fluid. The status was supplied by its activity, rather than its architecture.

Because there were so many programmes stuffed into the building, programme-makers could always rely on bumping into someone interesting. Even quite junior people could mingle with celebrities and ministers in the cheaply furnished entertainment rooms. Staff would come out of their offices if somebody really famous was in the building; though the only time the place came to a complete standstill was when the Osmonds were interviewed by *Nationwide*. The corridors were crammed with producers and executives lurking in the hope of catching a glimpse of the toothy Mormon pop sensation.

The Prime Minister and her rumbustious press secretary, Bernard Ingham, believed Lime Grove was stuffed with people who took great delight in dragging politicians through the mud. The previous year her defence minister, John Nott, had walked out in the middle of a live *Nationwide* interview with Robin Day, who was questioning him about defence cuts; always a sensitive issue for the Conservatives.

When Day snorted that Nott was 'a here today and gone tomorrow politician' who might not care about the defence of the nation, a silent explosion seemed to take place in Nott's head. He scuffled to his feet, announcing disgustedly: 'I'm sorry; I'm absolutely fed up with this interview.' He tossed his lapel mike on to the table with an electronic thud and stomped off, tracked by the cameras. 'Thank you, Mr Nott,' Day scoffed as the minister disappeared from view.

For the 1983 election phone-in Thatcher and Ingham set off for Lime Grove in the back of their chauffeur-driven Jaguar, with the Prime Minister's husband Denis in tow. As they approached Shepherd's Bush, the Prime Minister told the driver to pull up in a car park a few streets away from the studios.

Setting off early for appointments, making sure she arrived bang on time, was one of Mrs Thatcher's standard power ploys, and one she often used when visiting the BBC. She would sit in the back of the stationary Jaguar studying her brief, talking to her ministers on the car phone or just staring out of the window in grim and silent contemplation of the handbagging she was about to deliver.

The Prime Minister duly arrived bang on time and with a great flurry of activity. It had to be made clear that every second of her time was precious, and they were lucky to get her at all. She was escorted through the Lime Grove labyrinth to Studio D, to meet Sue Lawley, the presenter. Denis was steered into the hospitality room where there was an ample supply of booze and a TV monitor.

The show was going well enough for the Prime Minister until Mrs Diana Gould, a schoolteacher, appeared on the screen with a question about the sinking of the *General Belgrano* during the Falklands War. This should have been easy meat for Mrs Thatcher. Political pundits thought the Falklands had been her finest hour, and the moment when she had emerged as a politician of world stature. Talking about it could only do her a lot of good.

Mrs Gould wanted to know if the Prime Minister had ordered the sinking to make it politically impossible for the Argentine Junta to withdraw from the Islands without a fight. This was a theory popular with opposition parties. The allegation was nonsense, Thatcher replied, the *Belgrano* was a threat to our forces. Gould said that this was not true. The ship had been sailing back to port. 'You are quite wrong,' the Prime Minister replied, 'it was not sailing away from the Falkland Islands.'

At this point the Prime Minister looked as if she was expecting Lawley to pass on to the next question. Instead, with instructions from the editor crackling in her earpiece, she asked Mrs Gould to continue. 'That's not good enough, Mrs Thatcher,' Gould said. By now the phone-in caller was looking the more composed and statesmanlike of the two. Mrs Thatcher butted in stridently: 'But when it was sunk, it was a danger to our ships. You do accept that, don't you?' she insisted. But the caller was still allowed to stay on the line. 'No, I don't accept that,' Gould said calmly, and started quoting authoritative-sounding facts about the event. The Prime Minister was being humiliated in front of millions of early evening viewers.

In the control box Roger Bolton, who was directing events, was highly delighted. A clash like this was great television: 'I watched fascinated as these two iron ladies battled it out. It seemed to me to be democracy in action,' he later told the *Guardian*.

When the programme was over, the Prime Minister glared at Lawley, virtually threw down the lapel mike and stormed off, Nott style, to join Ingham and Denis in the hospitality room. Bolton arrived to thank her, offer a drink and round things off on a friendly note. There was no chance of that. Instead Denis launched into an extraordinary rant about Lime Grove being a nest of communists, poofters and long-haired Trots.

Ingham, taking a more professional view, thought the show had been a 'stitch-up'. The BBC had asked the Prime Minister to appear and there would have been no show without her. In return there was an unwritten rule that phone-in callers should be cut off if questions were too hard-edged, or if the guest became flustered. It was either Bolton or Lawley's fault. They had allowed Gould, obviously an activist of some sort, to keep going. The Prime Minister did not say much. She knocked back her whisky in one gulp and bustled out of Lime Grove, vowing never to return or speak to 'that dreadful woman Lawley' again.

The Prime Minister and her advisers thought the incident was typical of the BBC. She had featured as a standing joke on BBC comedy shows since the early 1970s, when *Monty Python's Flying Circus* carried a sketch saying her brain was the size of a pea and was located in her foot: character assassination dressed up as 'entertainment'.

Her habit of dusting off the Corporation's senior management also dated back to the '70s when she was education minister in the Heath government. People at the BBC still remembered her first visit, a lunch with the Board of Governors during the 1974 miners' strike that brought Heath down. She had not eaten a morsel, and instead spent the time laying into them about the way the BBC was reporting the strike and, generally, promoting sex, violence and left-wing views. The BBC's behaviour was, in a phrase she kept repeating, 'quite intolerable'. When she had gone the Governors heaved a collective sigh of relief and rushed for the brandy decanter.

Mrs Thatcher's view of the BBC did not improve as she made her way up the Conservative Party hierarchy. The Corporation had led the way in slaughtering her friend and intellectual mentor Keith Joseph when he made his famous gaffe to the effect that women from lower social groups should be discouraged from breeding. The coverage put paid to his chances of becoming leader of the Conservative Party, much to the regret of right-wing Tories like herself.

But what was really unforgivable, the Prime Minister thought, was the BBC's attempts to report the troubles in Northern Ireland as objectively as possible, instead of joining in as an arm of the war against terrorism. Here Mrs Thatcher's complaints were personal, and deeply felt. She had sworn she would never forgive the BBC for interviewing a gloating member of the Irish National Liberation Army who claimed to have organised the murder of her close friend and campaign organiser Airey Neave, a Tory MP.

Soon afterwards, during the 1979 election, she had been invited by the BBC to take part in a face-to-face interview with Jim Callaghan, in the style of the televised US Presidential debates. Bell and Reece, the image men, advised her not to do it. Her television retheming was then far from complete. Mrs Thatcher herself was undecided until Chris Patten, who was running the Conservative Research Department, told her a refusal would make the BBC 'very, very unhappy'. She made her mind up on the spot: 'Good,' she said, 'if it makes them unhappy, let's refuse.'

Matters were made worse by the Prime Minister's lifestyle. She rarely watched television or read the papers, relying instead on the Press Association tape machine installed in Number Ten by her distant Labour predecessor Clement Attlee so that he could keep up with the cricket scores. The tape was supplemented by official briefings from Ingham, and unofficial ones from Denis.

The Prime Ministerial consort had a lot of time on his hands, and spent much of it monitoring the BBC. His short periods with his wife over breakfast and supper would be spent detailing the latest outrages. If his wife was unavailable he would vent his spleen on anyone who was to hand. The papers reported how he accosted a television reporter at a conference while 'smelling of something which was certainly not Aramis'. When she told him she worked for ITN Denis grunted: 'That's all right then. As long as it's not the British Bastard Corporation.'

Denis was a dedicated listener to the *Today* programme,

the agenda-setting Radio Four early morning show. This was bad luck for the BBC, since the *Today* team were wedded to the idea that it was their job to hold the government of the day to account, whatever its political complexion.

The result was not pleasing to Prime Ministerial ears. Ingham later said: 'Most damage to Government-BBC relations was done between 6.30 and 9 am by my former *Guardian* colleague, Brian Redhead,' the *Today* anchorman. Eventually Ingham banned Mrs Thatcher from speaking to the programme after Redhead had called him 'a conspiracy' for the way in which he orchestrated leaks in the Government's favour, and then refused to apologise. Ministers would make a point of listening to *Today*, so that they could judge the Leaderene's mood in advance of cabinet meetings; or join in the ritual denunciations of BBC bias as people waited to get down to business.

Mrs Thatcher believed the people who ran the BBC had never had a proper job in their lives. They had gone straight from university to the BBC, and were immune to the rigours of the market. The BBC ridiculed her background as the daughter of a shopkeeper, and would not even recognise her sort of Britain or its people. Yet these people were being forced to pay a licence fee on pain of being taken to court. They thought the world owed them a living.

Alasdair Milne, the man elevated to the post of Director General of the BBC at the end of 1981, was never likely to get on well with a Prime Minister like Margaret Thatcher. When Milne was appointed his predecessor, Ian Trethowan, was invited to Number Ten for a farewell drink. Mrs Thatcher had asked him if the new Director General was 'One of Us'. Unfortunately for him, he was not. Milne was a prickly Scot who had made his name as a producer on legendary Lime Grove programmes like the *Tonight* show in the 1950s.

Milne had then helped create *That Was The Week That Was* and therefore became one of the gilded '60s liberal-minded radicals who had reached the peak of their careers, unfortunately for them, just as the new and relatively unknown doctrine of Thatcherism was about to grip the country with a mission to destroy all they held dear.

Soon after his appointment Milne was invited to Downing Street by Bernard Ingham. It might help things 'get off to a good start,' he said. When he arrived Milne found Thatcher friendly, but oddly intense. In the middle of chit-chat she became animated, and her voice quickened: 'I must show you something I saw in my boxes over the weekend,' she said excitedly, as though about to give him an unexpected treat.

The Prime Minister returned with a meaty report about the effects of TV sex and violence on children, prepared by a group of Conservative teachers. She thrust it into his hands: 'Read it. I know you won't like it,' she said brightly. The main idea was that the 'adult' 9 pm viewing watershed should be put back later in the evening. The rest of the document, Milne thought as he flicked through it, just seemed to put the standard Mary Whitehouse line.

'You are quite right,' Milne said. 'I don't agree with a word of it.' The Prime Minister said it was a shame that he had such fixed ideas and suggested he discuss it with Keith Joseph, now Education Secretary. 'There's not much point in that,' Milne shot back: 'for a start he doesn't have a TV set.' The Prime Minister looked at him wide-eyed: 'I don't believe you,' she said. 'It's perfectly true,' Milne explained. 'He told me himself. In fact he told me he keeps one downstairs for the servants to watch.'

The next year Milne was involved in much more damaging wrangles with Number Ten during the Falklands War. The BBC's editorial guidelines told reporters not to refer to British troops as 'our troops' because the literal meaning was 'BBC troops' and this was confusing, especially as BBC radio routinely used phrases like 'our correspondent in Buenos Aires'. The guidelines were picked on by backbench Conservative MPs who accused the Corporation of producing bulletins that were 'almost treasonable'. At Prime Minister's question time Mrs Thatcher was asked if she agreed.

'Judging by many of the comments I have heard from those who watch and listen more than I do, many people are very concerned that the case for our British forces is not put over fully and effectively,' she replied, adding: 'if this is so, it gives offence and causes great emotion among many people.' People at the top of the BBC guessed she was talking about Denis, and a horrible vision of him ranting with 'great emotion' about the Argie fifth column at the BBC came to mind.

Milne and the BBC Chairman, George Howard, were then called before a meeting organised by the backbench Conservative media committee where they were crucified by the 150 Tory MPs present. The MPs became steadily more angry as the two BBC chiefs defended the Corporation's work. The meeting ended in chaos with purple-faced MPs shouting abuse and thumping the table. Howard was called a traitor, to which he had replied: 'Stuff you!'

Mrs Thatcher was scarcely more polite when she gave a dinner at Number Ten just after the war. She complained bitterly to Milne about the Falklands coverage and repeated the charges of treachery. 'Do you know,' she said, 'I came down to breakfast one morning and I heard the BBC saying we had landed troops from the *Queen Elizabeth*. I was astonished that the BBC would give such information to the enemy. You are taking risks with people's lives.'

Milne thought about this for a moment and said, in bemused tones: 'You must have issued that statement yourself; where else would we have got it from?' Thatcher replied at once: 'You got it from your satellites.' Milne was taken aback: 'But we haven't got any satellites,' he pleaded, 'you've got them all.' But the Prime Minister refused to budge. 'I don't care, it is true,' she said. Denis would not lie to her.

Milne gave up and tried to change the subject. But Bill Cotton, an important BBC 'baron', soon to become Managing Director of BBC Television, interrupted. He had watched the Prime Minister's performance and the way Milne was trying to handle it with mounting unease. 'Excuse me, Prime Minister,' he said, 'but isn't it a little irresponsible to accuse

the BBC of outright treason?' Thatcher, irritated, replied: 'It
most certainly is not. I have said what I have got to say.'

Conservative Central Office meanwhile maintained a constant barrage of complaints about alleged bias in the BBC's
coverage. These had to be fielded by the Assistant Director
General, Alan Protheroe, whose job it was to look after news
and current affairs for Milne.

Protheroe, who had started his career running BBC News
in Wales, was a part-time soldier with an old-fashioned
military manner. He was known as 'the colonel'. His own
title for himself was 'flak-catcher general'. He had to deal
with complaints and saw it as his job to watch Milne's back.
Protheroe employed the traditional BBC strategy of keeping
a straight bat. Complaints from political parties, and
especially the Government, were to be expected. During
Harold Wilson's premiership the Labour Party had been just
as bad. In some ways the complaints were a source of pride:
evidence that the BBC was doing its job well and causing
equal offence to whoever was in power.

But during the 1983 election the sheer volume of complaints started to get to him. Ninety-five per cent, he
reckoned, were pure trivia. One was about the tone of voice
used by a newsreader reporting some surprisingly good trade
figures against the trend. Protheroe thought the item had
been read faultlessly. But Conservative Central Office had
detected a 'surprised' tone and rang to complain. 'How can
you identify a thing like that? And what do you want me to
do about it?' Protheroe had asked. He was accused of being
'unhelpful'. Finally Protheroe decided the Conservatives
were waging a form of psychological warfare which went far
beyond the normal party political axe-grinding. It got to the
point where he was relieved if a complaint had any substance.
It made such a change.

The whole unpleasant experience of the 1983 campaign
was rounded off on polling day when he bumped into the
spectral figure of Norman Tebbit in a dark Lime Grove
corridor during the election night special. Protheroe offered

his congratulations for the landslide victory, but Tebbit cut him dead: 'No thanks to you,' he said.

Now that Mrs Thatcher had won a second term some people were beginning to realise her complaints went further than the alleged left-wing and anti-British bias. The Prime Minister was criticising not only what the BBC said; but the very nature of the Corporation and the way it did things.

She saw the BBC, like so much of the public sector, as overmanned, dominated by trade unions and hopelessly unbusinesslike. Whenever a BBC crew arrived to film her they would always have far more people in tow than they appeared to need. Ingham once counted 55 names on the security checklist for a BBC team doing a live broadcast from Number Ten. Some of them might be coming along for the ride, Ingham thought, so that they could say they had been inside Downing Street. But even taking this into account, the overmanning was gross. 'What do all these people do, Bernard?' Thatcher had asked afterwards, genuinely mystified. Ingham had to confess he had no idea.

Instead of just complaining about what the BBC said, the Prime Minister opened up a new front. She was more and more interested in the way the Corporation worked and spent the licence fee. This new campaign was kicked off with a tour of Television Centre, the BBC's television 'factory' in White City, West London. Well briefed and in full hard hat, hand-bagging mode, she had gone through the studios like the proverbial dose of salts, exuding hostility and insulting everyone regardless of their rank or status.

When she reached the studios she set about production teams as though they were stereotypical idle British Leyland car workers. 'Why does it take you so long to make these things? Why do you need so many people? Isn't it terribly inefficient,' she demanded to know. One producer, on the set of the prestige drama series, *The Borgias*, replied: 'You have to understand, Prime Minister, the series is twelve hours long and the actors have to learn their lines.'

This standard defence of BBC thoroughness was dismissed

at once. 'Nonsense,' Mrs Thatcher said, 'when I'm campaigning I learn more material than all those actors put together and I don't take twelve hours.' The Prime Minister was whisked away through the corridors. Her next victim was the young producer of a language course which, her BBC minders thought, could not fail to impress. The programme represented exactly what governments had always praised about the BBC: commitment to education and public service and, since the course involved the sale of tape recordings and books, the additional Thatcherite virtues of private enterprise and technology.

But as the producer proudly went through his pitch, the Prime Minister became impatient. 'I don't know why you are bothering,' she butted in. 'If people want a language they will go and live in the country and learn it that way.'

The Prime Minister's entourage ended up in a conference suite for what was intended as an informal mingling session with about fifty programme-makers. By now the hostility was mutual. The BBC producers spent an uncomfortable half-hour huddled tightly near the door, leaving Director General Milne stranded with Thatcher and her advisers chatting uneasily in the middle of the huge room.

Wielding the handbag was one thing, but to make changes at the BBC would depend on changing the people at the top; starting with George Howard, the Chairman. Howard had been appointed in 1980 by his friend and shooting partner Willie Whitelaw, Thatcher's first Home Secretary and an influential representative of the Tory wets. For people on Whitelaw's wing of the party, the BBC was an important totem of 'One Nation' conservatism: a much loved part of the national heritage that ought to be preserved and protected. The Reithian ethic of civilising the masses, treating the audience as 'viewers' rather than customers and consumers was, after all, one of the purest forms of classic conservatism.

George Howard, a country gentleman with broad liberal interests and an eccentric arty streak, and famous for wearing kaftans in public, fitted the bill perfectly. But after the

1983 election the wets were summarily purged from government and public bodies as a new market-led attack on the establishment was unleashed. Whitelaw remained in the Cabinet as a practical link with the past and symbol of party unity. But a new breed of populist Tories came to the fore as the Thatcher Revolution of free markets and consumer choice began in earnest.

People like George Howard, who had been the President of the Country Landowners' Association but was not a businessman, had no role in the bright new enterprise future. When his contract ran out just before the 1983 election it was obvious that Downing Street would take the opportunity to appoint someone more to its liking. Director General Alasdair Milne asked the BBC's Board of Management to suggest a replacement. He was in no doubt the final decision would be made by Mrs Thatcher. But he would forward any suggestions and they might be considered.

The Board of Management was an important body in the BBC, responsible for the day-to-day running of the Corporation but answerable to the Board of Governors who were political appointees with the job of safeguarding the public interest. Milne and most other members of the Board of Management would have preferred a detached academic who would stand up to the rising tide of Thatcherism.

But Bill Cotton did not agree. He put forward the name of Stuart Young, a businessman who had recently joined the Board of Governors. The rest of the Board thought Cotton had lost his marbles. Young was one of two Governors whom, everyone believed, Thatcher had appointed because of their innate hostility towards what the BBC stood for and, possibly, to prepare it for privatisation.

Cotton explained his case. There was no way Thatcher would appoint a liberal in anything like the same mould as Howard. They had to box clever. It was true that Young was a Thatcher appointment, but since his arrival he had seen how the BBC actually worked and had come to understand and like it. 'We are going to get someone Thatcher approves of whether we want it or not,' Cotton said. 'With Stuart we will at least get someone we can work with.'

Young was an accountant and self-made man. His firm, Hacker Young, was one of the most successful corporate finance consultancies in the country. In 1980 he branched out into broadcasting, organising the finances for one of the consortiums bidding for the breakfast TV franchise. The bid failed, but a year later he was appointed to the BBC's Board of Governors at the relatively young age of 44.

Cotton won the argument. Young's name was put forward and he was duly appointed BBC Chairman, though Milne was never very keen on the appointment. At first there was more interest in Young's political connections than his experience of television and radio which, as with most of the Governors, was slight. Stuart Young's brother, David Young (later Lord Young), was chairman of the influential Centre for Policy Studies, where Mrs Thatcher herself had been Vice-Chairman in the 1970s.

By 1983 the CPS was one of a group of business-financed think tanks geared to 'thinking the unthinkable' about government policy. They were cleverly used by the Prime Minister as an alternative to the established, consensus-minded Whitehall and Tory Central Office policy-making machine. And because the think tanks were in the private sector, they could float politically risky policies that could be officially disowned if the resulting outrage was too damaging.

This was something new in British politics and was especially threatening to the BBC. In the past, whatever the intentions of the government, the BBC's top management could deal directly with the broadcasting department of the Home Office. Sharing the same Olympian outlook on life, the two interlocking bureaucracies could normally defuse any threat to the status quo at the research stage of policy-making.

If all else failed they could simply tie things up in redtape and wait for a change of government: just like Sir Humphrey, the fictional permanent secretary in *Yes, Minister*, which was about the only BBC TV show Mrs Thatcher seemed to like.

The privatisation of policy-making in this way represented by the new importance of the think tanks was essentially an American phenomenon. Many of the ideas they threw up were American too, especially in the field of broadcasting, where demands for US-style deregulation and 'marketisation' of the whole broadcasting system were now the norm. In the early 1980s some of these ideas were given powerful support by Rupert Murdoch, Mrs Thatcher's favourite media tycoon.

Unlike Milne, Murdoch was very definitely 'One of Us'. After buying the *Sun* and steering it to enormous success a decade earlier, Murdoch was back in London with a vengeance, moving to expand the British end of his empire, buying the ailing *Times* and the *Sunday Times* and trying to find a way into commercial or satellite television.

Murdoch's bid to buy *The Times* and the *Sunday Times* had been bitterly contested in Parliament, with the Labour Party still smarting from the way he had turned the previously Labour-supporting *Sun* into the most effective gun in the Tory media arsenal. Others snobbishly objected to the Dirty Digger, owner of the 'tit 'n' bum' *Sun* and the vulgar *News of the World*, taking over the self-styled Top People's Paper.

But Murdoch got what was seen as his reward for helping Mrs Thatcher get to Number Ten when the Government imposed a three-line whip in the Commons allowing him to buy the titles without reference to the Monopolies Commission. Murdoch bought the papers and promptly installed Andrew Neil, a truculent Scot, as editor of the *Sunday Times*.

Neil, or 'Brillopad' as he was to become known in tribute to his diminishing patch of wiry, rust-coloured hair, was not a particularly distinguished newspaperman. He was better known as the former editor of the *Economist* magazine's British pages, where he had campaigned for the new gospel of free-market economics and privatisation in the 1970s when it was less fashionable.

Since then Neil had spent time examining the American media, especially TV, which he admired enormously. Neil was something of a technology freak who loved electronic gadgets of all types, a trait which he combined with the hectic social life of an eligible bachelor. Those who knew him said: 'If he can't plug it in or screw it, he's not interested.'

Neil's thoughts on television were set out in *Look Here*, a documentary he made for LWT, dreamed up by one John Birt, a rising star in the world of commercial television. Neil found the British system riddled with overmanning and inefficiency. American news camera crews consisted of one or two people, often beefy youths straight out of college hired for their ability to elbow their way to the front of a crowd, pointing lightweight Japanese video cameras at the action. British TV news still used old-fashioned film cameras. Neil had been horrified to find that even the smallest American TV stations had installed the electronic Quantel system to produce graphics for programmes, while the British were still using old mechanical methods.

Neil's admiration for the American system extended to the programmes and what he saw as the extra choice it gave people. He was convinced the attitudes of the British public were just the same as the Americans. Every American consumer fad from nylons, chewing gum and hamburgers to rock and roll, denims and baseball caps had arrived first as an exotic novelty but quickly swept the mass market. Like most people in the world, the British could just not get enough of the American Way.

The transmission technology of fibre optic cable and satellite, able to connect viewers to dozens of channels offering everything from children's shows to raunchy movies, was already on its way in the US. Soon it would spread to the United Kingdom. Multichannel television masterminded by red-blooded tycoons like Murdoch and Robert Maxwell, and free from interference from the detested English 'establishment', would soon drag British television into the modern world.

In 1982 Neil returned to London and set out his case in a book called *The Cable Revolution*. The work caused a minor flurry, but was rubbished by what Neil called 'the broadcasting establishment'. Free-market competition, the critics said, had reduced US television to a diet of cheap game shows, ancient movies, glitzy greed fantasy soap operas and endless adverts. The real business of television was serious news and current affairs; worthwhile but popular natural history shows like *Life on Earth*; and prestige drama that gave a platform for writers like Bleasdale, Bennett and Potter.

You rarely got that sort of material on American TV, unless it was imported from Britain, the home of Quality Television, underpinned by the BBC licence fee and the ITV monopoly of television advertising.

# 2

## *The Last of the Great Cigar Chompers*

The BBC's reliance on the licence fee, set at a level determined by the Government, was always its political Achilles' heel. The fee was set at £46 in 1981. Since then the Corporation had expanded its local radio network, launched breakfast television and was planning a thousand extra hours of daytime programming to rival ITV. In January 1984 the BBC was beginning a year-long campaign for an increase in the licence fee and was, therefore, at its most vulnerable.

The BBC said the fee would have to go up to at least £60, an increase of up to a third at a time when the Government had declared 'war on inflation'. In 1983 inflation had dropped to five per cent; the lowest figure for fifteen years.

An early sign that the BBC would not have an easy ride came when Home Secretary Douglas Hurd complained about a lowbrow imported mini-series called the *The Thorn Birds* screened on BBC1. This was not the sort of thing the licence fee should be spent on, Hurd said, especially when ITV was investing in critically acclaimed drama like *Jewel in the Crown* and *Brideshead Revisited* at no cost to the public.

The BBC was continually expanding its activities at great

public expense and dragging its feet over new developments like satellite TV, despite being granted a virtual monopoly, Hurd complained. Now the BBC had its bottomless begging bowl out again, but was offering no guarantee that extra income would be spent on quality programmes instead of empire-building and imported mini-series.

The papers picked up the theme. Max Hastings, son of the legendary BBC reporter Macdonald Hastings, led the charge in the *Evening Standard*. WHO WILL HALT THE RUN-AWAY BEEB? Hastings asked, fingering Alasdair Milne and his director of programmes, Brian Wenham, as 'the forces driving the Corporation juggernaut out of control'. *The Thorn Birds*, Hastings wrote, showed the BBC's statutory 'commitment to excellence' had collapsed, to be replaced with 'remorseless mediocrity'. The series, he added, showed the leadership of the BBC was 'pitifully inadequate, bankrupt of ideas and lost for a course'.

After this opening shot, a hostile press campaign gathered pace all year boosted by more Government leaks hinting that the BBC might be made to take advertising to supplement the licence fee. The campaign produced a tidal wave of weak puns based on the BBC's initials. It was the BRITISH BONKERS CORPORATION, said the *News of the World*, claiming that 140 staff, led by David Icke, were employed covering two tables at the World Snooker Championship. That year's SDP conference in Buxton, the paper said, had been covered by 250 BBC employees, almost matching the number of delegates.

The *Daily Mail* said the initials BBC stood for (utterly) BIASED; (morally) BANKRUPT and (politically) COR-RUPT. Columnist Paul Johnson claimed BBC drama was being run by a Communist-style Production Politburo that acted like a 'sleazy pornographer', adding: 'alongside the sadistic sex, the BBC slips in the political message. It not only lies, it lies for the left. It not only rapes, it rapes for the revolution.'

Inside the BBC the press campaign was having a catastrophic effect. Producers and executives felt they were living in a bunker having the stuffing knocked out of them. If the BBC's management defended itself, as Milne had done during the Falklands War, that would be reported as evidence of a NEW BBC ROW and thrown back in their faces. They just could not win.

Milne and Wenham brazened it out. They knew effective competition with ITV was the key to public support for the licence fee. *The Thorn Birds* was a ratings hit, watched by more than fourteen million. If the BBC caved in and just showed endless current affairs and worthy documentaries, which was what the politicians seemed to be saying the licence fee was for, the BBC would be handing them a loaded gun.

If the BBC was not providing the sort of popular programmes people wanted they might start to wonder why they had to pay the licence fee. And in the early 1980s the BBC had fallen well behind ITV in the ratings battle. The Director General's attention turned to Alan Hart who, as BBC 1 controller, was held responsible for the problem.

Milne thought Hart lacked 'bottom' and was disappointed that the controller's job had not gone to the head of the BBC's current affairs department, John Gau. Gau was a controversial figure because of his involvement in the 1979 Carrickmore incident, when fledgling reporter Jeremy Paxman and a BBC camera crew filmed a staged IRA road block.

The Carrickmore footage was never screened but the *Financial Times* carried a report of the incident which Ingham drew to the Prime Minister's attention. She 'went nuclear' and caused a stink. Despite intensive lobbying from BBC managers, it seemed to some that the Governors held Carrickmore against Gau and they appointed the lacklustre Hart, then head of sport, instead.

Milne was able to use the ratings problem to put pressure on Hart. His position had never been very strong. In early 1984 Bill Cotton was promoted to the job of Managing Director of BBC Television, becoming Hart's immediate superior. Cotton shared Milne's assessment of Hart and had his eye on the perfect successor: Michael Grade, the former programme chief at LWT, whom he hoped to lure to the BBC from his latest job running a Hollywood TV production company.

Michael Grade was the nephew of Lew Grade, the famous cigar-chomping TV mogul. Unlike Hart, Grade was seen as someone who understood show business inside out. He had the contacts to attract big names to boost the BBC's ratings. Bill Cotton had known Michael Grade since childhood. Michael's father, Leslie, had represented Cotton's father, the band leader Billy Cotton Snr of 'Wakey Wakey!' fame. The relationship was so close that Bill Cotton was asked to read the oration at Leslie Grade's funeral.

After working briefly as a sports journalist on the *Daily Mirror*, Grade had become an agent handling stars like Larry 'shut that door' Grayson. At the age of 30, he moved from this base to join the buzzing frontier country of LWT where he helped to put together a BBC-crushing Saturday-night schedule. Three years later, in 1977, he became LWT's programme controller. Then in 1981 he moved to Hollywood to work for Norman Lear's Embassy Television for a reported signing-on fee of $1 million. Grade described this at the time as 'a living wage'.

But Grade had not always got on well with US network TV bosses and made a sideways move, setting up his own Los Angeles production company and making a six-part mini-series based on Jeffrey Archer's novel *Kane and Abel*. He was already contemplating a return to Britain when Cotton sounded him out for the BBC1 job. He was immediately tempted. The BBC job would enable him to escape from the nightmare of the American network system that, he later said, had convinced him that a completely deregulated TV system produced little more than an all-out chase for ratings driven by the power of advertisers.

But Grade still needed persuading. The first problem was the drop in salary. At the BBC he would earn only £50,000. This was a pay cut of around £200,000 a year. There was not much Cotton could do about that; but he was able to promise Grade a big budget, a lot of creative freedom and a potential place in TV history as the man who saved the BBC. Grade accepted.

This time it was vital that the Board of Governors did not block Grade's appointment, as they had done when Hart beat Gau to the controller's job four years earlier. So their agreement was secured in advance without any formal interviews with rival candidates. Hart was pushed aside to become Controller International Relations, and Grade arrived at Television Centre.

Grade attacked his new job with relish, providing a much-needed tonic for the rank and file after the press battering. His entrepreneurial streak and irreverent one-liners were not always appreciated by the 'suits' at Broadcasting House. But the programme-makers responded quickly to Grade's energy.

Grade's instinct for generating the right kind of publicity boosted BBC morale further. The new controller's first important outing was at a Royal Television Society symposium in Cardiff. He lived up to his reputation and grabbed the headlines by turning criticism that he would drive BBC 1 down market on its head. Grade said he would invest heavily in domestic drama and cleverly managed to make a virtue of the fact that the BBC had recently stepped aside, allowing ITV rights to the Miss World contest: 'These contests no longer merit national airtime,' he proclaimed, 'they are an anachronism in this day and age of equality, and verging on the offensive.'

Fleet Street lapped this up and, even better, he provided the tabloids with a ready-made story to feed the national obsession with the appearance of TV weathermen. 'I've been away three years,' he said, 'and they still don't look as though they wash their hair.'

On top of this unaccustomed wave of positive publicity, Grade brought something much more important to the BBC: a harder edge to scheduling, honed in the world of commercial television. Unlike the BBC, ITV had to sell specific slots to advertisers and the black art of scheduling was therefore much more developed. Massive market research was undertaken and fed into every decision about programmes. And Grade's LWT was renowned as the most aggressively commercial scheduler of all. It had only three evenings to hit the mark and 'deliver' specific audiences to advertisers. Unlike the BBC, the preoccupation was at least as much about when programmes went out as their content. At LWT Grade had won a reputation for an uncanny knack of deploying the right programme at the right time to inflict maximum damage on BBC 1's Saturday-night schedule.

It would be at least eighteen months before Grade could put his own programme commissions onto the screen, but there was a lot he could do by adjusting the existing schedule. An early success involved *Tenko*, a workaday drama series about women in a Japanese PoW camp. Grade moved it from Thursday to Sunday evening and the show took off. 'It smelled like a Sunday show to me,' he explained, 'it was just instinct.'

It would be much more difficult to assert his authority over the position of current affairs programmes in the schedule. The Lime Grove current affairs centre threatened to revolt over his plan to move *Panorama* from 8 pm to a new slot after the Nine O'Clock News. The rebellion was quashed when Grade lavished the famous charm. The change went ahead and *Panorama's* audience doubled.

After this brisk tightening up of the existing schedule, Grade limbered up for a major overhaul of BBC 1. He had the luck to arrive when an investment in programmes made three years earlier was about to bear fruit, providing him with *EastEnders*, a gritty new soap opera. For years the BBC had tried to come up with a rival to ITV's veteran soap, *Coronation Street*. There had been various attempts: *Compact*, a flawed saga of trendy media activity; *United*, a repetitious chronicle of goings-on at Brentwich FC, a fictional football club, where everyone was either 'sick as a parrot' or 'over the moon'; and *The Newcomers*, a prissy *Coronation Street* clone set in a nondescript London overspill town. None had worked. Taking its tone from the Governors, the BBC did not seem to have its heart in producing anything like *Coronation Street*.

Now the Corporation at last overcame its puritanical instincts with *EastEnders*, the secret scheduling weapon Cotton and Wenham had been developing since 1982. Publicity for the soap indicated an extraordinary cast of characters including a resident National Front skinhead, an unmarried mother who worked as a stripper and was drifting into prostitution, a heroin addict, a gay couple, a pregnant teenage schoolgirl and a 'Mr Nasty' publican whose glamorous but drunken wife had endless adulterous affairs.

The BBC had invested enormous resources in the soap, and had commissioned a purpose-built permanent set at the recently acquired former ATV Elstree studios, just outside London. It would be Grade's job to make sure the money was not wasted and that *EastEnders* was targeted to inflict maximum damage on ITV's domination of early evening viewing. Grade decided against taking on *Coronation Street* directly. Instead he put *EastEnders* on half an hour earlier at 7pm on Tuesday and Thursday when ITV was showing the 'sex, sheep and senility' soap, *Emmerdale Farm*. A new thrice-weekly chat show hosted by Terry Wogan would provide light relief for the rest of the week.

More than nine million viewers tuned into the first episode of *EastEnders* broadcast in February 1985. This was a satisfactory, if not brilliant start. But by May audiences had slumped to five million. This was lower than *Wildlife on One*, the Governor-friendly programme it had replaced. But then Grade had a brainwave. By repeating the two mid-week episodes together on Sunday afternoons, creating a supposedly distinct 'omnibus' edition, the audience figures could be added together, boosting the notional number of viewers to 12 million.

This put *EastEnders* right up there with *Coronation Street* in the top ten. ITV cried foul, but Grade was able to say the trick was already used by *Brookside* on its commercial sister station Channel Four, which was where he got the idea in the first place. Together with *Wogan*, which apart from the host's £350,000 salary was very cheap to make, the new schedule was a success. It stopped the BBC1 ratings slide, which at one point had gone under 35 per cent.

The battle to win back viewers was slow, but steady. It was not until 1989 that ratings peaked at more than 40 per cent. Best of all Grade was able to claim this triumph was being set in motion without abandoning quality standards. *East-Enders* might be down-market in some ways, but it was a resolutely British, or at least English, show. Cotton was pleased. Michael was doing fine.

The BBC's hand in the licence fee debate was strengthened by the ratings triumph. But the press campaign against the Corporation as an institution continued unabated. The idea that the BBC should take advertising to cover some of its costs, and so keep the licence fee down, now began to gain ground.

This idea had the enthusiastic personal support of the Prime Minister. She had raised the subject with senior BBC people during a lunch at Television Centre in October 1984, coincidentally a few days after the IRA had attempted to kill her by bombing her hotel room during the Brighton Conservative Party conference. Milne had expected to find her badly shaken by the experience. But, if anything, she seemed more self-possessed than ever.

The Prime Minister breezed in and immediately started dusting everyone off about efficiency, and the 'enormous' numbers of BBC technicians she had seen at the conference.

During drinks she pointedly ignored Cotton, who at their last meeting had dealt sharply with her over the BBC's supposed Falklands 'treachery'. Instead Milne chatted with her about the bombing. This, at last, seemed to bring out her human side. Milne was told the story of how she had put Denis to bed and was reading her Whitehall papers while sitting on the loo when the bomb went off. 'Good heavens. I must go and see how Denis is. He can't possibly go to hospital. He isn't wearing matching pyjamas,' was her only thought as the bathroom came crashing down round her ears.

After breaking the ice in this way, the Prime Minister turned to the topic of putting adverts on the BBC. Milne revealed that the Corporation had done a study showing there was not enough money to go around, and that ITV would be put out of business. 'If we started to take advertising, we'd take it all,' he said.

'Oh, I don't believe that,' Mrs Thatcher replied. 'I'm sure you can raise a little. I don't mean very much, just a minute or two around the Nine O'Clock News.' Milne repeated himself, and the conversation petered out.

The Prime Minister turned her attention to Cotton. 'Well, how is television getting on?' she asked airily. 'Very good, very good indeed,' Cotton replied. The Prime Minister returned to her advertising obsession: 'Well, if it's so good,' she said, 'why won't you take some advertising?' Cotton had anticipated the question and had a little routine all worked out.

'Did you get a chance to see any of the Olympics this summer, Prime Minister?' he asked. It was certain she had, if only to appreciate the enormous PR coup it represented for her friend Ronald Reagan. 'And did you see that marvellous moment when they took the discs from the seats, held them up, and it made the flags of all nations?' Cotton continued.

'Oh yes,' the Prime Minister effused, 'wasn't that wonderful?' Cotton then delivered the sucker punch: 'Well, the American audience missed that because they were on a beer commercial at the time.'

The room fell silent. The Prime Minister did not take kindly to being patronised like this, especially by people from the BBC. But there was no explosion. 'All that can be organised. It is detail,' she said. But Cotton would not give way. 'No, no,' he said sagely: 'That's deregulation for you. Oh yes! And we don't want too much of that, do we?' Now the

Prime Minister got angry. 'Nonsense,' she said and stabbed the food on her plate. 'Absolute nonsense.'

In the autumn and winter of 1984, after the Brighton bombing, the Prime Minister had more pressing matters than the BBC's finances to deal with. Top of the list was the year-long miners' strike. The BBC was caught up in the dispute in the normal way, accused by both sides of biased or misleading reporting.

One tactic being used by the employers was to say that the strike was slowly collapsing and that a 'drift back to work' was gathering pace. British Coal would provide figures of how many miners had decided to return to work. The phrase 'the driftback continued today' was regularly included in BBC news bulletins, demoralising the strikers and leading to furious complaints. At the same time the Government and employers objected to the way scenes of police violence were heavily featured.

The strike ended in February 1985 in humiliating defeat for the trade unions; and complete victory for Mrs Thatcher. The Prime Minister was now at the peak of her powers. British Telecom and British Airways had been privatised the previous year after massive redundancies. Now, with the power of the public sector unions broken, she could begin the process of making nationalised industries like British Gas, British Steel and, eventually British Coal, strike-free, profitable and ripe for privatisation.

All publicly owned ventures would be on the privatisation agenda, and that included the BBC. The problem was that the Corporation had no source of income, apart from the licence fee and the trickle of money from BBC Enterprises, the Corporation's commercial arm. The idea of introducing advertising to BBC 1 and Radios One and Two, with their mass audiences, and possibly turning BBC 2 into a subscription service, was the obvious way forward. But even then it was unlikely the BBC would ever generate the sort of profits needed to attract shareholders.

It was a knotty problem, and much discussed in Mrs

Thatcher's Downing Street Policy Unit, the driving force behind the privatisation programme. Unfortunately for the BBC the Unit had come under the direction of Brian Griffiths, a right-wing economist and Christian moralist. Others in Mrs Thatcher's circle, including Bernard Ingham, were alarmed by the strength of his views on the subject of broadcasting. He would rave about the 'bloody awful' BBC. The licence fee, he believed, was a denial of freedom of choice and, therefore, an offence against God.

Ingham thought Griffiths had become 'unbalanced' and had vastly overestimated television's importance and influence on people. Much later, at a think-tank meeting with Griffiths and like-minded thinkers, Ingham was incautious enough to describe the BBC as 'a cultural asset to Britain'. Shudders of disgust went round the room.

The Prime Minister admired Griffiths enormously. Like many of her most trusted advisers he was a convert from the intellectual left. A former grammar-school boy, he had supported Keynesianism as an academic economist. Then he joined the intellectual war on inflation, writing a treatise on Mexican monetary policy. *The Times* reported that his Whitehall enemies saw him as an ambitious schemer with a 'Svengali-like' grip on Government thinking.

Like Andrew Neil and his boss Rupert Murdoch, Griffiths was excited by the possibilities offered by cable and satellite television. Even more promising was the potential of satellite to broadcast across frontiers. This could provide a new weapon, Griffiths thought, in the Cold War against Communism. The peoples of Eastern Europe were already besotted with Western pop music. If satellites could beam down the beguiling view of life in the West presented in pop videos and television programmes like *Dallas* and *Dynasty*, the popular pressure on Stalinist governments would be immense.

The ideal solution would be for the private sector to launch a multi-national satellite service, generating profits from subscribers and advertisers in the United Kingdom, but with a broadcast footprint covering the whole of Europe, including the Eastern Bloc. Standing in the way was the BBC which, with its access to public money through the licence fee, would be an impossibly strong competitor for a new satellite operator.

Bernard Ingham, with his more pragmatic approach, would remind Griffiths and Thatcher that the BBC was still popular with the voters. For all Griffiths' intellectual arguments, there was no sign of a licence fee revolt. Despite evasion, people did not seem to think the licence fee was unreasonable, and were even patriotically proud of paying for the 'best television service in the world'. Abolition of the fee amounted to destroying the Corporation itself and that would not go down well with the voters.

In the meantime there were plenty of others who agreed that the BBC should be privatised. It would be much better if a campaign for privatisation, to which the Government could respond with legislation, was left to them.

# 3

## *Dialogue of the Deaf*

The year-long press campaign against the BBC reached a peak on the eve of the licence-fee negotiations in January 1985. An extraordinary series of three consecutive BBC-bashing leaders appeared in Rupert Murdoch's *Times*. This was a degree of editorial attention unprecedented since the abdication crisis of 1936. They were written by Peter Stothard, a former BBC graduate trainee later to become *The Times*' editor, and addressed directly to the Government.

'The BBC should not survive this Parliament at its present size, in its present form and with its present terms of references intact,' the paper said. 'Television is probably best at providing relaxation, undemanding entertainment and information that needs illustration with pictures,' the paper said, adding that a lot of people now used television as a sort of audio-visual wallpaper. There was nothing wrong with that, if people wanted it, but there was no reason why it should be paid for by a form of taxation.

This was followed by a withering attack on the key BBC idea of Quality Television. 'Suppose it were proposed,' the paper asked, 'that all cornflakes boxes have printed upon them the works of Shakespeare. Would that mean we had the highest quality cornflakes boxes in the world, or would it mean that we were rather foolish?' Quality ought to be defined by the consumer, rather than the producer, as in the American free-market system, the paper said.

The paper ridiculed the BBC's 'Best Bargain in Britain' slogan. 'A bargain is something that the buyer can leave on the shelf if he so chooses,' the paper said, adding: 'The Government should concede no increase in the BBC licence fee.' Instead it called for a 'radical and rapid inquiry' into what the BBC should be doing.

*The Times* advocated the BBC restricting itself to news and current affairs; education and, perhaps, some of the more unpopular arts. Advertising or sponsorship could pay for some of these programmes in the way private sponsorship supplemented Arts Council grants for opera. (Religious programmes were worth paying for out of public money, *The Times* said, if it could be shown that your neighbour was less likely to throw a brick through your window if he sometimes watched *Songs of Praise*.)

The paper's conclusion contained the most radical suggestion of all. It recommended the break-up of the BBC into a series of franchises that could be bought by commercial companies. These new channels would be financed by advertising, and possibly supplemented by a share of the licence fee to pay for public service conditions attached to the franchise.

There was no mention of who might want to bid for the franchises. But Alasdair Milne had few doubts. A week later he named Rupert Murdoch in a speech to the Television and Radio Industries Club. 'Who is the more likely to serve the public interest,' he asked, 'the BBC or *The Times*, whose recommendations if acted upon would have the practical effect of enabling its owner Rupert Murdoch to acquire some of the most valuable broadcasting action in the UK?' *The Times* officially denied Murdoch was directly involved in devising the leaders, and Milne apologised.

But the Government followed at least some of *The Times'* advice. The licence was set at £58; well short of the £65 the BBC said it needed. And part of this increase was withheld until a committee of inquiry into the BBC's finances reported to Parliament the following year. The committee was to be headed by Alan Peacock, an economics professor at Heriot-Watt University in Edinburgh.

Professor Peacock seemed certain to support the introduction of advertising, and might well go even further down the road to privatisation. He was an expert in the new science of introducing simulated free markets into public sector organisations, which was something of a boom industry under the Thatcher Government. He claimed to be 'a liberal in the tradition of John Stuart Mill, rather than the Austrian school.' This was a neat way of signalling to those in the know that, while he was completely sound on free-market principles, he was not as extreme as 'the carpet chewers', as some devotees of the Austrian philosopher Friedrich Von Hayek were called in think tank circles. *The Times* described him glowingly as 'a distinguished free-market economist who should relish an assault on the self-interested case law of the lobbyists'.

From the start Professor Peacock was decidedly cool towards the BBC. His first meeting with officials, an informal get-together at Broadcasting House in June 1985, was short and sharp. 'What do you want to ask us?' a BBC official enquired. 'Nothing,' Peacock replied. He was then asked when the BBC would have to submit its own evidence to his committee. 'August 31st,' he snapped, and with that excused himself. The meeting had lasted two minutes. Inquiries like this usually dragged on for ages. Now the BBC was being given just a few weeks to put together a case for its whole future.

There was more concern when the membership of the committee was announced. Peacock was joined by Sam Brittan of the *Financial Times*, the brother of Home Secretary Leon. Brittan was an apostle of market forces who had made a series of detailed studies on the broadcasting industry. The committee seemed hand-picked to recommend advertising. The list included two industrialists: Jeremy Hardie, a businessman with SDP leanings, and Sir Peter Reynolds, chairman of Rank Hovis McDougall; and Lord Quinton, a philosopher and former President of Trinity College, Oxford. The rest of the committee comprised Alastair Hetherington, an ex-editor of the *Guardian* and former controller of BBC Scotland, and Judith Chalmers, the TV personality.

Sam Brittan was to make all the running on the committee. He thought the stakes were much higher than a spat between Mrs Thatcher and Alasdair Milne over whether the BBC should take advertising. The Corporation was a publicly owned monopoly which, he believed, was failing to grasp new technology and offer consumers more choice.

The position was similar to British Telecom where, during decades of public ownership, the only concession to consumer choice was the introduction of the Trimphone, available in three tacky state-regulated pastel shades. After privatisation BT was forced to respond to the market, introduce new technology to cut costs and offer all kinds of new services like 'on line' information services, Micky Mouse handsets, computerised phone books and an entirely new network of digital exchanges. There was now great and excited talk of people like stockbrokers and bank managers turning their living rooms or golf clubs into 'remote data processing centres' so that they would not even have to go into the office.

In this bright vision of the future the boring old telephone socket was to be transformed into an 'entry port' to a consumerist electronic Utopia. The revolution was only being held back by the failure to dig up the country's pavements and install fibre optic cable capable of carrying much more information. Subscriptions to cable television services was the ideal source of capital for this activity. Standing in the way was the BBC which, working alongside ITV, was thus blamed for keeping British television back in the age of the Trimphone.

Brittan had developed his theories with Peter Jay, the former economics editor of *The Times* and presenter of LWT's *Weekend World*. Jay was not on the committee, but had strong thoughts of his own on the future of television. He and Brittan were to spend long sessions together at Jay's Ealing home, effectively forming their own private committee, and wildly exceeding Peacock's original brief. Together they developed a radical intellectual case for the future of television as an electronic version of newspaper or magazine publishing, with the ideal of dozens of subscription channels delivered by cable. Against this background it was positively dangerous to allow the BBC access to money from advertising.

The important thing was to ensure the BBC did not have enough money to become involved in new technology such as satellite TV. It would only block competition and extend the dead hand of state control even further.

Brittan, Jay and other radical thinkers about the BBC were cheered on by *The Times* and Murdoch himself. The publisher recorded a special interview with Alastair Burnet for screening at the September 1985 meeting of the Royal Television Society, the bi-annual TV bosses' jamboree in Cambridge. Murdoch was in New York at the time, applying for US citizenship so that he could start buying what became known as the Fox television network.

Murdoch laid into the BBC, saying the licence fee was 'wasteful, very unfair to the public, and unnecessary.' The Corporation's activities, he said, were 'bad for the country' because 'people should be trusted to choose what they want to watch' instead of having it given to them courtesy of a form of taxation. 'Now we have the Peacock Committee and the future of the BBC is being decided,' he added, 'I would privatise BBC1 and make it stand on its own feet.' If this happened, the channel could become a commercial operation like any other, Murdoch said, funded by advertising and sponsorship.

But there should be no half measures. Like Brittan and

Jay, he opposed the BBC taking advertising while it remained a public body: 'if it was privatised; yes. But for the Government to stay in the business and take commercials as well would be very unfair.'

Murdoch conceded that his idea of public service programmes should be preserved somewhere in the system, but it should be financed by subscription or charity on the American model. He gave a practical example: 'I myself have a place in the country here, and there's a wonderful classical music radio station I listen to. Every couple of months they appeal for money, and they get at my conscience and I send them a cheque for $50.'

Burnet asked him whether he really thought the BBC could be funded 'on the back of bring-and-buy sales,' living hand to mouth. Murdoch smiled: 'If they were a little more hand to mouth they would be more responsive; and a little less arrogant about their audience. Who are they to say what's good for the audience? The public should say these things.'

With Murdoch's advice ringing in their ears, members of the Peacock Committee embarked on a whistle-stop fact-finding European tour. They found foreign broadcasters in cities like Paris and Rome surprisingly well briefed. 'We hear you are going to destroy the BBC,' they would say. 'Please don't do it.' They would then provide substantial briefing papers. Peacock was convinced these were being boomeranged from Broadcasting House.

Returning to London, the committee found that evidence from the various lobby groups, trade associations and pressure groups was arriving by the lorry load in Whitehall. The Home Office organised a public meeting to sort through it all. The venue was Church House, Westminster, where England's bishops hold their synods. The meeting was an odd affair, with the echoing hall two-thirds empty. The Home Office seemed to have fixed the agenda in advance.

People from the broadcasting unions and the commercial watchdog, the Independent Broadcasting Authority, were told they would not be allowed to speak. This dialogue of the deaf was made all the more complete by the choice of chairman Jo Grimond. The former Liberal Party leader kicked off by announcing he was medically, as opposed to figuratively, stone deaf.

Grimond had another problem. His ignorance of the television industry meant that he mistook John Birt, LWT's fashionably attired programme controller, for a member of the public. Birt was curtly told by Grimond he had thirty seconds in which to make his point. The LWT programme chief, not noted for verbal economy, declined and returned to his seat, allowing Peter Jay to rattle through his electronic multichannel future scenario at breakneck pace.

Jay had no time for the BBC concept of 'universality', providing something that could reflect a shared culture. This was 'a pernicious ideal,' he said. He did not think much of Milne, or the way he was answering criticism from the Government. Milne was 'wrapping himself in the mantle of Lord Reith and telling the politicians and public to "fuck off",' was how he later described it. This was an 'insane' way of carrying on, Jay thought. Alasdair Milne was treating the BBC like a private toy and asking people to leave him alone.

Milne was allowed to speak and, for once, impressed observers with his robust defence of public service broadcasting. At the Cambridge RTS meeting a few months before, Milne had been torn apart by Paul Johnson, the upfront Conservative thinker who had accused the BBC of 'raping for the revolution' in his *Daily Mail* column.

After this sobering experience the Director General now put the BBC's case eloquently. Public service broadcasting entailed offering a stimulating range of programmes, Milne said, and did not mean giving people what the BBC thought was good for them, as Murdoch said, but what they wanted if they knew it existed: a whole country talking to itself.

By the time the Peacock Report was published in July 1986, Brittan and Jay had steered it well away from recommending advertising. Instead there was a wide range of suggestions, dealing as much with ITV as the BBC. Under-pinning it all was the Brittan-Jay vision of dozens of subscription channels, which the committee was realistic enough to say would have to be introduced gradually. More important was the suggestion that both ITV and the BBC should be required to take 40 per cent of their programmes from the independent sector.

The arrival of Channel Four, launched in 1982, had already undermined the Corporation's claim that only 'Rolls Royce' operators, like itself and the big ITV companies, could make quality television. All over Soho bright young programme-makers, armed with Filofaxes, word processors and designer ties, were offering an entrepreneurial alternative to what Mrs Thatcher regarded as the complacent fat cat attitude of British television.

These Young Turks were represented by the Independent Programme Producers' Association, an articulate pressure group. The Association got to work on the Peacock Committee, suggesting that the BBC and ITV should be forced to show a fixed quota of programmes made by their members.

The independents, used to making daring programmes for the officially alternative Channel Four, were typically left-wingers more used to defending the licence fee against the ravages of Thatcherism. But the prospect of a guaranteed slice of the ITV and BBC duopoly's £2 billion income transformed them into free-market storm troopers overnight.

The lobbying had the desired effect. When Peacock delivered his report in July 1986 it recommended the 40 per cent quota. Although this was later whittled down to 25 per cent when the BBC and ITV claimed it would put their programme-making departments out of business, the independents were delighted. It was not every day that a trade association won well over £500 million extra income for its members, a lot of which would have to be handed over by the BBC.

At the same time the licence fee was to be pegged to the retail price index. If the proposals went ahead, the BBC would have no extra money to pay the independents and was therefore locked in enormous and rapid cuts in its pro-gramme-making departments.

Curiously for a committee set up to examine how the BBC should be financed, Peacock's most explosive short-term pro-posal was selling off the ITV licences to the highest bidder with the potentially enormous sums going to the Treasury. In the past the IBA had awarded franchises on merit.

Even more unexpectedly the committee declined to recom-mend advertising on the BBC, which was supposed to have been its entire point. Mrs Thatcher was apoplectic and the Labour opposition gleefully exploited this rare slap in the face for the Leaderene. Bernard Ingham was despatched to tell journalists the committee had 'kicked the ball into the long grass' and would be ignored.

Peacock himself was called in to see Douglas Hurd, the Home Secretary, to explain himself. He found the session uncomfortable, rather like an oral PhD examination he might give to one of his students. Peacock had no idea what the questions would be. He thought Hurd might be angry about 'the advertising problem' as Peacock sheepishly described it.

Instead the meeting was dominated by discussion of a side issue. Peacock was personally opposed to any form of govern-ment regulation of what could be seen on TV. 'Are you really saying you want a position where anything goes?' Hurd asked. At the time the Home Secretary was embarking on one of the Conservatives' regular crusades for morality and family values. Peacock said there was a general law against obscenity on the statute book that could be used; but beyond this adults should be free to choose. Hurd scowled. Another boot into the undergrowth seemed certain.

At Broadcasting House there was relief that the advertis-ing threat had been seen off, but consternation about the size of the independent quota. BBC TV's chief accountant, Cliff Taylor, met Home Office officials and told them the 40 per cent quota was 'a hell of a shock' and completely impractical.

They were happy about using independents in principle, but the target was too high. The Government settled on 25 per cent to be phased in over five years. But even with this reduction the BBC would still have to sack a lot of people.

Milne had no experience of managing change on the scale implied by Peacock. He was a programme-maker at heart, who had been brought up in a continuously expanding BBC. Some said he never really settled in with the more mundane side of life at Broadcasting House, and pined for Television Centre where the programmes were made. Anticipating this, Stuart Young, the BBC Chairman, had insisted on management changes during the period when Peacock was deliberating.

Young was never the Tory hatchet man some thought him to be. He was essentially a non-political man. To the horror of Downing Street, it emerged that he had once voted Labour. But he thought the BBC had grown fat in the 1970s during the shift from black and white to more expensive colour TV licences. This had produced real annual increases in the BBC's income as more people made the switch.

The colour bonanza came to an end at the start of the 1980s, forcing the BBC to rely on licence fee increases which had to be wheedled from reluctant governments. Worse still, the BBC had been forced to find even more money to compete with Channel Four, commercial radio, ITV's expansion into breakfast TV, and the imminent arrival of daytime and all-night broadcasting; all of which were financed from advertising.

Young could see big changes were needed on the financial side of the BBC and thought Milne might need help to make them. Young's worries about Milne's lack of enthusiasm for cutting BBC spending became more intense through the summer of 1985. Noticing this, Bill Cotton suggested Young should appoint a Deputy Director General to work under Milne, but to take charge of finance.

After setting up Michael Grade to look after the ratings on BBC 1, Cotton now turned up just the right man to look after the money: Michael Checkland, the head of television resources and a professional accountant. 'Put Mike in charge of the factory,' Cotton had urged. Checkland would get on with making the BBC more efficient while Milne would be free to concentrate on programmes.

Cotton had worked closely with Checkland for many years and they had watched each other's backs. The partnership stretched back to the late '70s when Cotton was controller of BBC1 and Checkland had been in charge of television planning and resources. Checkland fought the internal battles to win the money Cotton needed to keep big-name acts like Terry Wogan (*Blankety Blank*: 20 million viewers) and *The Two Ronnies* at the core of his schedule.

Checkland had taken a more public role as a result. In November 1980 he surprised delegates at a Royal Television Society conference in Southampton by saying the BBC would have to increase productivity to find the money needed for expansion. In future, he said, there would be an 'explosion' of air time to fill, but television companies, including the BBC, could not afford to expand staff numbers at the same rate. The speech was a subtle attack on the broadcasting unions, then believed to be invincible. He talked about abolishing demarcation and the 'cosy standby arrangements' that had led to overmanning.

Checkland made such an impression that he was offered the job of Managing Director of Central Television in Birmingham. He found the offer very tempting. It would mean a big salary increase and the chance to run an entire television company, his 'own command', which was something he thought he would never achieve at the BBC. The job would also have enabled Checkland to return to his home city of Birmingham and be near his mother at a time when his personal life was becoming complicated after separating from his wife Shirley.

Checkland said he was going to take the job at Central, but Cotton persuaded him to talk it over with Alasdair Milne. This was difficult because Milne was on one of his frequent fishing holidays, this time on a remote Scottish river. Cotton tracked down Milne on the phone and explained the problem. 'What do you want me to do about it?' Milne had asked. 'Just make sure he does not leave,' Cotton replied. 'Every man has his price. You have got to find out what it is and give it to him.' Checkland flew to Glasgow and then on to Milne's hotel by helicopter for an emergency summit.

Checkland was elevated to Director of Resources for the whole of BBC television. The job made him the Corporation's top-ranking money man with a seat on the all-important Board of Management. From this position he had handled the financing of the Corporation's expensive move into Breakfast TV and buying the old ATV studios at Elstree, later to be used for the *EastEnders* set.

As Milne saw it Checkland was a BBC man through and through, but hardly one of the gilded, creative intellectuals he preferred to work with. Like Young, Checkland was a grammar-school boy, the son of a Birmingham ironmonger. But instead of going straight into business, he studied modern history at Wadham College, Oxford, where he was something of a hearty, keen on athletics and football. Although it was highly unfashionable at the time, in 1959 Checkland had signed up with an accountancy firm, joining the BBC in 1964 in a junior position, just when Milne was making his name as a creative wunderkind at Lime Grove.

Milne dismissed the suggestion that this man should now become his partner in running the BBC. This worried several members of the Board of Management. They agreed with Young and Cotton that the move was a good idea, in order to avoid a split between Milne and Young if nothing else. Alan Protheroe, the Assistant Director General in charge of journalism, went to Milne's villa in Holland Park one evening to secretly put the Board of Management's case and persuade Milne to change his mind.

When Protheroe arrived he found Milne in his dressing-gown, ill with the 'flu. The Assistant Director General had his own reservations about Checkland but said, on balance, it was better to accept the appointment, rather than risk falling out for good with the Chairman. Mike was easygoing, calm, loyal, sensible: an ideal number two. He was a capable guy, a very clever man, Protheroe pleaded, and not the dull accountant some people said he was. He had a first-class degree in history, a proper subject, and studied Oliver Cromwell in his spare time. The three of them would get on just fine.

Milne was not impressed. The appointment was unnecessary, he said. Young was making a fuss about nothing. Protheroe tried again. Mike could look after the money; he, Protheroe, would continue to be the 'flak catcher', as he called himself, dealing with Government complaints about bias, and Alasdair could continue to lead the whole team.

At that moment there was knock on the door. Protheroe's driver had been tipped off that Young had just set off from Broadcasting House and would be arriving any minute. It would have been fatal, Protheroe thought, if he and Milne were discovered plotting together. He rushed back into Milne's sitting-room: 'Stuart Young is on his way,' he yelped, 'Where's the back door?' Milne explained he did not have one. 'What sort of half-arsed house is this?' Protheroe screeched, 'I'm off!' He rushed out of the front door, and leapt into his car which shot off just as Young's was pulling up.

Protheroe's paranoia was due to a growing split between Young and Milne. Both men had tried to keep their differences secret, but could not stop them spilling out in public from time to time. That September executives at the Royal Television Society meeting in Cambridge were alarmed to see them arguing bitterly. Young was annoyed by Milne's attitude to finance, and the way the Director General was trying to keep him and the Governors at arm's length, working in a cabal with the Board of Management and refusing to tell the Governors what was going on.

Young entered Milne's sitting-room, mercifully unaware of Protheroe's visit, even though the chain-smoking Assistant Director General had left his customary blue haze behind him. Milne said he had changed his mind and was happy with the idea of Checkland becoming his deputy, but needed to talk to him about the exact division of power. He would do that the very next morning, so that it could be announced at the Board of Governors meeting later the same day. It was also important, Milne said, that the announcement came from him, and did not look as if it was being imposed on him. Young agreed.

The next day Milne went into Broadcasting House, still ill with the 'flu. He did not get a chance to speak to Checkland before the Governors' meeting started. Young called on Milne to speak about the Checkland appointment, but he said he was not ready to talk about it. Young was furious. He called Milne into his office and read him a letter of warning from the Board. 'We wish to show you every consideration,' it said, 'but things cannot go on as they are.' Milne returned to his office, tore the letter up and threw it in the bin. He had agreed to the Checkland appointment, what more did Young want? A new low in their relationship was reached. Milne wrote in his diary that he thought Young was 'crackers'.

Checkland was duly made Deputy Director General. He would go no further, Cotton believed, and could settle down into a job he would do well without undue stress. This was important at the time, because Checkland's promotion coincided with the death of his estranged wife Shirley, leaving him and Sue Zetter, his companion, with three teenage children to look after.

The combination of personal problems and financial pressure on the BBC meant he would have enough on his plate for the time being. After the licence fee freeze and the publication of the Peacock Report, Checkland's experience of managing the BBC's finances would be vital if the Corporation was not to be very badly damaged.

Unfortunately for all concerned, the first crisis to engulf the BBC after Checkland's promotion to Deputy Director General was not about money, but the editorial content of one of its programmes. The problem was *Real Lives: At the*

*Edge of the Union*, and it was to cause what was described as a 'constitutional crisis' at the BBC.

*Real Lives* featured Martin McGuiness, believed by many to have been a military commander in the IRA, who was interviewed at length in his living-room about his life and times. It also showed a Unionist extremist, Gregory Campbell, talking in a similar way. The idea behind the programme was to make the point that the people involved in The Troubles were not stereotypical psychopaths, who merely needed to be located and locked up in order to stop the fighting. Instead McGuiness and Campbell came over as people you might have as neighbours, complete with kids, mantelpiece ornaments and tacky three-piece suites. This laid-back, living-room-to-living-room glimpse into their psychology made 'great television'.

But the *Sunday Times* picked up the scent of a story from the programme's pre-publicity press release. Its reporter tracked down the Prime Minister at a press conference about Anglo-American relations in Washington DC and asked a hypothetical question about how Mrs Thatcher would feel if British television decided to screen an interview with a suspected IRA commander.

'I would condemn them utterly,' she replied at once, adding: 'I feel very strongly about it and so would many other people.' The *Sunday Times* ran the story big. Home Secretary Leon Brittan went into a spin and asked the Governors to preview the programme and consider banning it.

Milne was away on another one of his fishing holidays, this time in Scandinavia. He was stranded on a ship in the middle of the Gulf of Finland and would not be able to get back to London for several days. Checkland, as Deputy Director General and therefore Editor-in-Chief in Milne's absence, eventually contacted Milne on the ship-to-shore telephone and asked for instructions. Milne told him not to panic. It was not a good idea to show the documentary to the Governors. Nevertheless, Checkland organised a screening.

The Governors sat in a semicircle in the half-darkened

boardroom to view the film. Lips began to curl when McGuiness appeared. There was much tut-tutting when his recollections of the 1960s civil rights movement were intercut with archive footage of police hitting demonstrators with batons. Five minutes into the film heads started to shake vigorously. After twenty minutes the mood was volcanic.

The lights came up and the Governors sat in dazed silence.

'Well, what did you make of that?' Stuart Young asked tentatively. Nobody wanted to speak first. The ice was broken by the Earl of Harewood, an ex-POW. 'No, No, No,' he said slowly, pausing after each word: 'Never, Never, Never.' William Rees-Mogg, who as Vice Chairman normally spoke last, spluttered that he wanted a ban. Anything else was unthinkable. A vote was taken. James Kincade, the national Governor for Northern Ireland, abstained. The only governor to definitely oppose a ban was the Welsh Governor, Alwyn Roberts. The ban was duly announced, producing more bedlam in the BBC press office.

Milne returned from Scandinavia to the scene of the disaster and tried to get the Governors to change their minds. There was an unpleasant moment when he saw Norman Tebbit, the Tory hard man, striding down the corridor for a previously arranged lunch date. Milne had to break off from being crucified by the Governors over *Real Lives*, to be battered by Tebbit over the soup course about alleged general anti-Government bias, before returning for another dose from the Governors in the afternoon.

Milne failed to get the Board to support him over *Real Lives*. Instead they issued a long statement that began: 'The Board of Governors are the BBC and are therefore responsible for the editorial policy of the Corporation.' This was ominous. The Governors' statement was technically correct, but it ran against accepted practice. For as long as anyone could remember the Governors had seen their role as setting policy in broad terms.

The *Real Lives* documentary was eventually shown, with

minor changes. But the incident had irrevocably damaged Milne's relationship with the Governors.

Alan Protheroe was soon in the firing line as well, for an article he had written in *The Listener*. 'When the Home Secretary thanked the BBC's Governors for banning *Real Lives*, it resembled nothing more than the White Star Line congratulating the iceberg on sinking the *Titanic*,' he wrote.

Rees-Mogg complained bitterly about Protheroe's 'insubordination', but Milne took no action, even though Protheroe thought he might get the sack. Milne's relations with the Board were to become even more strained and the mutterings that he ought to go, which had been circulating for some months, began to grow more insistent. But only the Chairman, Stuart Young, could sack the Director General. Young might have taken action if he had not been seriously ill.

The Chairman had developed lung cancer two years earlier and was by now in great and almost constant pain. Board members noticed how the lines of agony would appear on his face ten minutes into Board meetings. Soon he found it difficult to concentrate and impossible to walk more than a few feet without taking a long rest.

Young's death in August 1986 gave the Government the chance to install a man who would make the changes it wanted.

# 4

## *'Tebbit has got us now'*

The death of Stuart Young sent the combined BBC and Whitehall rumour machine into overdrive. Who would replace him? Would it be a political assassin with orders to 'get' Milne? And, if so, would he be able to resist the famous BBC ethos that had captivated Young and drawn his teeth. Mrs Thatcher herself, still sulking over the Peacock Committee's failure to recommend advertising, had not pronounced on the matter, but Bernard Ingham was said to be lobbying very hard for Lord King, the chairman of British Airways.

King was a rags-to-riches ball-bearing magnate who had taken over the nationalised airline in 1980, sacked 23,000 of its 60,000 staff and steered it to a flotation as one of the first and most successful privatisations. Although many found him personally unpleasant, King was very influential in Whitehall, definitely 'One of Us' and the perfect person to see through the drastic changes implied by the Peacock Report.

Alasdair Milne went to visit Willie Whitelaw and Stuart Young's brother David, Lord Young, at the House of Lords to discover what was going on. David Young, the Prime Minister's favourite cabinet minister as employment secretary, said he would do everything he could to prevent King getting the chairmanship. The BBC might be in need of reform, but programme-makers were not baggage-handlers and the operation needed a lighter touch. Whitelaw agreed. He said King would stay at British Airways. But nobody had any idea who might get the job instead.

An appointment from within the Board of Governors did not seem very likely. Some had thought William Rees-Mogg, the Vice Chairman, would get the job. But he went off to become Chairman of the Arts Council instead. His replacement in the number two job was Joel Barnett, appointed a few weeks before Young's death.

Barnett was a former Labour cabinet minister, though hardly a man of the left, or even the liberal centre. As Treasury Secretary he had presided over an ultra-orthodox financial strategy with enormous public spending cuts, taking on the unions in the resulting 'Winter of Discontent'. Barnett could claim to be the man who introduced the key Conservative policy of monetarism into Britain's public finances, even before the Conservative Government came to power. His own daughter described him as being 'slightly to the right of Genghis Khan.'

Barnett broke with precedent at the BBC and insisted on having his own office and secretary. He had even persuaded Young to give him an official BBC car and driver. Milne knew Barnett wanted to play a bigger role in the BBC and, without much enthusiasm, he had suggested his name to the Home Office as a possible Chairman. At least he would be better than Lord King.

The idea was rejected, and Milne was not consulted about the final decision, or even told about it in advance. Instead he received the news while attending a conference at the National Film Theatre. Milne was passed a note with the simple message: 'The new Chairman is Marmaduke Hussey.' He had never heard of him. As Milne screwed his face into a puzzled expression the conference speaker, Channel Four's

Jeremy Isaacs, broke off from his text and asked if Milne knew who his new boss was. Milne said he did. 'Will you tell us who it is then?' Isaacs asked. Milne thought for a moment and said: 'No, you'll have to wait.'

Isaacs persisted: 'Well, are you pleased?' Milne descended into perplexed thought. Hussey? Wait a minute. Yes, he had heard of him. He was some sort of retired newspaper executive, wasn't he? Didn't he run a small commercial radio station in the West Country or somewhere? Certainly no tycoon. What the hell were they playing at? Isaacs again asked if he was pleased. Milne's face broke into a wry smile: 'I'm intrigued,' he said.

Back at Broadcasting House the Governors were eating lunch in the boardroom when they got the news. They were as clueless as Milne and one of their number was sent to look up their new leader in *Who's Who*. Marmaduke Hussey was meanwhile having his photograph taken on the street outside, cracking jokes with journalists.

The appointment had sent the hacks scurrying to their clippings libraries. Compared with the bulging files available on most public figures, the Hussey file was alarmingly slim. A few yellowing newspaper cuttings revealed he was married to Lady Susan, one of the Queen's Ladies in Waiting, and that he had led the management side in the disastrous 1979 strike at Times Newspapers. After that the trail went cold.

Hussey told the hacks he was as surprised as everyone else by the appointment. He claimed Douglas Hurd, the Home Secretary, had called him out of the blue. The new Chairman chuckled that he knew very little about broadcasting and absolutely nothing about the BBC. He even claimed he had not known where the BBC was based. Lady Susan had looked it up in the phone book and even then he was not sure whether to turn up at Broadcasting House or Television Centre.

The hacks cheered up. This was great material. With his inane grin, aristocratic bearing, funny name and, as they soon discovered, false leg, this cheery old buffer seemed like

the ideal candidate for the Monty Python Upper Class Twit
of the Year Award. He seemed bound to provide them with
reams of entertaining copy over the coming months.

Marmaduke Hussey was born in 1923, a product of the
comfortable interwar middle classes. His father, Eric, had
been a colonial administrator and Olympic hurdler. He was
educated at Rugby School and then went to Trinity College,
Oxford, for one year before being called up to join the
Grenadier Guards and fight in World War Two. He was a
platoon commander by the time he had his first and last taste
of action at Anzio in February 1944. He was almost killed by
machine-gun fire.

'I was only in action for five days,' he later said, 'but I have
spent the rest of my life celebrating the fact I came up against
the worst marksman in the German army.' Hussey's leg was
amputated in a German field hospital and then, with his back
still full of lead, he was sent to Colditz where he was fitted
with a false leg. Seven months later he was repatriated. The
camp commandant was convinced Hussey was about to die.

The injury and operation had left him in constant pain that
required considerable courage to overcome and work normally. But Hussey was philosophical about his war wound,
chirping: 'First they shot it off, then they put it back on
again. Doesn't make sense, does it?'

After the war Hussey was in and out of hospital for years,
somehow completing his degree and taking a management
training course. He had done well on the financial side of the
newspaper business and married into the aristocracy. His
wife, Lady Susan, was the sister of William Waldegrave, the
blue-blooded Conservative politician. Hussey played up to
the aristocratic image by shortening his first name to Duke,
and picked up the half-affectionate nickname 'Dukey'.

By the time he took the BBC job he was a regular visitor
to Buckingham Palace, where he would use the swimming-
pool, and was well known to the Queen. He told people the
story of how, when he once fell down the notorious Palace
stairs, the Queen had rushed over to ask if he needed a

doctor. 'No, no,' he replied, nodding cheerfully towards his artificial leg: 'I think I need a blacksmith.'

Hussey's newspaper career peaked in the 1970s when he moved from Associated Newspapers, publishers of the *Daily Mail*, to become Managing Director of Times Newspapers. He complained he spent 90 per cent of his time dealing with unofficial strikes. In November 1978 Hussey gave an ultimatum to the unions: either they agreed to stop the strikes, accept staff cuts and flexible working hours, or he would suspend publication of *The Times* and the *Sunday Times*. The unions called Hussey's bluff and the papers disappeared from the news-stands for a year before he was obliged to organise a humiliating retreat. The papers resumed production after some concessions on the union side.

The Thomson Group sold the papers to Rupert Murdoch soon afterwards and, surprisingly, Hussey was one of the few members of the old management to keep his job. But he was given the unimportant role of preparing for the paper's bicentenary; effectively a retirement posting. Hussey's Palace connections would smooth the way for the Royal visits that would be the climax of the celebrations.

Now that Hussey had turned up at the BBC there was immediate suspicion that 'Dukey' would operate as a fifth-columnist in Murdoch's campaign against the BBC. In reality Murdoch had played no part in Hussey's appointment. He was just as surprised as everyone else and rang Charles Wilson, the editor of *The Times*. 'You'll never guess who they've chosen to run the BBC,' he drawled with great hilarity: 'Old Dukey!'

Later, over lunch, Milne found Hussey genial, but oddly cool. The new Chairman went to great lengths to explain that the Prime Minister had played no role in his appointment. Milne had asked nevertheless if he knew what she was thinking. 'I've never met the woman,' Hussey said. Milne thought this astonishing.

Milne then turned the conversation to the subject of his own future and asked if there was any chance of an extension to his contract. He had been Director General for almost five years. He was contracted for six and a half but was promised an extension of at least one year when he took the job. Hussey was irritated by the request: 'We'll have to see about all that,' he said, directing the conversation back to the immediate future.

Hussey said he wanted to talk individually to each of the Governors and all senior BBC staff before he said anything about the future. Milne started to talk about arrangements when Hussey butted in. 'I shall book a table at Claridge's and have people for lunch every day,' he boomed. Milne, nonplussed, said that might be a bit expensive. But Hussey insisted: 'No, no. It is very important. It must be Claridge's.'

Hussey then said he was very unhappy about an edition of *Panorama* called *Maggie's Militant Tendency*, which dealt with alleged extremist infiltration of the Conservative Party. The programme had led to legal action from backbench MPs and the case was about to go to court. Milne said he was handling the problem; but that he could talk to the BBC's lawyers if he liked. This was bad news. The programme, at the time, was a major cause of friction between the BBC and the Conservative Party.

*Maggie's Militant Tendency* had been broadcast almost three years earlier and the story had its roots in the 1983 general election. Conservative Central Office had disowned Thomas Finnegan, its candidate for Stockton, after it was discovered that he was a supporter of an extreme-right political group. The story was covered by reporters working in the BBC's Election Special team who were later contacted by a group of Young Conservatives claiming they had an official report showing extremist infiltration was widespread and growing. When the report was endorsed by the executive committee of the National Union of Conservative Associations, *Panorama* was offered an exclusive.

The programme was meticulously checked and rechecked at every stage. A massive quantity of documentary evidence was accumulated, and sworn statements were gathered. The

BBC's lawyers went through it all for days, as did senior journalists and editorial executives. After the film was made it was shown to a meeting of the BBC's top editorial people including Milne's chief political adviser Margaret Douglas, Chris Capron, then head of current affairs, and Glenn Del Medico, one of the Corporation's most experienced lawyers.

Milne arrived back from a trip to India after *Maggie's Militant Tendency*'s screening to find the press again in full cry. The charge was led by the *Daily Mail* which headlined its story LIES, DAMN LIES AND PANORAMA. The Conservatives were demanding an apology for the programme and withdrawal of all the allegations. Party Chairman John Selwyn Gummer was livid.

Milne looked at the research for the programme, examined the evidence and pronounced it 'rock solid'. He and Alan Protheroe, the Assistant Director General, met Gummer and Conservative chief whip John Wakeham, who produced a list of forty alleged inaccuracies or examples of bias. These ranged from matters of fact to the way that film of present-day right-wing meetings had been interwoven with archive material featuring the German Nazis of the 1930s. Milne said he could answer all the points without much difficulty.

Gummer then introduced the menacing figure of Edward Du Cann, a leading Conservative lawyer, who came up with additional charges backed with talk of a libel action. The involvement of Du Cann showed the Conservatives were taking the matter very seriously. It soon emerged that the Prime Minister was also taking a personal interest. One of the backbenchers shown by the programme to be dealing with extremists was Gerald Howarth, the MP for Cannock. Howarth was later to become the Prime Minister's parliamentary private secretary.

Milne went through the complaints again, several times, and each time assured Gummer and his colleagues that all the accusations could be countered with facts, or were matters of opinion and fair comment. Back at the BBC he dismissed the complaints as an attempt at political intimidation, which was to be expected after a hard-hitting programme like this. Milne declared the matter closed, as far as he was concerned, and left Protheroe to deal with it.

Early official action against the programme came from Joan Mason, leader of an anti-immigration pressure group called Welsh, Irish, Scottish and English Association (WISE). She was featured organising meetings with Conservative MPs. Unable to get a libel action off the ground, Mason had taken the BBC to a Broadcasting Complaints Commission hearing. When things did not go well for her she flew into a foul-mouthed rage and had to be dragged from the room shrieking: 'You buggers, I'll get you buggers!'

After this harmless skirmish the BBC faced a much more worrying threat: libel writs from some of the Conservative MPs featured in the film. The first, from Harvey Proctor, was withdrawn at an early stage. The MP for Billericay agreed to drop his action soon after he started it. In return the BBC promised never to reveal he had given up his complaint. (He was later driven out of politics after involvement in a homosexual rent-boy 'spanking' scandal.)

The other two writs were from Gerald Howarth and Neil Hamilton, the Tory MP for Tatton. At first it seemed they might drop their action on similar terms to Proctor. Protheroe went to negotiate directly in a series of meetings at the Institute of Directors in Pall Mall. He went to the meetings 'wired up' with a concealed tape recorder. There was a tricky moment at one of the meetings when the tape ran out and began flapping about, making a terrible din. Protheroe explained it away as a new type of telephone bleeper and disappeared off to the lavatory to fix it.

Protheroe reported the results to Stuart Young. The Chairman was involved with a number of Jewish charities, and was genuinely horrified by the evidence of neo-Nazi activity uncovered by *Panorama*. He thought the programme was excellent, the perfect example of the BBC carrying out its public service role. Young was backing Milne's strategy of not giving an inch, and it seemed to be paying off. The case went quiet.

But then Stuart Young died. Lord Barnett took over as acting Chairman, and everything changed. Inside the BBC the programme was still thought to be, in Milne's phrase, 'rock solid'. But whereas Young had been keen on defending every word of the programme, his successors saw it more as a nuisance and liability that should be laid to rest as quickly as possible. Hamilton and Howarth began to press harder, and the case was scheduled to appear in court in October 1986; coinciding, as it happened, with the appointment of Marmaduke Hussey as BBC Chairman.

BBC journalists covering the Conservative Party conference were told by an indiscreet, but very well informed senior Tory that at least one of the Governors was dealing separately with Conservative Central Office and they were going to force the BBC to cave in the minute the case started.

The trial was now imminent and in the remaining couple of weeks Protheroe tried again, without success, to negotiate a settlement. The BBC's lawyers thought their chances of winning in court had dropped to 40/60, mainly because some of the witnesses had 'turned shy' and could not be relied on to turn up in court. But these were still very good odds in a libel case, and ought to be enough to deter Howarth and Hamilton from taking the risk of losing and paying the huge estimated costs. It was not to be. Protheroe was still pushing for a settlement hours before the case opened in the High Court on October 13.

Richard Hartley, Hamilton's lawyer, delivered a ferocious opening statement. It was the BBC and not the MPs who had behaved like fascists, he said. *Panorama*'s 'attempts to deceive were breathtaking. What we saw on the screen was trial by television at its worst.' The programme had painted a picture of widespread extremist activity and 'into this stinking cesspit of unbelievable evil the BBC has dropped a number of people including Mr Hamilton,' Hartley thundered. 'It was as if Madame Tussaud's were to put Mr Hamilton into the Chamber of Horrors.'

Hartley's opening statement was due to last four days, with the BBC being painted as a monstrous organisation, persecuting two innocent public servants out of pure political spite.

The opening statement was reported by a universally hostile press under banner headlines. DR GOEBBELS TACTICS BY BBC, roared the *Daily Mail*. A member of the BBC defence team's spirits dropped when he noticed the court correspondents surrounding Howarth in the court's foyer. One of the reporters was overheard telling him: 'You have got nothing to worry about. We are backing you all the way on this. Wait until the BBC's Governors read my paper tomorrow.' Barnett summoned Milne and Protheroe and told them he wanted the matter settled immediately on any terms Howarth and Hamilton wanted. The press coverage was so hostile that the longer the case went on, the more damage it would do, he said.

Milne protested, and Protheroe backed him. He still felt there was an excellent chance of winning. Having gone this far the BBC should at least offer a proper defence. The BBC's own QC had said it would be fatal to settle before cross-examining the witnesses. Barnett became angry. He turned on Protheroe and told him he had spoken to all the Governors and they wanted it stopped immediately: 'in hours, not days'. There would be no more discussion. This was an 'instruction'.

Protheroe dejectedly passed on the bad news to the BBC's legal team who were meeting downstairs in Broadcasting House. Glenn Del Medico, the lawyer who had prepared the BBC's case, could not believe the decision. They had followed the same strategy for six months. He told the meeting the decision was 'quite astounding' and 'wholly unacceptable.' The entire BBC hierarchy, including the Chairman, Governors and legal department, had been kept informed and had decided to back the programme 'to the hilt' as a matter of policy. Just what had changed?

Michael Cockerell, one of the reporters on the programme, supplied an answer: 'We have got a new Chairman'. Cockerell wondered if Hussey or the Governors had subverted the case as had been rumoured at the Conservative Party conference. There was no shortage of people on the Board with strong links to the Conservative Party.

Mrs Thatcher had taken a greater interest in the membership of the Board than most previous prime ministers. She had rigorously applied the 'One of Us' principle. A long list of useful people had been nominated by Milne and others, only to be vetoed by Downing Street. Names included Ludovic Kennedy's wife Moira Shearer and John Mortimer, the creator of *Rumpole*. He did not seem to stand much chance after being described by John Butcher, a member of the Government, as an 'upmarket punk' who 'based his career on running down Britain'.

Nominees like Mortimer were rejected in favour of people more acceptable to Downing Street. After the arrival of William Rees-Mogg, the classic Thatcherite appointee, most people thought, was Daphne Park of MI6, the Principal of Mrs Thatcher's old Oxford college, Somerville. In 1983 Park had severely criticised the refusal of her fellow academics to grant the traditional honorary advanced degree to the Prime Minister on the grounds that she had inflicted 'deep and systematic damage to the whole public education system in Britain'. Park had failed to reverse the decision. But the Prime Minister, who had been upset by the insult, could be assumed to be grateful for her support.

Downing Street did accept Milne's nominee for the job of Scottish Governor. This was Watson Peat, a farmer and amateur radio ham. Milne, a former controller of BBC Scotland and Gaelic speaker, took a great interest in this particular appointment. As part of his theatrical Scottishness he had twice appeared on the social fringe at broadcasting jamborees wearing a kilt and playing the bagpipes. Milne thought he could work with Peat but soon realised he had made a mistake. The Scottish Governor turned out to be a

dedicated right-winger of the 'hang 'em and flog 'em' persuasion, as Milne later put it.

Political balance on the Board was theoretically maintained by including a representative of the trade union
movement. But this turned out to be the oddball figure of Sir
John Boyd, the former president of the Confederation of
Shipbuilding and Engineering Unions. In Labour movement
terms he was about as far to the right as it was possible to
be: a Mary Whitehouse-type Christian and a keen member of
a Salvation Army marching band. Milne thought he was
'messianic'.

Del Medico said Hamilton's solicitors had been seen talking
to John Selwyn Gummer that week, doubtless discussing
tactics. The BBC had endured Hartley's opening and had no
chance of making a reply. The case was being handled in a
way that would inflict maximum damage. Everything Hartley was saying would go on the record without challenge.
'Tebbit has got us now,' he concluded.

Protheroe was depressed, but pragmatic. This was
obviously the showdown between the Government and the
Corporation they had all feared. But there was not much
they could do about it. 'The carpet has been pulled from
under us,' he said.

The case was settled. After all the fuss, the two MPs
received £20,000 in damages; which the BBC considered a
derisory sum considering the seriousness of the allegations
that had not, at the end of the day, been tested in court.
Howarth's and Hamilton's activities had, in any case, only
formed a small part of the allegations made in the programme. More important material had not been legally
challenged or contested at all.

*Maggie's Militant Tendency* became a byword for inaccurate and biased television journalism. Instead of the relatively
small damages paid, the press reported the £550,000 cost of
mounting the case, which the BBC also had to pay. One
hundred Conservative MPs tabled a motion deploring the
way the BBC had wasted half a million pounds and called for

Milne's resignation and 'restoration of proper standards at the BBC'.

The Director General tried to calm things down. He told the Board of Management that they should 'weather the storm' and wait for it to blow over. But only days after the *Maggie's Militant Tendency* settlement Norman Tebbit was on the warpath again, describing the BBC's coverage of the American bombing of Libya, fronted by Kate Adie, as 'a mixture of news, views, speculation, error and uncritical carriage of Libyan propaganda'.

The attack involved Milne in a wearisome exchange of letters but he was, for once, backed by the Governors. Otherwise the rift between Milne, Protheroe and the Board of Management on the one side and the Governors on the other had widened into an unbridgeable gulf.

# PART TWO

# 5

## *Men of Honour*

Alasdair Milne was sacked after a regular meeting of the Board of Governors on January 29 1987. The Director General's last ally on the Board, the Welsh national Governor Alwyn Roberts, had retired the previous evening, giving Milne resounding support in his farewell speech. Roberts had warned the other Governors against the dangers of giving in to Government pressure. The speech had not gone down well. One of the Governors, Sir John Boyd, was heard to mutter: 'This is all nonsense. You wait until tomorrow.'

The Governors were charged with steering the BBC on matters of grand strategy and generally representing the public interest as part of a ramified network of regional and specialist advisory boards. Led by the Chairman, their main power was the right to hire and fire the Director General, which they now exercised.

Marmaduke Hussey met each Governor individually and secured their support for sacking Milne. Hussey said he had spent all his time since arriving at the BBC talking to people and listening. Everyone who mattered inside the Corporation and outside wanted Milne to go.

Most of the Governors agreed without hesitation. They were still annoyed by the way the Director General had resisted the appointment of Checkland, the accountant, as Deputy at a time when it was obvious the BBC needed to concentrate on its finances.

Most of them did not like Milne's style. He rarely responded to criticism. They thought he was arrogant and complained that he passed the buck and was rude to his staff. In Board meetings he would just sit back, kick off one of his suede shoes and let Protheroe take the rap for any bad decisions. Whenever there was a crisis he seemed to be missing. During *Real Lives* he was off fishing in Scandinavia and nobody could get hold of him at first. The arrival of Hussey and Barnett, some Governors thought, gave him the chance to make a fresh start. Instead he had gone into a sulk.

The next day, knowing they were about to sack him, the Governors joined Milne and other senior BBC staff in the sixth-floor conference room at Television Centre. Not a word was said about the decision. The morning session of the meeting went ahead as normal. The Governors took their places and a discussion about programme strategy took place, led by Michael Grade, the BBC 1 controller.

Grade was keen to get through the agenda so that he could set off on a skiing holiday. When he finished, the Board took a coffee break and everything was sweetness and light. Grade said his goodbyes and Hussey boomed that he should enjoy his holiday and forget all about the BBC. With that Grade rushed off, picked up his anorak from his flat in Victoria and jumped in his car to catch the three o'clock ferry from Dover.

Grade was just passing Canterbury when the car phone trilled. It was Graeme McDonald, the controller of BBC 2: 'Michael, sorry to bother you. But Bill Cotton is going to ring you in a minute. I thought you ought to know the Governors have just fired Alasdair.' Grade almost swerved into the central barrier. 'Why? What's happening?' he yelped. McDonald said he did not have the details. 'Bill will call you,' he said, and rang off.

Grade was left clutching the steering-wheel, eyes bulging and wondering if he should get off the motorway and head back to London. Cotton rang a couple of minutes later and confirmed the news. Milne had signed a letter of resignation and had already gone home. Hussey was saying there would be no other immediate changes, and the job would be advertised in the normal way. There was nothing anyone could do. He should carry on with his holiday, but keep in touch.

Milne's 'execution', as he was later to call it, had taken place about an hour after Grade left Television Centre. The morning session ended at 1 pm and the Governors set off downstairs for lunch. Milne, still completely unaware of what was about to happen, went to collect Michael Checkland, his Deputy, and Bill Cotton from the Managing Director's office.

The three men were just about to join the Governors when Patricia Hodgson, the BBC secretary, appeared. 'Alasdair,' she said reticently, 'will you come and see the Chairman.' Milne thought this was odd. Hodgson was a prim and fastidious woman and had never before used his christian name in public. Her tone was very serious, as though she was about to announce the death of a close relative.

Milne left his two colleagues and followed Hodgson silently down the corridor to Hussey's room. He found the Chairman and Barnett standing awkwardly behind the desk. There were no pleasantries, and Hussey's lip trembled as he said: 'I am afraid this is going to be a very unpleasant interview. We want you to leave immediately. It's a unanimous decision of the Board.' Barnett added abruptly: 'We want to make changes. We can't under the present circumstances.'

Milne glared in silence. What was it all about? Could they sack him without any discussion or explanation? These two men had only been involved with the BBC for a matter of months. He had worked there for over thirty years. They had sat through the Board meeting all morning without saying a word. Hussey interrupted Milne's thoughts, his voice quickening: 'It is a unanimous decision. You might prefer to resign, er, for personal reasons.' Barnett added: 'We are men of honour. If you resign it won't affect your arrangements.'

Milne said nothing. Since arriving as Chairman, Hussey had been oddly cool towards him; but the Director General thought this would change in time. In his own mind Milne was still the bright young man who had enjoyed a rapid rise to the top through sheer talent. In a daze, Milne asked for a piece of paper, leaned forward and began to write his resignation letter. He had to ask what the date was. He handed the letter to Hussey.

The meeting had lasted less than five minutes. The ex-Director General went to his own office, picked up his briefcase, told his personal assistant, Ros Sloboda, he had been fired and went to see Cotton and Checkland, who were still waiting to go down to lunch.

'What was all that about?' Checkland asked with mild concern. 'They've fired me,' Milne replied. Cotton knew Milne had asked for an extension to his contract, and was unlikely to get it. 'You mean they aren't going to renew your contract when it comes up?' he asked. 'No, no,' Milne said, 'they want me out.'

Cotton and Checkland glanced at each other. 'When?' they asked. 'Now' Milne replied, adding emotionally: 'I am not going to give them the pleasure of sacking me. I have resigned.' He said they could discuss it later. Then he left. Milne was driven to his home in Holland Park Avenue. Half an hour later a letter arrived formally accepting his resignation and thanking him for his many years of service.

Back at Television Centre, Checkland was called in to see Hussey, who asked him to run the Board of Management until a new Director General was found. He was then told to join the Governors for lunch, which he did. Cotton was called in next as, effectively, number three in the hierarchy. 'I expect you want to know why this has happened?' Hussey asked. Cotton said he did not. If the Director General had resigned, he had resigned. Cotton did not want to talk to them about it until he had seen Milne first.

Next into Hussey's office was Michael Bunce, the BBC's

satin-tongued public relations man. He had been completely unaware of what was going to happen. After the morning session with the Governors he had left Television Centre for a lunch in Cavendish Square, only to be called back to see the Chairman on urgent business. Hussey handed Bunce a statement and told him to release it to the press at once. With that the Chairman went downstairs to join the mixture of Governors and senior staff who were by now finishing their first course.

The Governors, and now Checkland and Cotton, knew what had happened. But the rest of staff were still as clueless as Milne had been. Hussey had gone to the length of instructing the catering staff not to put place names round the table, as was normal, so that there would not be an embarrassing gap next to him at the top of the table.

Hussey called the gathering to order by tapping on the side of a wine glass with a spoon, like the best man at a wedding reception. 'The Director General', Hussey announced, 'has resigned for personal reasons.' He looked round the table and added: 'Now there's a conversation stopper.' And with that Hussey sat down and started eating. The Governors stiffened and the staff were dumbstruck. Some took the announcement at face value. Everyone knew Milne's wife Sheila had been ill with cancer for a long time.

All eyes turned to Checkland. He looked excited, and preoccupied with the new responsibilities suddenly thrust upon him. But he was saying nothing, and everyone else followed suit. Most people were wondering what would happen to them; and who was going to get what job in the inevitable reshuffle.

Within minutes Alasdair Milne was history, soon to join the portraits of other ex-Director Generals hung on the walls of the council chamber in Broadcasting House. Alan Protheroe excused himself and went straight round to see Milne. The former Director General had arrived home to an empty house. Sheila was out shopping and did not arrive back until later in the afternoon.

Protheroe found Milne pacing the floor, still in deep shock and barely able to talk. Another nasty aspect of the affair hit home. Hussey had wanted Milne to go quietly. He had obviously worked out that people who knew about Sheila's illness might well believe Milne had resigned for the 'personal reasons' mentioned in the official BBC statement.

Milne and Protheroe were soon joined by Michael Bunce, the public relations man who had issued Hussey's statement. He gave Milne a copy so that he would at least know what the BBC had said about him when the inevitable pack of journalists arrived on his doorstep. It was a hard moment for Bunce. He would have liked to have handled the press for his old boss, but knew this would be impossible in the circumstances. Instead he arranged for a former colleague to keep the hacks at bay.

The next morning most of the papers reported the story in full and gleeful detail. MILNE QUITS BBC IN CRISIS OF CONFIDENCE was how *The Times* headlined the story, quoting one Governor saying: 'I am not aware of his being pushed. It was his personal decision.'

When the importance of what had been done began to sink in there was amazement at the degree of cool and ruthlessness Hussey had shown. Years later all those involved would remember the event, and the tinkling sound of someone tapping a wineglass would still set their teeth on edge.

Inside the BBC manoeuvring for the succession to Milne began at once. The BBC could be like the court of an Eastern potentate where all claimants to the throne were slaughtered when one Emperor replaced another. Outgoing Director Generals usually took great pains to ensure they nominated an heir. The man seen as Milne's natural successor was Brian Wenham, the Managing Director of BBC Radio.

Wenham had been recruited to the BBC from ITN in 1969 and placed in charge of Lime Grove for a while, where he developed a reputation as the BBC's in-house intellectual. Milne had wanted to make him Assistant Director General with special responsibility for trouble-shooting in current affairs. But Wenham, showing the intelligence for which he was famous, decided the job was a bed of nails and turned it down. The job went to Alan Protheroe.

Wenham had since been involved in the public slanging matches about the BBC, putting the case for a higher licence fee and writing the BBC's reply to the Peacock Committee. In 1984, during the row over *The Thorn Birds,* Max Hastings accused Wenham of being one of the 'forces driving the BBC out of control'. Wenham had set about Hastings in reply, reeling off a long list of the BBC's achievements, and dismissing most of the criticism.

Wenham's tussle with Hastings made him popular inside the BBC, and might have been seen as staking a claim to the Director General's job after Milne. But it did not go down so well with Downing Street. William Rees-Mogg opposed Wenham's promotion inside the Corporation, calling him a cynic and a man with no conviction.

Now, after Milne's abrupt departure, an advertisement appeared in the papers inviting applications from 'suitably qualified candidates' for Director General of the British Broadcasting Corporation. Both Wenham and Checkland put their names forward, fulfilling a prophecy Wenham had made some five years earlier. After Milne's arrival Checkland had been promoted to become Director of Resources for BBC television, working alongside Wenham as Director of Programmes. At the time Checkland told colleagues how he had overheard Wenham saying they would one day have to fight it out for the Director General's job. 'I don't know where Brian gets his ideas from,' Checkland said at the time. 'They'll never have someone like me as Director General. Anyway I don't think about these things, I just get on with my job.'

Hussey did not want either of them. His own choice was David Dimbleby, the famous BBC presenter and a member of the Dimbleby broadcasting dynasty. Most of the Board of Management thought this was a barmy idea. Although he was one of the BBC's best-known faces he was, in practice, an 'outsider' who worked as a contracted freelance and had never been on the staff. Most of his experience was in Lime Grove, where he was not always popular with colleagues.

Other executives were worried about Dimbleby's lack of organisational experience. He was the owner of a chain of local newspapers in South West London. But in 1984 he provoked a year-long strike by moving the papers to a non-union printing plant. Labour movement figures like Neil Kinnock refused to be interviewed by him, which meant Dimbleby had not been able to cover the Party conferences. The dispute spilled over into the BBC where a meeting of about 100 members of the Lime Grove branch of the journalists' union had debated 'blacking' him altogether. This had not happened, but the vote was very close. The whole affair had caused an emotional and damaging split amongst the staff.

Hussey evidently did not care about this. The Chairman had endured a similar experience during the strike at *The Times*. If anything Dimbleby's robust union-busting was to his credit. Dimbleby was his man, and he was determined to have him.

Michael Grade arrived back from his skiing holiday horrified to find that David Dimbleby was the front runner for Director General. Realising candidates from the existing Board of Management, including Wenham, stood little chance, Grade and Bill Cotton looked for an alternative and sounded out Paul Fox, a former BBC1 controller who had moved on to run Yorkshire TV. Fox made his name in sports journalism, then edited *Panorama* and was controller of BBC1 between 1967 and 1973. Fox was remembered at the BBC as a managerial bull in a china shop, but had since evolved into the industry's elder statesman.

Fox told Cotton and Grade he would not apply for the job, and would certainly not subject himself to an interview. But he would be happy to talk to the Governors if Hussey invited him to apply.

Cotton and Grade went round to Hussey's Chelsea flat to get him to consider Fox. Cotton said Fox was a substantial industry figure. He had immense management experience and had helped transform the fortunes of Yorkshire TV at a difficult time. He would be a reassuring figure after the traumas of the Milne period, and would be the ideal choice to lead a more commercial BBC. Hussey listened politely. He gave nothing away, but agreed to meet Fox.

A few days later the Chairman invited Fox to meet the Governors and then consider putting himself forward as a candidate. Fox refused. 'If you want to draw up a list of candidates,' he said, 'that's fine. But I am not going to be on it.' Fox warned Hussey against appointing David Dimbleby. He was an excellent TV performer, one of the best in the business, but a man incapable of running the proverbial whelk stall. He then bowed out of the contest.

With Fox out of the frame, Cotton encouraged Grade to make an application himself. Both men knew he had no chance of getting the job. Grade was mainly interested in using the interview to establish his claim to become Managing Director of the Television Service. Cotton was due to retire in eighteen months and he wanted Grade to take his place. He told his protégé: 'Let them see the colour of your money. It'll be good experience for you.'

Grade duly put in his application, joining the five other candidates whittled down from the 130 hopefuls who applied. The other 'insider' candidates were Brian Wenham and Michael Checkland. They were up against Dimbleby, still the bookies' favourite, and two other outsiders: Tony Smith, Director of the British Film Institute, and Jeremy Isaacs of Channel Four, who started out with the backing of the Vice Chairman, Joel Barnett.

The interviews began at 10 am and a result was expected in time to provide an exclusive for BBC 1's Six O'Clock News. Checkland was interviewed in the morning. This was a distinct advantage. The Deputy Director General had a contingent of supporters on the Board. And they all knew that he had been highly thought of by Stuart Young. They were grateful for the way he swept up after Milne. The down side was that he was not an editorial man and, some thought, did not sound like or have the look of a Director General. The consensus was that Checkland was an able but rather dull man, an ideal Number Two but not a real leader.

Checkland prepared his application very carefully to counter these negative points. He came with a complete organisational blueprint for the BBC's future, the 'Five Year Plan' he had been working up to ever since becoming Director of Television Resources in the early 1980s. Checkland also seemed prepared to get on with the large staff cuts implied by the Peacock Report. Again, he seemed to have a workable plan of how to bring this about. Another proposal involved the merger of the BBC's news and current affairs departments into a single journalistic unit. This, he said, would both save money and make central control easier. Hussey was especially keen on this.

The Governors were pleasantly surprised. This was no mere technician, as some had thought. Checkland was a man of vision, who had a complete strategy for the future and, after Milne's arm's-length attitude, was keen to involve them in the detailed management of the BBC.

Brian Wenham performed well at his interview, but this did not help him much. He could claim some credit for the BBC 1 ratings triumph two years earlier when he was Director of Television Programmes. Wenham got the feeling the 'hard right' faction on the Board, led by Boyd, Daphne Park and Hussey himself, were not at all impressed. There was some interest when Hussey asked him about the idea of merging BBC news and current affairs. Wenham was opposed to the plan.

The existing, separate news and current affairs operations were already very powerful, he said, and they had an endless appetite for money and access to the schedules. A merged news and current affairs directorate would hugely outweigh the other departments. It would become a black hole, its sheer gravity soaking up more and more of the licence fee and leaving little money for anything else.

Wenham later said the merger would end up costing 'an arm and a leg', which was an unfortunate turn of phrase with the monopede Hussey pressing for the change. It would be very bureaucratic, creating a new line of management that would cut across radio and television. Wenham's opposition to the merger finished off his application. He was written off as backward-looking and wedded to the status quo.

The Governors listened politely to Michael Grade. Although he did not think he would get the job, Grade prepared his application meticulously. He went to the lengths of getting some television chums, including John Birt of LWT, to come round to his house and rehearse the interview.

Grade told the Governors he supported the merger of news and current affairs. The existing system, he said, was deeply flawed because one department was responsible for commissioning the programmes and another for transmitting them. The channel controllers needed more power over the departments that made programmes, including current affairs. Above all, the BBC needed a strong Managing Director for the Television Service, the job he planned to apply for next year. They nodded, thanked him and crossed his name off the list.

Tony Smith was the candidate least likely to succeed. Some Governors thought he gave the best performance of all the candidates on the day; and it was agreed that he had run the British Film Institute very well. But the BFI was a much smaller organisation than the BBC, and Smith did not have much recent programme-making experience.

The Board moved on to the bookies' two front runners: Dimbleby and Isaacs. Both of them ran into difficulties on the day. Isaacs had done well at Channel Four, a 'publisher-broadcaster' with no production resources of its own, almost entirely screening programmes made by independents. Issacs' experience with independents was useful, but he struck most of the Governors as being just as arrogant as Wenham and Milne. He mentioned he had already been offered the job of running the Royal Opera House, which was very attractive, and behaved as though the Governors ought to be trying to persuade him to take the BBC job. He was unruffled when Sir John Boyd, the 'messianic' right-wing trade-union moralist who had given Milne so much grief, interjected: 'You do not seem to me like a man who takes kindly to discipline. Now I see by your smile that you take that as a compliment, but I can assure you some of us here see it as a criticism.' The odds on Isaacs lengthened.

The Governors were impressed by David Dimbleby's grasp of television but realised he knew next to nothing about radio and the commercial side of the BBC. They were also worried that as a television presenter he would have difficulty coping with the fine detail and office routine of managing a huge organisation like the BBC. This had been part of the problem with Milne, and the Governors did not want to appoint another reluctant administrator.

The last interview finished at 4 pm and the Board began to debate the relative merits of the candidates. Of the two favourites, Jeremy Isaacs was the first to be rejected. Some of the Governors spoke in his favour, but they could not overcome the hostility of Boyd. And the signals coming from Downing Street were clear enough. The Government did not care who they appointed so long as it was not Wenham or Isaacs.

Hussey was pleased. It seemed that his man, Dimbleby, was going to have a clear run. But the Governors were annoyed that Hussey was pushing so hard for his favoured candidate. After the months of division on the Board it was important, they thought, that the Governors worked as a team in the interests of the BBC.

The result was deadlock, and the meeting went on for hours after the 6 pm deadline. Individual Governors kept ringing down to reception to rearrange official cars booked to whisk them away. Dimbleby, who had gone up to Eton to see his son perform in the school play, kept calling in to see what was going on. But nobody knew.

Outside on the street the rumour had begun to circulate

amongst the shivering journalists that Paul Fox had made a late application and the Governors had gone on speaking to him late into the evening. The story was based on a tip-off from Yorkshire TV that Fox had left Leeds that very afternoon for an evening meeting in London. He was obviously going to be a surprise appointment. What other explanation could there be?

They were wrong. Fox was at a London club having dinner with the head of the Halifax Building Society. When the dinner finished at about 10 pm Fox ordered his chauffeur to drive to Broadcasting House with the wicked idea of sneaking in the back door and emerging through the front, just to wind up the hacks and get his picture in the papers. But eyeing the scene through the car window he thought better of the idea and set off home.

Inside Broadcasting House the Governors were wearily coming to a conclusion. Some had started arguing for the appointment of Michael Checkland the minute the discussion started. The Deputy Director General had performed well at his interview and there was a feeling that an organisation man was needed at the top. He could be given the normal five-year term to put his plans into operation. When the BBC was put on a firm financial footing they could look around for a younger man to 'inject a bit of editorial dynamism', as one of them put it.

Hussey hung on to the end, but finally realised Checkland would have to be appointed, and that the decision would have to be unanimous. Switching his vote was a painful decision and explaining it to Dimbleby might be difficult. Then he had a clever idea. He would soften the personal blow by offering Dimbleby the job Checkland was vacating: the Deputy Director Generalship.

Checkland would be appointed Director General, but Dimbleby could still be in charge of journalism, as intended, as Deputy Director General with Checkland looking after the money and the rest of the organisation. The decision was made, and the news was held back for a few minutes, until 10.30 pm, to stop ITN's News at Ten getting the story.

Checkland was called into Hussey's office and told he was to be Director General, but Dimbleby would still be in overall charge of the important business of news and current affairs as his deputy. But Checkland asked if accepting Dimbleby was a condition of his own appointment. Hussey had to confess he had not agreed that with the Board. Checkland's appointment was about to be announced to the nation. It could not be changed now. Hussey had to concede that it was not a condition. Checkland said he would think about it.

Marmaduke Hussey seemed less than impressed by the appointment. Telephoning Jeremy Isaacs to tell him Checkland had got the job, the Chairman confessed: 'The fact is I am slightly surprised by what we've actually done.'

# 6

## *The Vision Thing*

A lot of people in the television industry were distinctly underwhelmed by the elevation of Michael Checkland to Director General of the BBC. Journalists camped outside Broadcasting House on the evening of his appointment wondered if the BBC TV news crew would even be able to recognise their new boss.

Liz Forgan, a rising star at Channel Four, wrote in *The Listener* that the appointment showed 'no obvious sign of human inspiration'. The Governors, she thought, had taken the easy option: 'I have never heard anyone utter a bad word about Michael Checkland,' she wrote, 'but, offered a choice among the giants of broadcasting, the fact is that the Governors, in the public interest, have chosen a candidate of lesser stature.' One of the fallen giants was Jeremy Isaacs, Forgan's mentor at Channel Four, who now left the television scene and went off to run the Royal Opera House.

The *Daily Mail* described Checkland as MR NOBODY, a 'safety first' appointment. There was sympathy from his local paper in his home town of Birmingham, which proudly ran a 'local boy does well' story with the headline MR SOME-

BODY COMES HOME when he went to visit his mum to tell her about his new job.

But after Alasdair Milne's tetchy encounters with Fleet Street, Checkland's first press conference as Director General seemed like a blast of fresh air. Sue Zetter, described by the papers as his 'companion', had rushed out to Marks and Spencer to buy him a pink shirt to wear at the press conference. There was a momentary flutter of excitement as some of the papers ran TOP TELLY BOSS LOVE NEST type investigations. But it was soon discovered that Checkland's marital status was unremarkable, and that he planned to marry Ms Zetter as soon as his divorce came through. Otherwise his personal life was just as humdrum, apparently, as his career had been.

Checkland replied to the jibes that he lacked the heavyweight status of his defeated rivals, claiming he had been 'the outstanding candidate.' Complaining that he had been branded 'Michael Chequebook', the dull accountant, he was at pains to explain that, strictly speaking, he had not been an accountant for years. He was a 'management accountant', which was entirely different and much more glamorous. Over the past ten years, he said, his job had been 'making programmes happen'. He was 'more rounded than the stereotype would indicate.'

Now, as Director General, his activities were much more visible and effort was needed to sell his ideas to the Government. From now on the BBC was to be run like 'a billion-pound business', he said. Licence payers were to be regarded as 'shareholders' in the BBC plc. The idea of the Corporation as 'a billion-pound business' was a favourite phrase of Hussey's but anathema to many of the BBC's senior managers. One of them groaned: 'If Checkland wanted to run a billion-pound business, why the bloody hell didn't he go and find one?'

That weekend Checkland and the Boards of Governors and Management decamped for a think-in at the Ettington Park country hotel in Warwickshire, graced by a visit from

Douglas Hurd, the Home Secretary. There was great interest in a speech delivered by Tim Bell, the bouffant-haired image king who had helped retheme Margaret Thatcher for television. Bell had been hired by Milne to improve relations with Downing Street during the row over the licence fee, and Checkland now inherited the arrangement.

Bell launched into an extraordinary rant against the BBC 'old guard'. The BBC's problems, he said, were like those of all the public sector. It was 'producer driven'. They needed to see the public not as viewers, but as customers and shareholders. More attention would have to be paid to public presentation. Advertising was needed to tell people how good BBC programmes were, and how much they enjoyed watching them. PR companies, Bell explained, had transformed the public perception of public sector organisations like British Rail, where prices had increased but passengers were now called customers.

As others applauded loudly Brian Wenham, present as Managing Director of Radio, buried his head in his hands. He had heard this sort of talk before and thought it was poppycock; the old trick of sweet-talking the punters with a tremendous amount of blather. Corporate branding, like the soulful oil companies who ran advertising campaigns boasting how they had saved a few English country hedgerows while destroying other parts of the environment, was essentially a confidence trick. The BBC did not have an 'image problem' with the viewers, Wenham maintained, so long as they liked the programmes.

Wenham noticed Checkland was looking nervous but very pleased with himself amidst all this flattering talk of new dawns and broadcasting revolutions. The proceedings were supplying him with what US President George Bush, another man with a 'charisma deficit', was calling 'The Vision Thing': a plausible-sounding path to the future which he could repeat to show he was an exciting leader of the modern enterprise culture that was transforming the country.

Checkland joined in the giddy atmosphere by repeating

that the BBC was 'a billion-pound business' and that he intended to run it like one. Checkland said nothing to contradict Bell, and it even appeared he wanted to go further. This was the 1980s and the Director General of the BBC had to operate like the Chief Executive of a major company. His job had always been to 'make things happen'. Now he could lead from the top, hunting out economies, redirecting money into programme-making.

A lot of this talk was derived from Hussey and explicitly aimed at Downing Street. Grade had always seen the value of having Bell, with his political contacts, on the payroll. But he had been an outside consultant. Checkland was now to fortify the lobbying link to Whitehall with the appointment of another political mover and shaker, this time at the heart of the machine with a seat on the Board of Management.

Howell James was appointed as Director of Corporate Affairs partly on the strength of his political contacts, which were brilliant. He arrived fresh from the Department of Trade and Industry, where he was personal adviser to Stuart Young's brother, Lord Young.

The precocious James, still in his early thirties, was close to Mrs Thatcher's charmed circle. Before joining the DTI, he had worked as a glad-hander for Capital Radio and then TV-am where he had managed to keep smiling as the wreckage of the Peter Jay régime collapsed around his ears. He had handled the public relations challenges presented by Angela Rippon ridiculing the management live on air and Anna Ford throwing a glass of wine over Tim Aitken, the TV-am chairman, with great aplomb.

Lord Young made the DTI 'where it was at' in the world of public relations. He unleashed a tidal wave of television, newspaper and poster adverts, backed up with millions of leaflets, glossy brochures and 'bullshit packs', as they were known in the trade. Some of his campaigns, like the 'whoosh factor' Enterprise Initiative, seemed to be little more than advertising campaigns giving the impression that the Government was 'doing something' when, really, very little was happening. One leaflet blitz involved sending two million copies of a forty-page glossy booklet called *Action for Jobs!* to thousands of Post Offices at a cost of £3.5 million. Unemployment went up shortly afterwards.

With James's arrival Milne's 'straight bat' for handling criticisms was well and truly thrown out of the window. In future the BBC would 'streamline responsiveness to public criticism and provide an integrated and up-to-date package of customer services.' The Corporation, James added, would soon start 'communicating confidently and coherently to licence-payers and opinion-seekers alike the BBC's commitment to value-for-money programmes and accountability in its performance.'

Few people had the slightest idea what this might mean, but it did indeed make the BBC sound more like a multinational coporation. James's additional promise to 'develop functional international links with broadcasters and non-broadcasters, particularly Europe', struck some as odd.

With the public relations offensive beginning to take shape, it was important that Checkland was not undermined by another dust-up with the Government over current affairs programmes like *Maggie's Militant Tendency*. Checkland had seen how political rows over programmes had undermined Milne and he was anxious to avoid the same problem. The danger was especially great because he had little experience of editorial matters. And he had declined to take David Dimbleby as his deputy, in effective charge of the journalism, as Hussey had wanted.

Checkland knew that having the Chairman's candidate for Director General as his Number Two would lead to endless trouble. He told Hussey he would look for another deputy: someone from outside the BBC who could sort out news and current affairs. Checkland sought advice from Bill Cotton and Michael Grade. They suggested John Birt, programme controller at Grade's old company, LWT, and the man who had helped Grade rehearse his own application for the Director Generalship a few weeks earlier. The advice was backed by a phone call to Paul Fox, the 'missing candidate' for Director General.

Fox told Checkland that Birt was the perfect man to end the 'internecine warfare' between the separate news and current affairs fiefdoms and push through the merger of news and current affairs that Hussey wanted. The merger would inevitably leave 'blood on the floor' and it was better if the bloodletting was done by an outsider. Birt, Fox said, would not be afraid of 'knocking heads together'.

The idea of bringing Birt to the BBC was not new. Grade had suggested it at least six months earlier when he realised the Governors had lost faith in Alan Protheroe, Milne's assistant in charge of journalism. Milne thought the idea was 'crackers'. Checkland was prepared to be more open-minded and began negotiating with Birt. He told Grade he would offer him the post of Managing Director of the merged news and current affairs directorate, with a seat on the Board of Management.

When Grade heard about the plan he phoned Birt to persuade him to take the job. The salary, about £70,000, was not too good. But this was the BBC, still by far the biggest, best and most important broadcasting company in Britain, probably the world. They could rekindle the great working partnership they had enjoyed at LWT.

Grade would look after the channels as Managing Director of Television; John would mastermind news and current affairs which, in the current climate, was one of the most important parts of the operation. News and current affairs spent a lot of money and was, in many ways, the real centre of gravity in the organisation. They would have the experience and backing of Bill Cotton. Checkland would sort out the money, as he had always done. 'What we don't know about television between us is not worth knowing,' Grade enthused. 'Come on over. You'll love it. We can have a great time together; there's a big job to be done.'

Birt said he would think it over and agreed to meet Checkland at the Howard Hotel on the north bank of the

Thames, opposite the LWT tower. Birt played hard to get. One problem was money. Birt was 'enormously well rewarded', as he put it, at LWT and was about to discuss a new long-term contract which would have made him a very rich man.

Birt was especially reluctant to give up a lucrative share option scheme which, with ITV advertising revenue booming, might be worth millions. And he was still worried about what the job Checkland was offering him entailed. He had not monitored much of the BBC's current affairs output, especially on radio, for some time. But from what he had heard, it was a disaster area. To put things right, he would need absolute authority.

A few days later Checkland told Grade that Birt was on the point of accepting the job. But instead of settling for Managing Director of News and Current Affairs he wanted the title of Deputy Director General. In theory this meant Birt would outrank Grade, a reversal of the old pecking order at LWT. Did he mind? 'Not at all,' Grade replied, 'it's not a problem.' He would have too much on his plate over the next couple of years to worry about titles.

Birt then rang Grade at home to make absolutely sure he would not be slighted by the apparent role reversal. Grade again said he was not worried. All it meant was that Birt would take on the formal role of editor-in-chief when Checkland was away. 'You are going to be in charge of news and current affairs anyway,' Grade said, 'and you deputise for Mike when he's away. Great. Off we go.'

After this Birt and Checkland went round to Hussey's Chelsea flat. The three men discussed the BBC's problems. Birt shared Hussey's low opinion of BBC news and current affairs. The problems, he suspected, were the result of poor management, rather than lack of talent. He would not come as a 'firefighter', as he later put it, dealing with problems one by one. He told Hussey a complete new structure and approach to the way the BBC made its programmes was needed. Birt got the job.

Checkland announced Birt's appointment to the Board of Governors and gave them a sheet of paper outlining details of his career. He had a lot of experience in current affairs, but in recent years had been more involved with light entertainment. When he was offered the BBC job he was on course to become Managing Director of LWT at the young age of 42.

John Birt was far from the typical BBC management personality. Born into a working-class, Catholic family in 1944, Birt spent his early years in inner-city Liverpool where his grandfather had worked in the docks. After serving in the RAF, Birt's father had made something of himself as a tyre salesman. Birt was still a boy when the family bought a house in the Liverpool suburbs.

Birt was educated at St Mary's College, a Catholic school, gaining A-levels in Physics, Maths and Advanced Maths. 'It was a highly regimented form of education, underpinned by corporal punishment,' Birt later said. 'Beatings with the strap, on the hand usually, and in extreme cases on the bottom. I wasn't often beaten. I was a good pupil and did my work.' Laurie Taylor, another St Mary's pupil who later became a leading media pundit, said the school made boys sycophantic to their superiors and aggressive to those below them in any hierarchy.

After this Birt went to St Catherine's College, Oxford, in the 1960s where he studied Engineering. Oxford was a revelation to Birt. He was not to shine in his subject, ending up with a third class degree, partly because he spent so much time watching 'art house' films and taking part in the sort of cultural activities he had missed as a teenager.

His guide to the alien world of the arts was to be Jane Lake, an American art student studying at Ruskin College. Birt met her in his first term and they were married before they graduated. With Jane's help Birt became a great fan of New Wave film directors like Jean-Luc Godard, whose point was that films were an extension of the egos of their makers.

Birt eventually made his own New Wave-style film called *The Little Donkey*, inviting the London film critics to the premiere. None of them turned up. There was some admiration from Nigel Rees, a fellow undergraduate later to become a minor member of the literati, but it was spoiled by being 'full of clichés and facile symbolism', as Rees recorded in his diary at the time.

Birt was too provincial and gauche to become part of Oxford's charmed arts and media circle, centred on the Oxford Union, the traditional recruiting ground for BBC high-flyers. As he later confessed, Birt knew nothing about foreign affairs and even less about economics, which was one reason why he was rejected when he applied to the BBC for a traineeship.

Instead Granada took him on as a production trainee. He worked as a researcher on *World in Action*, by then established as a televisual version of the new vogue for newspaper investigative journalism. Birt brought a new approach to the programme, moving away from traditional journalism towards a more experimental style based more on stunts and gimmicks.

Birt made his mark in July 1969 by persuading the editor of *The Times,* William Rees-Mogg, Bishop Trevor Huddleston, and Frank Soskice, an ex-cabinet minister, to meet Mick Jagger, who was on trial at the time for possessing cannabis. Jagger was flown to the meeting straight from court in a helicopter, with Birt squeezed between the rubber-lipped hipster and his girlfriend Marianne Faithfull, who spent most of the journey writhing in sexual ecstasy.

The Men in Suits were there to discuss the 'generation gap' with Jagger. Rees-Mogg had already come to his defence, saying the pop star was being pilloried for his beliefs and not for his crimes. Years later Birt revealed the thinking behind the show in a *Listener* article. 'The young had thrown away their Burton suits,' he wrote, 'and abandoned the limitations on self-expression and were set to explore new ways of living and relating to one another; there was outrage among the young. I felt it myself.'

Birt had by then replaced his own suit, if he ever owned

one, with jackets trimmed with crocodile skin, loon pants, granny glasses and long hair. He explained he 'felt no solidarity' with dope-smokers, but thought Jagger's sentence had been 'an assault on our values, the vengeance of one generation on another.'

(The Rees-Mogg and Jagger show was a hit and made a lasting impression on *The Times*' editor, who remained a great Birt fan. When Birt got his haircut in the 1970s and teamed up with Peter Jay, another *Times* man, Rees-Mogg's admiration knew no bounds. Birt became, according to one admiring LWT colleague, a 'punk monetarist'.)

Birt followed the Rees-Mogg and Jagger helicopter triumph with a chat show called *Nice Time*, brimming with the psychedelic preoccupations of the time. It launched the TV careers of Kenny Everett, later to be reincarnated as Sid Snot, and Germaine Greer of *Female Eunuch* fame. The show was remembered as a self-conscious attempt to subvert conventional TV entertainment shows, in many ways a precursor of Channel Four's *The Big Breakfast* and other examples of '80s and '90s 'anti-television'.

*Nice Time* featured such bizarre items as an orchestra composed entirely of musical-saw players; a backwards-walking race over the Derbyshire hills and a choir of ventriloquist's dummies singing 'The Legend of Xanadu'. The oldest member of the production team was 24.

To ensure things did not get out of hand, Birt created a substantial bureaucratic structure to keep the *Nice Time* team under his control. 'Without the apparatus of meetings, memos and hierarchy that he imposed, *Nice Time* would probably have dissolved into giggles,' Andy Mayer, Birt's partner on the series, later wrote in the *Guardian*. At the time Birt said: 'One day we'll look back and think that this was the best time we ever had in television'.

After two series of *Nice Time,* Birt stopped being silly to become joint editor of *World in Action*. But it was the silly stuff that made Birt stand out to the LWT bosses as the ideal man to breathe life into potentially worthy and dull material.

He joined LWT in 1971 as a producer, rescuing the ailing *Frost Programme*. Birt's work with Frost impressed the LWT heirarchy. His task was to mastermind the station's new current affairs show, *Weekend World*. Birt had now become one of the fastest rising stars in ITV. He was not yet 30.

In 1974 he became LWT's head of Current Affairs. Like many young men, Birt found he needed the support and patronage of a more powerful figure. This was provided by David Frost. In 1977 the two pulled off a coup by landing the first interview, a world exclusive, with the disgraced US president Richard Nixon. In the same year Birt added 'features' to his LWT responsibilities, helping to launch the *South Bank Show*.

Birt then really started moving further into frontier territory, setting up the London Minorities Unit in 1979. The unit was to make programmes like *Asian Eye* and *Black on Black*. Extra lesbian input to the Unit's gay programme was demanded after LWT's headquarters were besieged by an army of outraged dykes.

Some thought Birt was using the Unit to limber up for his application to become the first Chief Executive of Channel Four, due to go on air in 1982. Ever since 1973 Birt had lobbied for the creation of a 'publisher-broadcaster' fourth channel, which fitted with his broader manifesto for the future of television drawn up with Peter Jay, the economics writer.

Birt was devastated when his application for the job of running the channel failed. It was the only job he had applied for, as opposed to being offered, since he started in television. He remained at LWT and began to climb further up the hierarchy.

When Michael Grade, the other young LWT superstar, left for Hollywood in 1981, Birt took his job as Director of Programmes. He emerged as a dedicated ratings chaser, moving money away from expensive programmes like drama and children's television and shifting it into game shows. His greatest success was the derivative *Blind Date*. The show was an immediate hit, rarely out of the top ten and peaking with 18 million viewers.

Birt's move to the BBC, especially to revamp news and current affairs, was unfathomable as far as a lot of people in LWT were concerned. It did not seem to fit with anything in his recent career, and showed an inexplicable and wholly uncharacteristic willingness to take a drop in salary. Nevertheless his friends at the top of LWT saw him off in typically extravagant style, with much joshing about how he would rough up the down-at-heel hacks at the boring Beeb.

LWT said goodbye to Birt by 'kidnapping' him and holding him in a West London hotel. Birt was bundled into a car, driven to Heathrow and put on a plane to Vienna so that he could see the European Cup Final (FC Porto 2; Bayern Munich 1). Afterwards the merry pranksters dined in fine style. In a last gesture ITV's channel controllers asked him what he wanted as a farewell gift. Birt asked for an Armani suit.

Birt's appointment to the BBC caused some raised eyebrows on the Board of Management. He was obviously an able man but, in many ways, an odd choice to set up and run a merged news and current affairs directorate. He had no track record in daily news production, which was an entirely different animal to current affairs, and no experience of news and current affairs in radio, which was different again.

There was confusion about Birt's exact job description. Checkland gave the impression to some members of the Board that Birt was basically a replacement for Protheroe: a political flak catcher with an additional brief to sort out the current affairs department. Others doubted that Birt was ever going to be just the 'new Protheroe', and Brian Wenham knew more about him than most. Wenham and Birt had been on the opposite sides of an intellectual argument about television journalism, and the very nature of television itself, that had rumbled on for more than ten years.

In 1975 Birt and Peter Jay had written a series of articles for *The Times* that said television journalism had a 'built-in bias against understanding'. The need to provide pictures meant that news and current affairs programmes could warp news values, giving priority to material that looked interesting and beefed up the ratings. Over-reliance on visual material, Birt and Jay argued, was squeezing out what Jay was later to call television's 'mission to explain'.

This thinking was put into action with *Weekend World*, LWT's current affairs flagship, with Jay as the presenter. *Weekend World* was regarded as an often enlightening, but usually boring TV programme. Detractors said it consisted, in effect, of a long straight-to-camera lecture by Jay, illustrated with snips of film called up like slides in a magic lantern show. In TV jargon this was known as 'lexpo', meaning 'long exposition'; as opposed to 'bexpo' ('brief exposition') which was a brief summary of complex issues inserted into the middle of filmed reports. But, according to one joke, Jay and Birt were the inventors of flexpo, meaning 'fucking long exposition'. This would be followed by a long interview with a Very Important Person, often a cabinet minister.

Subjects chosen for *Weekend World* were generally whatever was at the top of the formal political agenda. The show rarely featured what journalists would think of as a story. A lot of people in the industry thought it was basically a radio programme in the old-fashioned BBC tradition of worthy 'talks' explaining difficult subjects to its small, meritocratic audience. It certainly did not make much use of the medium and struck some as a bit like reading a long newspaper article out loud on television. *Weekend World* did have the advantage of being popular with politicians who thought it was very important, not least because it featured them. After the 'success' of the show Jay turned his thoughts to the BBC.

Jay was watching *Panorama* one fateful day at his house in Ealing when he suddenly rounded on his wife, Margaret, who at the time was a *Panorama* producer. 'How is it that *The Times*, which has only a fraction of the BBC's resources, can afford to employ a man like me,' he asked, 'who has a lifetime of expertise in economics; whereas *Panorama*, which you work for, puts out this drivel?'

The hapless Mrs Jay explained that it was because *Panorama* only had six reporters, and they had to cope with all types of stories. Using the economic prowess he was so proud of, Jay at once worked out that the problem was organisational. The journalists saw themselves as working for the programmes they made; and no single programme was big enough to carry specialists like himself, and some other very sharp thinkers he knew, who could be relied upon to rise above the drivel level.

The answer was to create a centralised structure, like the staff of a newspaper, with expert correspondents in areas such as education and the arts who would fill up the programmes like separate sections of a quality newspaper. Together with their idea about television's bias against understanding, Jay and Birt wrapped in the need for more specialist journalism into a blueprint for the reform of the BBC.

In 1975 the two men presented their plan to Michael Swann, the BBC Chairman and a relative of Jay's. Swann was a distinguished academic administrator who ran the University of Edinburgh prior to becoming BBC Chairman in 1973. He thought the BBC should be run like a university; so what Jay and Birt had to say had considerable appeal. It also had the advantage of steering the BBC away from the politically risky '*J'accuse*!: We Name the Guilty Men' type of journalism that was being developed at Lime Grove in competition with ITV current affairs programmes like *World in Action*.

But Charles Curran, then Director General, was less impressed. He talked over the Jay-Birt blueprint with Wenham, who was running Lime Grove at the time, and decided it was essentially a sociological theory and had nothing to do with journalism as they understood it. There was a place for the sort of thing Jay and Birt were advocating, but it should not be allowed to dominate.

Wenham had then been alarmed to bump into Jay and Birt at Broadcasting House, clutching folders containing The Great Plan, apparently on their way to have lunch with Swann and the Governors. Following this chance encounter Swann called in Curran and Wenham to discuss the Jay-Birt proposals in detail. Wenham saw off the threat by saying that Jay had entirely misunderstood the way people watched television.

The BBC's own audience research was used to demolish Jay's analogy with newspapers and magazines. It was true that newspapers like *The Times* and *Financial Times* could survive with small specialist readerships, but in television the composition of the audience did not change much with its size. If LWT's *Weekend World* got a much smaller audience than *Panorama*, this did not mean LWT was getting an expert, up-market audience like a broadsheet newspaper. It just meant that it was not good television, or occupied a weak spot in the schedule, or both.

Swann rejected the Jay-Birt theory, and the merger of news and current affairs programmes that it entailed, and decided to stick with the more conventional journalism in which Lime Grove specialised. There was one concession. Swann told Jay the BBC would add 'context and perspective' to journalism whenever it could. Jay thought this was 'pathetic' and 'dangerously vague.' But he later claimed that the BBC's launch of *Newsnight* in 1980, which involved news and current affairs people working together to analyse the day's news, was a direct result of his conversations with Swann.

Now that Birt was inside the BBC, and was about to be given the job of merging news and current affairs, Wenham knew he had lost the battle and would soon have to leave. Wenham's *Private Eye* nickname had been Brian Wen-will-I-be-DG-ham. Checkland's promotion and Birt's arrival seemed to answer the question: never. Radio news and current affairs would be taken from him and included in the new merged directorate, leaving him with very little to do. Wenham negotiated a substantial pay-off and left. (After a slack period he resurfaced at LBC, the commercial London news station, and subsequently at Carlton Television.)

Alan Protheroe was another casualty of the new régime. At the 1986 Christmas party, just after the *Maggie's Militant Tendency* settlement, Milne had gloomily told Protheroe both of them would be gone by Easter. Milne was disposed of ahead of time in January. Now, in March, it was Protheroe's turn.

He was hosting a dinner to thank the BBC's Scottish lawyers for the work they had done on a current affairs series produced by BBC Scotland called *Secret Society*. The series was researched and presented by Duncan Campbell, one of the country's leading investigative journalists and an amazingly controversial figure in his own right.

Protheroe was alerted late to *Secret Society* because it was made by BBC Scotland. He began to worry about a programme that proposed to blow the whistle on the existence of a secret spy satellite codenamed Zircon. Funds to buy the satellite, Campbell discovered, had been moved from one part of the defence budget to another in order to mislead Parliament.

Protheroe did not think this was much of a story. Ministries and public bodies, not least the BBC, were always moving money around in this way. But he was more worried that information about the satellite might break the Official Secrets Act. He took his concerns to a regular meeting of the D-Notice Committee, the self-regulatory body set up by the Ministry of Defence to prevent journalists inadvertently printing military secrets.

Protheroe did not mention Zircon during the meeting, but asked the committee's chairman, Clive Whitmore, if he could stay behind for a little chat. Whitmore said that would be fine, but it would have to be quick because he had a dinner appointment. At the mention of the word Zircon, Whitmore's jaw dropped. 'Oh my God!' he yelped. He locked the door. Protheroe spent an hour telling him about the proposed programme. Whitmore listened intently before saying: 'Alan, you are really on very dodgy ground here. Very difficult ground indeed. Lives might be at risk. Let me think about it.'

After a meeting with the head of GCHQ, the government electronic bugging centre, Protheroe told Milne to pull the programme. When he did Campbell went bananas and started showing the film in Parliament and elsewhere, forcing Protheroe to take out a legal injunction against him. Soon the legal furore surrounding the programme extended to BBC Scotland's Glasgow headquarters, which were raided in an ultimately futile attempt to find leaked Zircon documents and bring a prosecution under the Official Secrets Act.

Protheroe briefly ended up in jail for refusing to co-operate with the search. He was then mauled by the Governors for allowing the programme to be made in the first place. He believed Zircon, along with *Real Lives* and *Maggie's Militant Tendency*, was one of the reasons they had demanded Milne's head.

Checkland now told Protheroe that Birt was taking over his job as the executive in charge of BBC journalism. The Assistant Director General was surprised that Birt had been appointed, but there was no reason, he thought, why Checkland should have discussed it with him. Protheroe asked to be released from his contract. Armed, like Wenham, with a generous pay-off he left the Corporation to take charge of British Forces Broadcasting in Buckinghamshire.

Protheroe's departure completed stage one of a clean sweep of the BBC's leadership. Bill Cotton was still on the Board of Management running television. But he had already announced he was going to retire on his sixtieth birthday, just a year away in April 1988. The Board of Governors, led by Marmaduke Hussey, was now dominated by people appointed after Mrs Thatcher's arrival at Number Ten.

The revolution in the BBC boardroom, that had started with the appointment of Hussey and the execution of Milne, was now destined to spread to the programme-makers themselves.

# 7

## *Year Zero; Anno Birticus*

John Birt was rarely seen in Lime Grove or the TV Centre newsroom during his first few weeks at the BBC. When he did turn up the new Deputy Director General would hover quietly, gnomically jotting impeccable little notes on a clipboard, blinking behind his David Hockney specs as he surveyed his new domain.

The way Birt dressed was an immediate topic of conversation. At LWT he had displayed a penchant for expensive Italian tailoring. For the BBC he switched at first to sober and expensive grey double-breasted Katherine Hamnett suits; affecting the Young Fogey style which was fashionable at the time. Nobody had ever seen such elegance at Lime Grove. People reckoned Birt's tassled Gucci loafers must have set him back £300 a pair. Michael Grade liked to wear red braces and luminous socks: but he was in show business. Checkland had set the tone for public service chic with his crumpled Marks and Spencer suits and Hush Puppies.

Birt made a habit of sitting in on editorial conferences, quietly observing people at work. During a session with the Radio Four *Today* team he said he did not listen to the radio all that much. Jenny Abramsky, editor of the Radio Four morning sequence, was aghast. But Birt explained: 'I've been fighting a television ratings war. What did you expect? Do you want me to lie?'

Invited to a weekly news and current affairs lunch at Television Centre, Birt revealed he had not watched the BBC's coverage of that weekend's historic visit by Mrs Thatcher to Moscow. The BBC was very proud of the coverage, believing it had been far superior to ITN's efforts. But Birt had missed it all. One of the journalists whispered to a colleague: 'What do you think of our new boss? I wouldn't give him a job as a sub-editor on Radio Bedford, would you?' The colleague hissed back through clenched teeth: 'Not fucking likely!'

At another session a producer asked Birt which BBC current affairs programme he liked. 'To be honest,' he replied, 'there's nothing I like.' Birt might drop the odd bombshell like this on fairly junior people but, like Hussey, he was much cooler to people higher up in the organisation.

With their new boss saying very little, people began to scan his writings for clues about what he might do. There were the 'bias against understanding' articles, reprinted at the time of his appointment. But these were highly theoretical and not much use for working out what he wanted now.

In a *Listener* article published when he was appointed to the BBC, Birt had praised Network 7, an LWT-backed youth venture, for showing the way. This featured anorexic post-pubescent youths interviewing people in a beaten-up caravan scavenged from a scrapyard and lit with two dustbins containing aircraft landing lights. 'Not a few mainstream current affairs programmes could learn something from Network 7's pace and vigour,' Birt thought.

Otherwise he was telling the papers he would be looking at news and current affairs 'from top to bottom' before announcing his plans. The information vacuum was filled by the Corporation's many rumour-mongers. In turn Birt was cast as a Zen Buddhist, a Tory hatchetman, a trendy lefty, a fundamentalist Catholic, a vegetarian fitness fanatic, a tee-totalling aesthete, a secret ex-hippy hedonist and an anally retentive 'control freak'.

It was known for certain that Birt had never been a news reporter, down at the 'sharp end' of journalism, cultivating contacts, working to tight deadlines and pushing his exquisitely shod foot in the door.

An anonymous poem was pinned to the newsroom notice-board in tribute to Birt's rarefied career and theories:

> *He says a single grain of concept*
> *Is worth a field of facts;*
> *So he loves the poets and thinkers,*
> *And despises hard-worked hacks;*
>
> *For how can one impress the Board,*
> *With mud upon one's shoes?*
> *In fact John Birt, the DDG,*
> *Doesn't really like the news.*

There were various conspiracy theories about Birt's appointment, many centring on the departed William Rees-Mogg. The two men had known each other since the famous *World in Action* drugs stunt with Mick Jagger. It was also thought Rees-Mogg had been involved in steering Marmaduke Hussey to the Chairmanship. After the hiccup over Dimbleby, Birt was turned up as the most experienced television journalist on the Hussey-Rees-Mogg-Jay circuit based around *The Times*. But Birt himself simply told people he, like Hussey, had been appointed 'out of the blue'. Not many people believed this.

At first he said virtually nothing to Ron Neil and Peter Pagnamenta, respectively the heads of news and current affairs. They began to worry about their jobs. Neil seemed to have the most to lose. He was one of the BBC's complement of acerbic Scots and an unabashed populist, very keen on making sure the Nine O'Clock News had its quota of Royals stories and other material Birt thought of as trivia. In 1983

Neil had been responsible for the launch of the sofa-bound *Breakfast Time*, in competition with Peter Jay's 'mission to explain' at TV-am. The cerebral head of current affairs, Peter Pagnamenta, seemed much more likely to get on with Birt. He was a heavyweight documentary-maker who had been put in charge of Lime Grove by Bill Cotton with a mission to tighten things up.

Neil and Pagnamenta took Birt to lunch in the Japanese restaurant at the Shepherd's Bush Hilton, an old BBC haunt, to try and pick his brains. Birt said he was still studying the BBC and doing a lot of listening. Neil and Pagnamenta knew this was true. But instead of listening to them he was meeting people outside the BBC, including politicians from all the parties, and listening to their complaints.

Birt was definite about one point. The news and current affairs merger would go ahead. It had been decided at Board level. They would have their say at a conference he was organising for all thirty or so senior news and current affairs executives to discuss the merger and how to bring it about. He had already chosen the venue: the Woodlands Park Hotel, Stoke D'Abernon, near Leatherhead. Until then, Birt said, there was not much point in him saying anything more.

In the meantime there was plenty to do reporting the general election that was due to take place in June 1987. Birt said he would play no role in organising the coverage, which was mainly to be handled by *Newsnight*, and specially extended editions of the Nine O'Clock News, culminating in the election night programme itself.

The BBC opened its Election Special by predicting a narrow Labour victory, based on an exit poll. Vincent Hanna, who was with Neil Kinnock in his Welsh constituency, noticed how the Labour leader's spirits lifted when the prediction came through. The reaction was exactly the opposite in Downing Street. Norman Tebbit found Margaret Thatcher tense and worried about losing.

But from the minute the first real result came in from Torbay it was obvious that the poll was wrong. Frantic recalculation showed the Conservatives were heading for a triumphant 100-seat majority. The Prime Minister cheered up, but the political damage was already done. Unforgivable upset and anxiety had been caused to the Prime Minister. Tebbit complained that the BBC had ignored 'the unwelcome truth' and 'deluded itself into believing what it wanted to believe; that we were sliding to defeat.' Birt sat in on the programme until the early hours, silently making notes. A BBC internal inquiry later found that the poll had contained a 'rogue' result and an inconclusive argument about whose fault this was followed.

Two weeks later the BBC's news and current affairs hierarchy set off for the Woodlands Park Hotel, Leatherhead, for Birt's merger conference. Apart from the eerie silence of Birt's first few weeks, the main attraction was the oppor-tunity to size up John Birt at close quarters and, maybe, get in his good books. Some thought the conference would run along similar lines to other television industry events: an axe-grinding session where people would defend their own corner.

People turned up to find the venue was not as bad as some had feared. The Woodlands Park Hotel was a refurbished Gothic folly built by Bryant of the Bryant and May match empire, complete with gardens, tennis courts, swimming pool, clay pigeon shooting and croquet lawns. The rooms were named after Edwardian showbiz stars. Its slogan was 'ele-gance and luxury in the seclusion of the Surrey countryside'. It was discovered that most of the conference would take place in a marquee on the lawn, complete with all the paperwork, adding a bizarre touch to proceedings.

From Birt's opening speech on Wednesday, it was clear to everyone that 'Leatherhead', as the event was known ever after, was not to be another inconclusive BBC talking shop. The Deputy Director General set the tone with an opening speech outlining his 'conclusions so far after five weeks at the BBC'. The talk was a detailed and highly flavoured critique of every aspect of news and current affairs. Despite what he had told Neil and Pagnamenta, it was obvious from the start that Birt was not very interested in listening to what the senior journalists arrayed before him thought.

Instead he spoke for more than an hour about the need to increase the number of specialist programmes and hire expert journalists from the broadsheet newspapers. BBC TV News, he said, was doing fairly well, but was not competing with either ITV or the broadsheet papers. The Nine O'Clock News and other bulletins were too superficial, and at times trivial. Reporters and editors needed to select items on the basis of their significance to the nation; rather than pander to the viewers. Important political events that would affect the future of the country had to be given priority over material like Ron Neil's Queen Mum stories.

There was 'too little real journalism', Birt said, and far too much 'access for opinion'. Reporters should get out and about more often. Increasing the 'authority' of BBC news was an absolute financial priority. That was what the licence fee was for. In current affairs, Birt said, there were even more serious problems. Many of the programmes, he said, appeared to be 'languid, lacking in pace and seem to be made by people with too much time on their hands.'

This was a problem not only for the BBC, but for television current affairs as a whole. It had failed to move with the times. Thames' *This Week*, he said, was 'a sad little programme' which was 'beached' in the age of film-making and had ignored the possibilities of new mould-breaking electronic production methods.

*Panorama* and other output from the Lime Grove current affairs centre left much to be desired, Birt said. They were using the wrong 'methods and tendencies'. They gave too much attention to 'accusers' who were making complaints against powerful people; while 'defenders' were given a hard ride. BBC interviewers were often straightforwardly 'rude' to politicians, he said.

'Rudeness' was a common complaint about the BBC in Whitehall, and one supported by William Rees-Mogg, who thought BBC journalism was much better in the 1950s. In those days interviewers had fawned over their subjects, and never asked anything embarrassing. A more combative approach was pioneered by Robin Day after the launch of ITN, and was being pushed further by younger interviewers like Jeremy Paxman. The great Paxo, as he was known in tribute to his stuffing abilities, soon revealed his interviewing method was based on keeping the thought 'Why is this bastard lying to me?' in mind at all times when interviewing politicians.

It was not the fault of individual journalists that things were going so badly wrong, Birt said. There were 'flaws' in the system of management control. Production teams were not being given clear enough briefs by their bosses. In future, Birt said, there would have to be much more discussion with senior managers before people were allowed to start making programmes.

With investigative journalism, it was especially important that lawyers checked programme ideas right from the start and not 'shortly before transmission'. This struck people as a reference to *Maggie's Militant Tendency*, which was very annoying. Lawyers were involved at all stages and the programme had been meticulously checked and approved in exactly the way he was advocating.

Anyway, over the years the BBC had attracted surprisingly few libel actions considering its vast journalistic output. The average for the whole of the 1980s was to work out at 17 a year covering the whole of television, national and local radio and the World Service broadcasting in dozens of foreign languages. This was at a time when papers like the *Sun* and *News of the World* were sometimes handling this many at any one time. The main problem was what was known as 'the live loony syndrome': where local radio producers were too slow to pull the plug on a phone-in that had gone off the rails.

Others used the libel laws to make a nuisance of themselves, or in the hope of getting a windfall pay-out. The BBC had once been sued when Gary Glitter appeared on *Top of the Pops* in a flashy American car painted with the number plate GG-1. The owner of the real number plate claimed that his reputation had been destroyed by being associated with such tastelessness. He was awarded £250 to compensate for the trauma. The stakes were much higher when it came to investigative journalism which, by its very nature, aimed to expose wrongdoing in high places.

The executives listened with a mixture of shock and anger. Some of them thought he was 'libelling the past', writing off everything they had done, good and bad. One of those present scanned the gathering and thought everyone looked mesmerised. Pagnamenta was particularly distressed by the way Birt was making these criticisms without first consulting him.

Some thought Birt's ideas were a reasonable, if ill-informed, starting-point for a debate. But at the same time their new boss could not hide a deep distaste for the BBC, and clearly did not want to listen. There was no warmth about him, and he did not respect what people had done.

For years they had worked for crummy wages, turning down lucrative offers from commercial television, because they really cared about the Corporation. It was so unfair. BBC news had just won a major ratings battle during the general election, outstripping ITN by two to one with its election special, despite the mix-up over the exit poll.

After the shock of his opening salvo, Birt introduced the BBC's head of research, Peter Maneer, who was one of the few BBC executives Birt had consulted. Birt had dragged Menneer over to his office at LWT and loaded him with research tasks. Most of these concerned looking at the 'segments' in the BBC's audience, which was usually of more interest to ITV than BBC, because of the need to deliver particular audiences for advertisers.

Menneer noticed the change of emphasis at once. Previously he had supplied figures for the BBC's reply to Peacock. In contrast these were used to show that the TV audience was very uniform, especially when compared with newspapers and magazines. This simple fact, supported by independent research by Professor Ehrenberg of the London Business School, was used to counter the Peter Jay view of television as an 'electronic magazine stand' with different groups of viewers prepared to pay for highly 'targeted' programmes.

The figures Menneer provided at Leatherhead showed that news and current affairs was viewed very frequently by the public. There was a tendency for the middle classes to watch more current affairs than the rest of the population, a fact seized upon by Birt to 'prove' that more informative, rather than audience-grabbing, material was needed.

Menneer finished his talk and Birt thanked him profusely, saying the presentation had been 'excellent work, full of insights'. Menneer looked embarrassed by this over-the-top show of gratitude. He stumbled into thanking Birt in equal measure for helping him put it together.

Looks flashed round the room. Everyone assumed Birt had seen and approved the presentation in advance and the audience was being treated to yet more of Birt's own views, this time relayed through Menneer. This was not strictly true, but everyone knew that conclusions drawn from statistical information had to be treated with great scepticism and, in this case, depended to a large extent on the questions Birt had framed.

Peter Ibbotson, the editor of *Panorama* at the time of *Maggie's Militant Tendency* and since promoted to become Michael Grade's 'batman' as the Chief Assistant to the Director of Programmes (Television), decided to tackle Birt about this. 'Ibbo' had worked with Brian Wenham on the BBC's and Professor Ehrenberg's response to Peacock. He wanted to know why the Deputy Director General was suddenly contradicting what the Corporation had always said about the nature of its audiences. Birt replied that the BBC had got it wrong during Peacock and should not rely on Ehrenberg: 'He was always wrong,' Birt said.

That evening the assembled executives formed into the

normal cabals, still reeling from what they had heard. Over
dinner Peter Pagnamenta looked worried and glumly compared what was happening to Stalinist Russia: a new party
leader was changing the official ideology. A purge of devia-
tionists was bound to follow. Pagnamenta said he would
speak up and put the BBC's case during the next morning's
session.

Everyone reassembled in the Big Top at 9.15 am. The
weather was hot, giving the event the feel of a Surrey
wedding, crossed with a three-ringed circus and a Moscow
purge trial. The marquee's door flap was rolled up in a
pointless attempt to cool things down. Then, when a loud
plane flew overhead, drowning out the proceedings, the
precise young man from the BBC secretariat who was taking
notes for Birt jumped up and closed the flap, producing hoots
of laughter at the futility of the gesture.

The session itself was simply called 'The Programmes'. Birt
had set a series of questions that Pagnamenta and Ron Neil
were required to address: 'What is the best blend of news,
news analysis, specialist journalism, programmes of reflection and journalism?' Pagnamenta spoke against overdoing
specialism, Birt's main preoccupation. Programmes only
worked when they had their own identity and were made by
their own teams. If they were seen as a vehicle for a central
group of specialists, there was a danger of creating a 'sausage
machine'.

If anything, Pagnamenta said, there needed to be more
variety and not less. He was not defending 'some strange and
ancient craft', but that was how television programmes
worked. As Pagnamenta tried to deal with Birt's accusations
point by point, the Deputy Director General would butt in,
using the phrase: 'I have a problem with that argument'.
This, people were soon to discover, meant he had formed a
different opinion and would not change it, no matter what.

Ron Neil spoke next. The Scot was known as a stout
defender of editors' right to stamp their own personality on
their programmes. This was fundamental to the BBC way of

doing things, but the technique was directly opposed to the Birt view.

Since the time of the inauspicious sushi session Neil had often talked to Pagnamenta about Birt. Neither man was happy about his appointment and, if anything, Neil was the more worried and hostile of the two. Now that Birt had apparently attacked Neil's approach head on, everyone was expecting him to give a stinging response. But to general astonishment, he did exactly the opposite; agreeing with most of Birt's thesis, and banging on about the need for specialist input as though he had invented the idea himself.

More people began to make Pagnamenta's Eastern European comparisons. It was like a show trial, with Neil denouncing himself for thought crime in the hope of being rehabilitated by the Great Leader. Over lunch Pagnamenta was even more gloomy and said morosely that he wouldn't mind a new job as a 'specialist expert' in agricultural programmes.

The afternoon session dealt with news and current affairs on radio, with Birt supplying egg-sucking platitudes like 'journalism is not about what you know, it's about what you don't know'. He criticised Radio Four for having no journalism in the morning after the *Today* programme.

Birt's personal style struck people as very odd. The Deputy Director General would often purse his lips in a pained expression when people said things he disagreed with. He bit his nails and was always looking at his watch, taken off his wrist and placed in front of him at the start of each session. Each speech was timed down to the precise second and then he moved the discussion on to the next point on his agenda.

By the end of the session it was abundantly clear that Birt had made up his mind about what should be done. Discussion was a formality: a way for those like Neil who had evidently decided to work with the Birt 'régime' to express loyalty; and for those who had not to be smoked out.

There was more unpleasantness to come later in the day when Checkland, who was not at the conference, arrived as

guest of honour at dinner. By now paranoia was such that
the seating plan was being scrutinised for signs of changing
fortunes. Birt sat at the head of the table flanked by Ron Neil
and Tony Hall, a relatively young journalist who had organised in-depth coverage of the election for the Nine O'Clock
News. Next to them sat Checkland who was placed, in turn,
next to Richard Tait, the editor of *Newsnight*.

Jenny Abramsky, editor of Radio Four's morning news
sequence, the *Today* programme, was included in the in-
group. It was also noted that Tait and Neil had been
instructed to bring their sports gear. Birt, a fitness fanatic,
insisted on playing tennis with them. All seemed to have
been singled out for greater things.

Checkland made a short speech saying the BBC was 'a
confident organisation' now that it had a master plan. This
included the news and current affairs merger. He was confident about that too; confident about Birt and confident about
the future. He was confident that the Board could be persuaded to part with more money for news; and very confident
that current affairs would be provided with a new building to
replace the squalor of Lime Grove.

The amateur Freudians in the audience decided that a man
who went round saying how confident he was so often
obviously had a chronic lack of confidence. Others thought
Checkland, the *Daily Mail's* 'Mr Nobody' with his crumpled
suit, inappropriate tie and nasal Brummie accent, still did
not look or sound like a 'real Director General'.

The next day's session began with another Birt lecture,
this time about the plan for more specialist reporters in the
areas of politics, economics, home and foreign affairs. These
people would 'drive' the whole range of BBC news and
current affairs, he explained. He confessed he had a liking
for programmes of 'great seriousness'. The BBC, he said, had
'failed to impress thinking people' and was 'not entering into
the policy debates in society'. There was too much concern
about securing a big audience. Programmes like *Panorama*
had become too sensationalist, dealing with issues by merely

saying 'Gosh, isn't that terrible?' without looking at solutions.

This was too much for Pagnamenta. It was ridiculous to say the BBC did not have serious programmes, and the schedule had to be looked at as a whole. Birt was advocating 'brownie point' television designed for a metropolitan élite, he said. Pagnamenta was referring to Birt's *Weekend World* which even people at LWT admitted was introduced in the early '70s mainly to impress the Independent Broadcasting Authority, the body that granted LWT's licence.

*Weekend World* was carefully targeted on the 'metropolitan élite' of politicians and broadsheet newspaper journalists. It was screened at Sunday lunchtime, in the middle of the slowest news day of the week. Politicians would appear in the knowledge that what they said would often be reported in the serious papers on Monday morning, because there was nothing else going on. This produced an impressive sheaf of press clippings from papers like *The Times* and *Guardian* that could be waved about as evidence of the programme's importance.

Some thought this strategy was fair enough; impressive, even. But it was unfair and misleading to compare it with *Panorama* or the Nine O'Clock News, which were in the business of winning mass audiences.

Birt's structure of four specialist areas was very neat and logical, which was another Birt trait, believed to have been inherited from his training as an engineer at Oxford University. Even his admirers thought that he was more of a 'programme engineer' who assembled and marshalled information rather than a journalist who knew how to develop and tell a story.

Peter Ibbotson listened to Birt with increasing alarm. He thought back to the last time they had met. It was at Michael Grade's flat when Birt had helped Grade prepare for his unsuccessful application for the Director Generalship. As they were leaving Birt confided, in an offhand way, that he really must start watching TV current affairs again. He had seen hardly any in the last six years. Now, three months later, he was lecturing the entire BBC hierarchy on the subject and re-inventing television journalism from scratch like some sort of student media studies project.

'This man is off his head,' Ibbotson whispered to his neighbour. 'It just ain't going to work.' Journalism could not be pre-planned like this. What if there were no interesting stories about finance or home affairs one week? Would the reporters have to go and find something just for the sake of it? Like Wenham, Ibbotson thought the plan would be ruin-ously expensive to put into practice. He had nothing against specialist journalists, in their place. But given too much power they would produce narrow and boring programmes few people would want to watch: except other specialist journalists.

The next day there was more evidence of the huge role John Birt was carving out for himself in the BBC. During a session about World Service news, led by the venerated figure of John Tusa, Birt announced that he did not like the direction the World Service was taking. Tusa was one of the BBC's most highly respected and experienced journalists, and did not take kindly to interruption from the man from commercial television, and replied briskly.

But Birt persisted. 'What audience are you aiming at?' he demanded to know. 'And what cultural assumptions are you making?' Tusa blinked with surprise. The session was sup-posed to be on the narrow subject of news, over which Birt could claim some authority, and not the service as a whole. Concerned looks once again flashed around the audience.

Birt was no mere replacement for Alan Protheroe, the Director General's news and current affairs troubleshooter, as some had been led to believe by Checkland. Here was a man who expected to have a say about what was going on at every level in the BBC. Tusa's speech ended the main business of the conference but Birt had organised a final dinner at a nearby hotel.

People had chilled when, at the start of the morning

session, Birt had announced the evening would be a 'fun' social occasion. People would be expected to tell a joke or an amusing anecdote. The previous evening people had been left to their own devices and there was riotous laughter on the lawn as people told their stories about Birt, *Weekend World* and the BBC. Now the Deputy Director General wanted to hear them and join in the hilarity.

Pagnamenta and Ibbotson escaped from the formal dinner to attend Brian Wenham's leaving party in nearby Weybridge, filling him in on the horrors taking place a few miles down the M25. The rest of the hierarchy clambered into a coach and set off with great trepidation for Birt's 'fun evening'. They got lost on the M25. There was a final effort to get Birt to change his mind about the story-telling. Jenny Abramsky found the courage to tell her boss the jokes were a bad idea. But Birt was adamant: 'I've decided we'll have jokes, and that's what we'll do. I can't be seen to be changing a decision,' he said, adding with a grin: 'The BBC is far too gloomy anyway.' Abramsky reported the bad news.

The party arrived at the hotel, hours late, only to find a wedding reception in progress. They were nevertheless found seats, amid more moans that there was no point in leaving the original hotel. After dinner Birt ordered everyone to tell their joke. Birt told a long rambling story about working with David Frost on the Nixon interviews, which struck people as more of an exercise in name-dropping than humour. The punchline fell flat but everyone managed a tactical chuckle. The guffaws were saved for a Kate Adie impersonation; one of the evening's highlights. But the ritual had its awful moments.

Some thought the process was little more than a naked demonstration of Birt's power to force them to perform to order like circus seals. Others thought Birt really did want to be popular and have a good time. The operation was just an example of his shy and strangely mechanical way of doing things. Either way the whole evening provided a surreal climax to the conference.

People came away from Leatherhead with very mixed feelings. Most thought the BBC was in need of a change of style after the complacency of the Milne era. Birt was the first person in a senior position at the BBC to come from the post-1968 'Me' generation. He was a big fan of Bob Dylan and Neil Young and had affected the style of the permissive society as a young man. LWT was swamped with such people, who gave the place a much younger, sexier image. The LWT tower block was described in the business as '22 floors of heaving copulation'.

But at the same time everyone realised the conference was a punctiliously organised series of seminars with more than one purpose. The executives grumbled and wondered what it all meant and the phrase 'I don't mind being told what to do; but I'm buggered if I'm going to be told what to think' was attributed to more than one of them. Afterwards it was never clear if these words had actually been spoken. But it seemed to sum up the mood of the BBC's officer class.

The event was obviously a landmark of the sort Birt needed in his own mind. It marked the end of his clipboard investigation stage. He had come up with his plan for the future and everything in the past could be mentally buried. It was Year Zero, Anno Birticus.

# 8

## Is there Life on Mars?

On the Friday after Leatherhead Peter Pagnamenta received a call from a reporter on the *Daily Express*. 'I hear you have been fired,' he said. 'Have you got any comment to make?' Pagnamenta said it was the first he had heard of it. He made an appointment to see Birt first thing on Monday morning.

At the meeting Birt coolly told Pagnamenta his job as head of television current affairs had disappeared in the merger of news and his department. The new management team would be announced later that day, and it did not include him. 'I'm sorry,' Birt said. 'But I have to tell you there will be no place for you in the new directorate.' It was not up to him whether Pagnamenta was found another job elsewhere in the Corporation. 'That's the BBC's problem,' Birt said, 'not mine.'

Birt and Ron Neil spent the week after Leatherhead putting the finishing touches on the executive structure of the merged directorate and holding meetings with individual members of staff. Tony Hall, who had so impressed Birt with his work on the election coverage, was one of the first to be called in.

When Hall went into the room to meet Neil and Birt he saw a pyramid diagram on the wall, displaying the intended structure of the directorate. He scanned the lower and middle reaches hoping to see his name. Instead, it was near the top, next to the grand title of Editor, News and Current Affairs (Television). He was flabbergasted. The position ranked him number three in the whole of BBC journalism.

Hall suspected he was well regarded by Birt. But this was extraordinary. He was working his way steadily up the BBC ladder and had reached the position of assistant editor on the Nine O'Clock News at the age of 35. Now he was being promoted over the head of Pagnamenta and other high flyers in news and current affairs, including a raft of more experienced people who had, in effect, taught him all he knew. Instead of taking charge of *Newsnight* or the Nine O'Clock News, he would now be responsible for every minute of nearly 3,000 hours of television each year. It was a hell of a responsibility, but Hall took the job.

Meteoric rises like this were more common in ITV. But over the next few days Birt was to change the rules of the BBC promotion game. Except for Ron Neil, who was the same age as Birt, the Deputy Director General decided to skip a generation. His senior team was to be a mixture of older people in areas like editorial policy and regional broadcasting and younger people like Hall in more central areas. A third element was to be the outsiders: thrusting, if sometimes inexperienced, young people hired from LWT.

News about Leatherhead reached the lower ranks of the BBC by the time-honoured method of newspaper leaks. More and more lurid accounts circulated as time passed. The gossip machine had already transformed Birt's painful evening of joke-telling into The Great Joke Test, with the Deputy DG marking people out of ten. Others were calling it Katyn Forest, a reference to the wholesale slaughter of the Polish army officer class by the Red Army.

At Ron Neil's suggestion Birt reluctantly agreed to call a meeting in Studio D at Lime Grove to answer questions from the troops. Birt and his team sat facing the audience like guests on *Question Time*. Peter Kenyatta, the son of the Kenyan Mau Mau leader Jomo Kenyatta, and the man chosen to be Birt's special assistant in news and current affairs, took the chair. Tony Hall and Ron Neil sat next to him, looking excited. Birt sat in the middle bolt upright. All these people were familiar to the audience. But there was one newcomer: Samir Shah, a new recruit from LWT.

It was explained that Shah would have special responsibility for weekly current affairs programmes, including *Panorama*. Like Hall, Shah was only 35, and people felt affronted that such a young and inexperienced journalist was to have so much power in the new set-up. Shah was the editor of *The London Programme*, LWT's regional current affairs show. This was respected in a way, but was outranked by all of the network programmes made at Lime Grove. Shah looked uncomfortable and embarrassed to be at the meeting. He sat with his back hunched, said very little and avoided eye contact by sheepishly staring at the desk top.

After the introductions Birt launched into a potted version of his Leatherhead manifesto. His delivery was slow, full of hesitating ums and ahs, but extremely measured. This betrayed a basic shyness and, above all, caution about making an injudicious remark. Although he was very proud of being a northerner, Birt's accent had now been toned down and was essentially nondescript with the occasional flat vowel, a bit like *Coronation Street's* Ken Barlow.

Birt ran through some of the Lime Grove programmes and said he had 'some harsh thoughts' about them. Overall they lacked authority and there was a need for more analysis. He spent a lot of time talking about *Newsnight* which, he thought, needed to be more analytical. It had a budget of £7 million, which was a lot, but Birt said he could not see 'value on the screen'. Neil helpfully butted in, saying the programme's budget was a third of the total for BBC news.

Birt was asked to define 'value on the screen', but became vague, and turned to Neil for help. 'What was the name of that bloody conference they had the other week?' he sneered. The 'bloody conference' was a reference to Ettington Park, the seminal think-in where Checkland had marked the start of the New Age and unveiled his vision of the BBC as a 'billion-pound business.' Birt said *Newsnight's* lack of value for money had been discussed there and something had to be done about it.

The Deputy Director General moved on to Lime Grove's working methods. As part of his mechanical style Birt spoke in a series of bulletin point headings like 'Impartiality', 'Programme Method' and 'Investigative Journalism.' Impartiality came first. 'Contentious issues must, I feel, be sensitive to the arguments on all sides of the question. And quite frankly there is not always that sensitivity shown.'

'Programme Method' came next. 'There are too many films of varying lengths which are seemingly made before the outline story is clear to the reporter.' There were murmurs of discontent, but Birt said he would answer questions later and pressed on with his list. 'Investigative journalism,' he said, taking a long pause and fiddling with his designer specs. He continued with immense seriousness, like a headmaster lecturing naughty schoolchildren. 'Nobody should be in any doubt that the BBC is still in that game. We are ready to tackle difficult subjects. But they must be accurate; the evidence must stand up even if the case goes to court.' Hackles rose at this point. Those involved knew this was obviously a reference to *Maggie's Militant Tendency*. Sensing opposition Birt added: 'Let's be frank, some changes will be necessary. The merger is a fresh start. It is an opportunity to get our working practices right.' A lot of those present thought they had been getting it right for years.

Birt finished his introduction with some good news. He announced his plan to close Lime Grove and replace it with purpose-built headquarters near Television Centre in White City. 'You will have pleasant, modern working conditions. The sooner we can get you all out of here the better,' he said. Neil added he had just been to the lavatory, which was in a disgusting condition: 'If anything proves the need for a new building, it's that,' he said.

Kenyatta asked for questions from the floor. The main preoccupation was forcing Birt to define some of the slogans and phrases that had been in circulation since Leatherhead.

Charles Wheeler, the veteran *Newsnight* reporter, was the first into the fray. 'These very general things you say are being interpreted in totally different ways and wild stories are flying around,' Wheeler warned. 'When you say "analysis"; when you use these words, how soon are you going to define what you mean? Because we have been analysing issues on *Newsnight* for about six years.' A chuckle went round the room.

Birt was indignant: 'I agree that you have provided analysis. Nobody has ever suggested that you haven't.' Wheeler persisted: 'Well, can you spell out precisely what form your idea of analysis would take and how it would contrast with what we are now doing?'

Birt tried to change the subject: 'If you had listened to what I said. My remarks were about the news and not about *Newsnight*.' Wheeler arched his eyebrows as Birt launched into a long digression about the Nine O'Clock News. Birt came to a halt and Wheeler dragged the conversation back to the point: 'About *Newsnight*,' he said, peering at his shorthand notes: 'you did say ... I wrote it down actually ... "*Newsnight's* role should be more tightly defined to provide news analysis of the day and the past few days".'

Birt floundered: 'Er, I did indeed say that. But I was not suggesting for a moment that *Newsnight's* business has not been news analysis, and very often effectively; though less effectively than it might have been.' Birt's difficulties were being relayed throughout the building on a closed-circuit television system, allowing the more enterprising to video bootleg editions for posterity.

Birt then repeated the separate accusation that *Newsnight* was somehow wasting money. Another member of the *Newsnight* team piped up: 'The message we are getting is "Analyse,

Analyse, Analyse." Who is going to set the agenda for original news stories?' This was a reference to *Newsnight's* speciality of screening filmed reports about things that had not yet reached the daily news agenda; such as profiles of rising but not yet newsworthy politicians.

'I want to drive towards programmes that are driven by specialists and contain more rigorous and original journalism than they do at present,' Birt replied. 'Sorry. Yes,' the questioner said sarcastically. 'It's great that we should be more specialist, be more rigorous and all that, but it sounds like it will be our job to see what's on the Nine O'Clock News and then analyse it. That's what it sounds like to me. Is that right?'

Birt's answer was defiantly vague: '*Newsnight* is at its best when it comes up with a story that feels like it's much more important than anything the Nine O'Clock News has put out.' Tony Hall added: 'The Nine O'Clock News is constrained by having to cover the news of the day.' This struck people as a bit crass, since everyone already knew that it was a daily news bulletin.

All the talk of 'Analyse, Analyse, Analyse' worried people. 'Do you mean you want us to make boring programmes?' someone asked. Everyone knew this was a reference to *Weekend World*, Birt's baby at LWT. But he did not rise to the bait. Instead he had some rare praise to offer. 'There is a programme made at Lime Grove of great integrity and professionalism: *That's Life*,' Birt said. 'It has brought a magic blend of consumer journalism and high-quality entertainment. So I hope there will be the odd laugh in our output, yes.' He leaned back and flashed a crooked grin at Neil in tribute to Leatherhead: 'Everyone knows that I am in favour of jokes.'

It was odd that Birt should single out the old Esther Rantzen warhorse for praise. Some later realised it had been direct competition for LWT on Sunday nights. Birt, therefore, must at least have watched it from time to time. This was not the case with the BBC's midweek output.

There was some praise, too, for *Breakfast Time*, now it had moved away from its original 'bright 'n' breezy format', and was carrying fairly heavy news. Ron Neil, the man who had launched the show, seized the chance to lighten the atmosphere. 'It is quite clear the first editor of *Breakfast Time* got it wrong, if he doesn't mind me saying so,' he quipped to lukewarm laughter.

Birt was then asked about his plans for weekly programmes. This was where he wanted to make the biggest changes, and where Samir Shah, the new boy, would be most involved. There was a pause as Birt considered his answer. But again he was vague. 'The balance is not quite right,' he said, and then gave his standard line about how specialism was a good thing.

'How will these specialist programmes relate to each other,' a voice shouted from the back, 'and what will *Panorama's* role be? Perhaps Mr Shah, as the man in charge, could tell us a bit about that.' So far Shah had been frozen to the spot and had said nothing. He replied quietly and hesitantly, flashing the occasional worried glance at Birt in search of approval. 'I think it's very difficult to answer. I will start by finding out how these programmes are put together,' he mumbled.

The questioner persisted: 'Do you have a vision of what sort of *Panorama* you would like to see in terms of the stories that are being covered this week?' This was a standard question put to candidates for junior jobs on programmes. And Shah gave the standard junior interviewee's reply: 'Well, er . . . Ha! That's a bit difficult. I've only been here for a few days and I think it's a bit premature to start talking about visions for *Panorama* . . .'

Birt rescued him. 'You are looking too much into the future,' he told the audience, though this was precisely what he had asked them to do. 'When we've got the top tier of management, the next stage will be translating these forward ideas into specific programmes.'

Some thought this answer, though casually given, was the most revealing of the whole session. It showed Birt was mainly interested in creating a neat management structure that, somehow, would create better programmes by virtue of its neatness. The more traditional view was that quality came from the journalists, and the management existed to make this happen, and not the other way round.

The Deputy Director General tried to end the meeting on an upbeat note. More money would be available once the problems, as he saw them, were solved. After that there would be a bright future and 'unparalleled opportunities' for all. 'Let's build a future together. And let's not hark too much on the past,' he said. The meeting broke up amid much unhappy muttering.

That evening in the many rival pubs and restaurants used by the Lime Grovers, there was real anger about the way Birt had handled himself. All his talk about the need for impartiality was highly insulting. They knew their job. The only people who thought they were biased were the Government and the Tory press. But governments always thought that; even before the elevation of Denis Thatcher and Norman Tebbit to the joint role of bias-finder general. Opinion surveys showed, if anything, the BBC was thought to be biased against the opposition, not the Government.

The main complaint was that Birt showed no signs of humility in coming from a small company like LWT to the BBC. Judging by his performance Samir Shah was obviously going to be his right-hand man and a total loyalist. There was sympathy for Shah as they laughed drily about his promise to investigate 'how current affairs programmes are put together.'

Less amusingly, it was decided that Birt's thinking still owed a lot to Peter Jay. Since the 1970s Jay had developed his theories about the nature of news even further. He explained in a very long and abstract speech to the Royal Society of Arts that even a sentence like 'the cat sat on the mat' contained bias. 'It is not "just a fact",' he had insisted. It was a point of view involving 'analysis, explanation and interpretation.'

Journalists and film-makers at the BBC and elsewhere thought this approach was hare-brained, to say the least. At the mention of Jay's name they would tell, with great hilarity, the story of how his 'mission to explain' at TV-am had resulted in a ratings disaster and virtual bankruptcy that had to be reversed by the arrival of Anne Diamond and Roland Rat.

Jay was also famous for having told a *Times* sub-editor, who could not understand a word of one of his economics columns: 'I write for three people in this country; and you are not one of them.' Jay had later tried to qualify the remark, but it was still insulting that a man who shared Peter Jay's ideas should be telling them how to do their jobs.

Dissidents who had left *Weekend World* had given it the nickname 'Weekend Warp', because of the way the facts were bent to fit the script. *Weekend World* once sent a camera crew to interview the Shah of Iran a few days before his fall. The script, written in London, followed the fashionable American view that the Shah was solid and Ayatollah Khomeini was a nobody with little support. When the team reported that a revolution was imminent, they were told that riots in the streets were ten a penny in countries like Iran. Less rigorous programmes, with their addiction to sensational pictures, could be left to film them; they were engaged in the authoritative business of interviewing the Shah. A few days later the mullahs stormed the palace and installed Ayatollah Khomeini. It is a legend in the industry that Birt basically missed the story. And this was the man who was now in charge of BBC journalism.

There was a more immediate concern about jobs. Peter Pagnamenta, their old boss, had not been present at the Studio D meeting and Birt had not mentioned his name once. It was as though Pagnamenta had become an Orwellian unperson. The idea of importing specialist journalists who would be given their own specialist shows was worrying. Who would go to make way for them? And what role would

*Panorama* have? There was a genuine fear that it might be simply axed.

The only chink of optimism was the vague promise that Birt would spend the next few weeks talking to the programme-makers in detail. Birt agreed to meet the editor of *Panorama*, Tim Gardam, and some of the programme's senior journalists to discuss the future. In the private surroundings of the *Panorama* office both Birt and the hacks felt free to talk more frankly, and the meeting soon degenerated into a slanging match.

There was a difficult moment when Birt announced he intended to hire a team of 'fact-checkers', a semi-journalistic job common on American newspapers like the *Washington Post*, whose role it would be to research and challenge the journalists on every point of fact. In the UK the only publication to use such people was *Reader's Digest*; in the view of many *Panorama* hacks, Britain's Worst Magazine. This, they thought, was an outrageous slur. Getting the facts right went to the core of their professionalism.

They told him he was working on prejudices dating back ten years to his own time as a *Weekend World* producer. 'Birtism', they said, was based on a myth that you could intellectually arrive at the truth of a story first and then go out and film it later. 'Well,' Birt said finally, 'this is typical of the defensive, inward-looking BBC culture. You are not prepared to realise you are being criticised. You can't go on as you have been.' Birt did seem to give ground on one point. The idea of employing fact-checkers was quietly dropped.

Leatherhead and Studio D left many Lime Grove journalists with difficult decisions to make. Would they stay and adjust to the 'Birtism-Jayism', or would they fold their careers in the BBC and take their chances in the commercial sector? There was no third option. The result was to be a wave of defections to ITV and independents. The team working on *Panorama* soon became polarised between the newly arriving 'Birtists' who replaced them and 'anti-Birtists', who were the more experienced Lime Grove reporters and producers. *Panorama* became the first battleground in the campaign to 'Birtise' BBC current affairs.

The programme-makers' dealings with the new hierarchy were channelled through Samir Shah, who became 'Birt's representative on earth'. The old guard, as the more experienced reporters were called, did not find him easy to deal with. One of the programme's most senior reporters was lectured by Shah for forty-five minutes about the philosophy of programme-making. At the end of the session, he decided he had not understood a single word.

One of the first shows Shah supervised was a complicated tale about the links between Oliver North's Irangate arms deals and the capture of Terry Waite and other Western hostages. It was a good story, later to be confirmed by North himself. When the programme was previewed Shah looked unhappy. He obviously did not like it, but found it difficult to fault. But that was often the way with Shah. He would go around muttering that the 'old guard' were obstructing change, and there would have to be a purge. But when they asked him what was wrong, and what exactly it was that he wanted, he just could not say.

Paul Woolwich, the 'old guard' *Panorama* deputy editor, was reduced to pleading with him for instructions. 'You've got the key to the door,' he told Shah, 'you are the boss. Open the door, walk through it and tell me what you want me to do. If I can say: "yes! I understand", then I'll do it.'

Shah responded by producing a pro-forma 'kit' for programme-making. This included detailed instructions on permissions to be gained before a subject could be tackled, including a document similar to a flow chart complete with boxes where producers were required to fill in the questions they intended to ask. Everything had to be done much more slowly, and programmes had to be prepared a week in advance of transmission so that Shah, and if necessary Birt, could see them and suggest changes.

The new approach to 'prescripting' programmes, as Shah put it, produced some bizarre scenes. One of the big stories of

1987, coinciding with Birt's arrival, was the saga of Peter Wright's book *Spycatcher*, and the Government's ham-fisted attempts to suppress it. Wright had disappeared to Tasmania and was not talking. But *Panorama's* John Ware was finally promised an interview. Ware's instinct was to get straight on the plane. He could not predict what Wright would say, but was sure he could get him talking. The bottom line was that almost anything Wright said about *Spycatcher* was news, and would provide an exclusive.

But to Samir Shah this smacked of 'cutting-room journalism'. Ideally he wanted a researcher to interview Wright first so that a script could be written and shown to Birt for approval. Ware was unimpressed. 'Look,' he told Shah, 'I know the guy. He trusts me. If I write a script he's going to change his mind and say something else anyway. He's very old. He might die. I've got to get out there while he's still a story.'

But Shah insisted. A script was written and redrafted several times with Birt helpfully supplying the phone numbers of some intelligence officers he knew. The interview eventually took place, but it took hours of filming to get Wright to confess he had invented the main allegations in his book. This was the story Ware was working on anyway.

The more bureaucratic approach to programme-making was anathema to journalists like Ware, brought up on the idea that stories had to be done fast and broadcast immediately if they were to have any impact. The new system led to a series of soul-destroying wrangles throughout 1987. Almost every programme became a battlefield.

Woolwich finally got fed up and decided to take his chances with an independent company, making a series for Channel Four. John Birt's activities in news and current affairs were by now causing alarm in other parts of the BBC, fuelled by articles in the trade press with front-page headlines like BIRT IS KILLING CURRENT AFFAIRS and BIRT PLAN SPARKS MUTINY marking the steady outflow of talent.

Birt was furious about the way 'anti-Birtist' film-makers,

led by Peter Pagnamenta, had fled from Lime Grove to be welcomed with open arms by the BBC's documentary department at Kensington House. The religious series *Everyman* briefly became a surrogate *Panorama* in exile, making current affairs shows about subjects like the politics of Iran on the grounds that it had some mullahs in it. Other ex-Lime Grovers found sanctuary on shows like *40 Minutes* and even *Horizon*. But Birt was determined there should be no escape.

People were surprised by the scale of Birt's territorial demands, which seemed to grow by the day. The Deputy Director General cheerfully admitted that he knew nothing about radio. Yet he already planned to annex *Analysis*, the Radio Four version of *Panorama*. The Talks and Documentaries Department (Radio) that produced the show said it would resist incorporation into Birt's directorate, but it was quickly overrun. David Harding, head of the separate Current Affairs and Magazine Programmes (Radio), that made *Woman's Hour*, told *Broadcast* magazine he was looking for a new name for his department that did not include the fatal words 'current affairs'.

In response to all the bad publicity about his dictatorial style Birt invited a reporter from the *Daily Mail* round to his Wandsworth house for an exclusive interview. 'When I was asked to join the BBC,' he moaned, 'I was under no illusion about the difficulties, or that there would be flak. But it was impossible to estimate just how much flak. It's no fun, but I just have to get on with the task.'

The piece was headlined IT'S NO FUN TAKING THE FLAK and featured a photograph of a relaxed-looking Birt sitting in a tasseled armchair in his front parlour. A separate strapline described him as the MOST FEARED MAN IN TELEVISION, and yet another quoted him saying: 'There are some people in the BBC who think I come from Mars.' Birt also complained about BBC leaks, saying: 'I do wish those people who are quoted anonymously would stand up and be named.'

Bill Cotton, the head of the television service, was stung

by the *Mail* article and decided to tackle Birt during a lunch for managing directors at Broadcasting House. 'About this article,' he said, brandishing the *Mail* feature. 'You accuse the BBC of leaking, when you sit in your house with these people talking about the BBC and its staff.' Birt puffed himself out and bristled: 'I am used to being in meetings where important decisions can be taken with absolute certainty about confidentiality.'

Cotton was annoyed by this automatic assertion of the superiority of the LWT way. 'You are playing in a different league now,' he growled. 'Before you came to the BBC you had probably never been in any important meetings.' Before Birt could reply Cotton launched into another complaint, this time about his pompous declaration that he would see his 'task', or mission as he often called it, through. 'Just what is your bloody mission, anyway? Nobody seems to be sure.' Birt, who hated public confrontations like this, backed off and the conversation fizzled out.

Cotton brought up the incident with Michael Grade, the man who had first advocated bringing Birt to the BBC. 'Are you sure about this Birt bloke?' he asked. 'I think he's a bit of a creep.' Grade assured him that it was just Birt's manner, and that everything would be fine. John had a big job on his hands in news and current affairs and needed to present himself as an outsider if he was going to get anywhere.

He was being fought all the way by the *Panorama* mob and so he could be forgiven for not exactly loving the BBC at the moment. The oddball style was familiar from LWT where Birt talked repeatedly of corporate goals and strategies, and the importance of sticking to plans once they were decided. It did not amount to much in the end.

The *Mail* article was a bit over the top, but that was John's style too. He was a shy man, and not very good at manipulating journalists. Instead of subtly giving hacks the odd off-the-record nugget, his mechanistic style led him to either say nothing at all, or blurt out everything he was thinking in a way that was, if anything, too honest.

Some people had always detected a faintly neurotic streak in the way Birt went about things. His critics said he was a 'control freak' who could not operate without the security and neatness of rigid plans governing every aspect of his life. When he had described himself to the Board of Management as 'a man from another world' people laughed at him behind his back, saying: 'Yeah, made by Martians who almost got it right.' According to gossip his personal life was just as regimented as his professional activity, with every minute of the day accounted for on a personal computer.

Dinner parties at the Birt residence in Wandsworth could be a harrowing experience for more chaotic personality types. Like everything else, they were run to a strict timetable and would often involve preplanned entertainment, like the joke test at Leatherhead, sprung on people without warning. At least once visitors finished dinner to be herded into the sitting-room where Birt had meticulously laid out the scripts of a play that they were expected to read out for 'fun'.

Birt was a health fanatic who dieted to a target weight measured every day. The story circulated of how there was a daily computer print-out stuck to the fridge in his kitchen instructing himself on what he was to eat that day, and when he should eat it. Most Friday afternoons he played football with his chums from LWT. They treated it as a harmless kick-about to jog off the excess from the week's power lunches, but Birt dealt with it like a European Cup final, becoming a scheming tactical genius with an iron will to win.

The competitive approach extended to everything he did. In the summer of 1986, just before he had joined the BBC, Birt and Grade had starred in a simulated game show called *The Ratings Game*, at the annual Edinburgh TV festival. Everyone thought this was a great joke, with Grade riding high on the *EastEnders-Wogan* ratings triumph and Birt the coming man in ITV. If the two men had not been great friends it might not have worked so well.

Even so Birt had prepared with immense seriousness and consulted endless demographic research and market segmentation profiles, while Grade did it all off-the-cuff, filling in the silences with one-liners; buying and selling programmes on a series of hunches. Grade, who was just as competitive in his own way, won by a narrow margin.

Now, with both men at the BBC, they were potential competitors once again. Grade still wanted to be Director General one day, and was being groomed for the job by Cotton, but would think about it again in three or four years' time, when the traditional jockeying for position would begin. Birt might turn out to be a rival then; but he was not that much of a threat.

Sorting out current affairs would bog him down for years. The MD-TV job would put Grade in pole position. He would build on the ratings success he had already achieved and, according to plan, emerge in a few years' time as 'the man who saved the BBC.'

With Grade in the top job, John Birt would make the perfect Deputy Director General.

# 9

## Giving the
## Shop Away

The new régime of Hussey, Checkland and Birt was unpopular with a lot of people at the BBC. Few wanted to speak out directly, but the message was spread samizdat-style by defectors and their supporters outside. An edition of *World in Action* called *The Taming of the Beeb*, made by Dave Mills, an ex-Lime Grove producer, cast Hussey as the Tory hatchet man sent in to get rid of Milne; Checkland was the dull accountant prepared to do his dirty work. And Birt's mission was to neuter BBC journalism, making it acceptable to Downing Street. Mills claimed he was deluged with phone calls from people still suffering at Lime Grove, congratulating him on the exposé.

A few days later Donald Trelford, the diminutive editor of the *Observer*, was invited to give his thoughts on the state of television journalism at a Royal Television Society dinner. Trelford mildly attacked Birtism as 'mechanistic' and 'joyless' and received a withering response for his troubles. William Rees-Mogg accused him of 'anarchism'; Brian MacArthur of the *Sunday Times* said his speech showed he was opposed to getting the facts right; while LWT's Brian Walden accused

him of being part of a 'metropolitan anti-Thatcherite establishment swimming in its own bile'.

Soon afterwards Milne published his memoirs, saying the
way he was 'executed' would 'stand high in the annals of
broadcasting infamy.' The Government campaign about bias
in the BBC, he said, was like Hitler's advice on propaganda
given in *Mein Kampf*: 'the great masses of people will more
easily fall victim to a big lie than to a small one.'

Whatever the truth of the 'tamed' accusation, the people
now running the BBC did agree with Downing Street about
two important points: BBC journalism was biased and deeply
flawed; and the Corporation was overstaffed and should
rapidly reduce the size of its work force. Birt was sorting out
the first problem; and Checkland was talking about his
Billion Pound Business. Political attention switched to ITV.

Mrs Thatcher's attitude towards the commercial network
was scarcely less hostile, despite the fact it did not rely on
public money. It was part of the duopoly that worked with
the BBC to keep out new players. And like the BBC, the
current affairs departments at the ITV companies were
regarded with great suspicion.

The Downing Street Policy Unit study group on broadcast-
ing, looking at both the BBC and ITV, and chaired by Mrs
Thatcher herself, was getting to work licking the Peacock
Committee's recommendations into shape. This would
involve a consultation period followed by the publication of a
White Paper and then a Broadcasting Act.

The process started in September 1987 when more than
twenty television executives were summoned to a Downing
Street seminar on the subject. They sat in semicircles facing
Mrs Thatcher, who was at the top table, flanked by Nigel
Lawson, Douglas Hurd and Brian Griffiths, the satellite
enthusiast. The BBC was represented by John Birt and
Michael Grade. Birt was already highly thought of in Downing Street, but Grade's relations with the Conservatives were
more complicated. He was friendly with Tim Bell, a Thatcher

public relations adviser. But Grade had also been involved in *Real Lives*-type arguments about BBC drama.

One of the most serious of these was a skirmish over an abortive drama about Mrs Thatcher's role in the Falklands War. Grade had gone to Number Ten to discuss the feasibility of the play with the Prime Minister's private office, and to see what access the BBC would be given to official records. The advisers were much more interested in who Grade would cast as the Prime Minister. Grade said it was such a huge role that he would have to use either Vanessa Redgrave or Glenda Jackson, the two leading actresses who could pass for being the same age as Mrs Thatcher.

But Redgrave was a leader of the Trotskyite Workers' Revolutionary Party; and Jackson was about to be endorsed as a Labour Party parliamentary candidate, appropriately enough, for Hampstead. There was no chance, Grade thought, of using lesser actresses or a look-alike. That would reduce the play to farce.

The casting was a problem, but Grade was already thinking of abandoning the play. Milne had offhandedly commissioned the work from writer Ian Curteis, whose previous dramas about Anthony Eden and Winston Churchill were great successes. But when Grade saw the script he was disappointed. The project was quietly dropped. Curteis was furious and leaked the story to the right-wing Freedom Association, which printed an article in its newsletter claiming the BBC had 'banned' the play because it was too nice to Mrs Thatcher. The article was picked up by the *Evening Standard* and followed up by the rest of Fleet Street including the *Daily Mail* which ran another THE BBC IS OUT OF CONTROL editorial.

The row over the Falklands play was followed by press outrage over Alan Bleasdale's series, *The Monocled Mutineer*, about a First World War deserter. Although it was drama, the BBC publicity department promoted it as a 'true story'. Grade at once admitted the mistake, but was still lambasted for passing off left-wing fiction as objective fact.

In an attempt to improve relations with the Conservative Party, Grade and Jonathan Powell, the head of BBC TV drama, invited Norman Tebbit to lunch at Television Centre. To their surprise, the BBC team found Tebbit was a likeable and very funny man. He sat at the head of the table cracking jokes while making his complaints. He had obviously been well briefed and attacked each person in rotation with a series of cheeky verbal punches.

When Powell's turn came Tebbit said: 'I know all about you. You're the man who makes all this bloody rubbish; all these left-wing plays. How can you possibly justify it all?' Powell had been briefed to be polite at all costs, but decided Tebbit was a bruiser who would not mind frank talk. 'That's bollocks,' he replied. 'Absolute bollocks. We make a drama called *Howard's Way*. That's not left-wing. It's right-wing: they're all Thatcherite people, doing well for themselves.' Powell then asked if Tebbit had bothered to watch the show. He said he had not, but added: 'You are lying. I know you are lying because you work for the BBC.'

Now, some months later, Grade was relieved to find that BBC bias was off the agenda at the Downing Street seminar. Instead most of the discussion was about ITV and Peacock's suggestion that the network's franchises should be auctioned instead of being awarded on the basis of merit by the Independent Broadcasting Authority.

Professor Peacock gave a short talk. Privately he was amazed by how quickly his recommendations were being taken up. He had served on government committees in the past and had a realistic idea of what they could do. After he had failed to recommend that the BBC should take advertising he was expecting his report to be 'strangled at birth', as he put it. Instead it was to form the basis of a major piece of legislation. Peacock told the seminar that to find the money needed for the auction ITV would have to become more efficient. If the companies could not do that, mainly by reducing their wage bills, they would have to make way for more entrepreneurial operators.

The ITV people grumbled that this would be difficult because of the power of the unions. Television programmes had a very short shelf life and the unions' threat to pull the plugs at the last moment gave them tremendous power. Richard Hooper, head of the pan-European Superchannel, complained that profits were already being hit by the need to pay repeat fees negotiated by Equity, the actors' union. The Prime Minister, stung by this reminder of union power, rose to her feet. 'You gentlemen are the last bastion of restrictive practices,' she said. The Prime Minister spent the rest of the meeting asking hostile questions.

Birt and Grade left the seminar relieved. With luck, the proposed White Paper would leave the BBC alone. But this was only likely if the changes Birt and Checkland were making continued to move forward. The Deputy Director General was now beginning to play a big role in the 'repositioning' of the BBC in the new more free-market broadcasting system the Policy Unit wanted. This was to bring him into conflict with Grade and Bill Cotton, the head of BBC TV, who thought Mrs Thatcher would not dare move against the BBC so long as the ratings were good. The key to this was entertainment, which had always had to fight for money and attention against the high-spending news and current affairs departments now merged and led by Birt.

As the weeks passed during the autumn of 1987 Grade found John Birt, his old friend, strangely distant. He started getting official memos from Birt, on the Deputy Director General's headed notepaper; prim and proper as though addressed to a complete stranger. One was about a Frank Bruno boxing match Grade had bought, but which had turned out to be a bit of a shambles. 'Is this really the sort of programme the BBC should be spending its money on?' Birt wanted to know.

At first Grade thought this might be a temporary brainstorm. At LWT, Birt was famous for his annoying habit of sending memos when a friendly word, or bit of informal advice, was all that was needed. Melvyn Bragg had once found himself descending in the lift with Birt one Monday lunchtime and had chatted pleasantly about the progress of his *South Bank Show*. When Bragg got back to his office he found a barbed memo written by Birt ten minutes earlier burning a hole through his desk. But Birt only did this sort of thing to people, however eminent, whom he regarded as his formal inferiors in any sort of management hierarchy.

When more memos followed, asking about the justification for running particular programmes at this or that time, The Great Scheduler realised, to his horror, that Birt thought he had the right to pull rank and tell him what to do.

Eventually Grade went over Birt's head and showed Checkland a clutch of offending paperwork. 'This is just silly,' he said, and he repeated the pitch he had originally used to attract Birt to the BBC: 'what the three of us together don't know about broadcasting isn't worth knowing. We have got to make this work; because it's not going to work if John carries on like this. It's just causing confusion.' Checkland wearily told him not to worry. He would tell John to stop sending the notes. They were not necessary.

Grade found the meeting strange. Checkland did not seem to appreciate where the confusion might lead or, at least, give any impression that he could do anything about it. He returned to Television Centre with the distinct impression he had been fobbed off. He was worried about the power base Birt was building. Grade knew Checkland was terrified of news and current affairs, that it would 'bite him in the bum' as Grade put it. The new Director General had seen how complaints about programmes had destroyed the Milne régime. Birt had evidently put a stop to all that. Checkland was deeply grateful.

When the memos continued to arrive Cotton and Grade began to realise a showdown with Birt was inevitable. The issue was to be the appointment of new controllers for BBC 1 and BBC 2, left vacant by Grade's impending promotion to Managing Director and Graeme McDonald's retirement from BBC 2. Grade regarded the appointments as crucial, and was determined he would make the decisions, advised by Cotton and cleared by Checkland.

Birt had already interfered in the process, but only indirectly. Grade's first choice for controller of BBC1 was Ron Neil. Despite his recent conversion to Birtism, Neil was still thought of by Grade as one of the country's leading 'tabloid television' enthusiasts. Assuming Neil would accept the BBC1 offer Grade had gone round smoothing the feathers of others in BBC Television who might think they had a claim on the job.

This had included Jonathan Powell, the head of TV drama who had commissioned *EastEnders*, but was equally successful with series like *Casualty* and *Tinker, Tailor, Soldier, Spy*. Grade and Cotton called him in for dinner at Television Centre. The two executives seemed a bit fidgety as they heaped praise on Powell. When the drama chief finally asked what was on their mind Cotton came straight to the point.

'We know you have ambitions and we think you are doing marvellous work,' Cotton said. 'We want you to keep doing that work. You know that the BBC1 job is coming up, but I have to tell you we can't give it to you.' Grade joined in the flattery, and was achingly sincere. He promised Powell he still had a great future and was desperate to keep him as part of the team, which was why they were going to such lengths to make sure he would not be upset. Powell was amused. He told them he was enjoying his job, was not thinking about promotion to controller and had no plans to go to another company. There were laughs all round and the matter was closed.

But a few weeks later, when Powell returned from a holiday, he got another call asking him to go and see Grade. He found the Managing Director (designate) in a jovial back-slapping mood, waving about one of his fat movie mogul cigars. 'Remember how I told you Ron Neil was going to be the new controller,' Grade said. 'Well, that's all changed.' Powell asked: 'Who is it going to be then?' Grade took a long puff on his cigar and then theatrically jabbed it towards Powell's face: 'You!' he cackled.

'This is a bit of a bummer,' Powell thought to himself. He was second choice and, anyway, would have preferred to keep his existing drama job. The meeting was over quickly and Powell was left to ruminate. Was he up to it? He knew he could do well with drama, and thought he could probably handle comedy quite well. Sport was a mystery to him, but he could get help. News and current affairs might also prove difficult; Powell had little appetite for this part of the schedule.

The meshing of news and current affairs with the channel was tricky at the best of times and the conflict between ratings and 'public service' that it represented went to the heart of what the BBC was about. When there was a strong controller, like Paul Fox, current affairs was kept in its place and worked as a service operation, providing programmes to order to help the schedule succeed.

At other times the tail wagged the dog and Lime Grove, in particular, was a law unto itself, seeing the channel as a vehicle and constantly pushing for longer and better slots. This power relationship would be much more difficult now that Birt and Neil, the first choice for controller, were running the directorate.

On the plus side, Powell got on well with Grade and knew he would be a powerful counterweight to Birt. He would have to lean a lot on Grade at first, but he would learn all the time and the whole experience might be very good for him. Powell agreed to be interviewed for the job.

At the same time Grade set about lining up Alan Yentob for the BBC 2 controller's job. Yentob had joined the BBC as a general trainee in 1968 and moved through television via the old *Omnibus* arts show to become editor of *Arena*. As a former hippy, like Birt, his view of what constituted art was coloured by '60s counter-culture. This entailed a deep intellectual appreciation of mass culture. One of his most famous films for *Arena*, the BBC 2 arts programme he had edited, was a paean to the Ford Cortina. By the time Grade approached Yentob with the BBC 2 proposal he was running BBC Television's music and arts department.

Grade was sent details of the appointments board, listing himself, Checkland, Hussey, Barnett and, amazingly, John Birt as members. Birt was there, but Cotton was not; which Grade thought was outrageous. He phoned Checkland and told him if Cotton was not on the panel he would not join it either. He could go ahead if he liked, but it was out of the question that he would take part without Cotton. Checkland gave in at once and Cotton was put on the list.

Grade then asked about Birt. Why was he there? What had the director of news and current affairs got to do with running the channels? Birt's presence would undermine him at a time when he was trying to establish his authority. It would give people the idea that Birt had the real power in the television service. They were dealing with a very sophisticated work force who could 'sniff a power shift at twenty miles'. Checkland listened patiently and said he would talk to John and get his views. Grade reported the conversation to Cotton, who was naturally furious. He called Checkland and, struggling to keep his cool, said he would like to discuss the matter in person at Television Centre.

When Checkland arrived later that day Cotton ushered him into his office, closed the door smartly behind him and let rip: 'Look, I do not need a man who has been in charge of programmes for a three-day company like LWT to tell me and Michael Grade who should be the controllers.' Checkland seemed more concerned about the leak than anything else. 'Where did you hear this?' he demanded to know. 'That doesn't matter,' Cotton glared back. 'Just so long as you tell me it isn't true.'

Cotton regained his composure and firmly said Checkland should be on the board as Director General, and there needed to be a member of the Board of Governors. Together with Grade and himself that was all that was needed to do the job.

Checkland said he agreed, and would look at the problem. 'Don't worry,' he said, 'I take your point. Consider it fixed.'

A couple of days before the interviews were due to take place, Checkland called Cotton and Grade to a meeting in his office. 'I know you are taking an interest in this,' he said, 'I have to tell you that John Birt will be joining the appointments board. The Deputy Director General has a right to be there.' Cotton took a deep breath and sighed: 'Well, I thought we'd agreed he wouldn't.' Checkland called Birt in from the adjoining office.

There was an awkward silence before Grade tried a personal approach. 'I beg you not to do this, John. There are enough problems,' he said. 'Already people don't really know what your position is. If I am going to be Managing Director, I really don't want them to be confused about where the authority is. It will make life more difficult for us both.' And he said again: 'I beg you, don't do it.'

Birt was stern. It was obvious he was not going to back off. 'I have got a contract and I intend that it should be fulfilled,' he said in a clipped voice. Checkland was silent. Grade and Birt looked each other in the eye. At that moment Cotton knew that Birt intended to replace Checkland as Director General, and wanted Grade out of the way. He and Michael, Cotton thought, had 'caught a tiger by the tail.'

Eventually Checkland proposed a compromise. He wanted John to be on the board; but Grade would make the final decision. Birt nodded abruptly. Cotton and Grade said they were not happy, but they would go along with that.

'That's me finished,' Grade thought to himself as he walked out of Checkland's office. 'I know when I am not wanted.' Grade decided he would see through the appointment of Powell and Yentob but would leave the BBC as soon as possible after that, by Christmas at the latest. He did not tell anyone about his decision, not even Bill Cotton.

Cotton was just as sickened, and started looking forward to his own retirement in April more than ever. Why had Checkland, whom he had done so much to help over the years, let him down like this? Why was he doing what this man Birt wanted? He took the Director General to one side for a quiet word.

'Have you given the shop away?' Cotton asked disgustedly. 'Because if you have given the shop away you had no right to apply for the job.' Cotton calmly reminded his old colleague how he had opposed his application for the Director General-ship in the first place. 'You certainly should not have applied for the job if you were not prepared to do it,' he added.

Checkland insisted he was still in control. 'But I've got to tell you the truth,' he confided. 'If I had stood up to Birt on this, he would have taken it to the Board and won.' Check-land seemed to expect sympathy. Instead Cotton exploded: 'What sort of an arrangement is that? Is Birt running the show, or are you?'

The interviews for the controllers' jobs went smoothly enough. Birt was grim and did not say much. Powell momen-tarily tripped up when he was asked if he would cut horse-racing. He didn't have the foggiest idea. But thinking on his feet he blurted out that his grandfather had kept horses and racing was one of his mum's greatest passions. Mercifully the panel collapsed in laughter and passed on to the next question.

Alan Yentob likewise cruised through his interview, show-ing that Grade was in charge as Checkland had promised. It was known that Birt would have preferred the appointment of Will Wyatt, the uncharismatic documentary chief. Yentob, at the time, was a completely un-Birtian figure: highly creative, but a notoriously indecisive man who operated by instinct and did everything at the last conceivable moment. Colleagues complained that 'getting a decision out of Alan is like trying to juggle with soot.'

Both Powell and Yentob got the controller jobs according to plan and, naturally, proclaimed themselves 'delighted'. They were less happy a few days later when Grade, the man who had backed their appointments, walked out of the BBC.

Grade had been talking to Richard Attenborough, the

Chairman of Channel Four. He knew 'Dickie' was in the process of finding a new Chief Executive for the channel, and expressed interest in the job. An interview was arranged to take place in secret as soon as possible, which was Saturday morning. The offer of a job was not absolutely certain, so it was important that nobody in the BBC found out what Grade was up to.

That weekend Grade was scheduled to fly to Los Angeles for one of the regular purchasing meetings with Hollywood production companies. The trip provided the perfect cover for the secret interview. Instead of going to Heathrow, Grade went to Attenborough's house in Richmond, south-west London, leaving his assistant, Peter Ibbotson, stranded in the departure lounge. Ibbotson began to spread the word that Grade was missing and a search was launched.

Grade had meanwhile been offered the Channel Four job and was hiding in his sister's Hampstead home, waiting for the decision to be ratified by the Channel Four board on Monday morning. Eventually he cracked and phoned Bill Cotton. Grade had rarely made a career decision without consulting Cotton first and he wanted to talk it through. Cotton was devastated. He knew that Birt was causing problems but thought Grade should stay and fight him. He had the backing of the staff and he was on the side of viewers. But, like the father figure he was, he told him to do what he thought was best for his future.

When the phone went down Cotton summoned Jonathan Powell and Alan Yentob to the Halcyon Hotel near Television Centre. The new controllers were sworn to secrecy. Cotton then told them what was going on. Powell was distraught. Grade had persuaded him to take the BBC 1 controller's job. They had always seen the future as a team effort. Powell was not sure he could handle the job on his own. He and Yentob, who had never worked at Television Centre, would have to face life as controllers with L-plates on.

The Channel Four board met on Monday and confirmed Grade's appointment. At the time Checkland and the rest of the BBC's Board of Management, with the exception of Cotton, still thought Grade was missing, or had gone to Hollywood on his own. But it was inevitable that the story would soon start to leak. The first editions of Tuesday's *Daily Mail* carried the news as its front-page splash: ANGRY GRADE MOVES TO CHANNEL 4.

There was pandemonium in Television Centre, with the public relations machine attempting to limit the damage as the *Mail* and the rest of Fleet Street started sniffing around the spats that had taken place between Grade and Birt. At Broadcasting House, where the mandarins had never really taken to Grade's swashbuckling style, the mood was generally one of 'I told you so'. But Marmaduke Hussey was incandescent, spluttering with rage at Grade's treachery.

Hussey had plenty to be upset about. Earlier in the year he had sat through Grade's pitch for the Director General's job, listening to him pontificate about the future of the BBC. Grade was always telling him what he should and shouldn't do, sticking his nose in the Board's business and sounding off to journalists, presenting himself as Mr BBC. Annoyingly, Grade and Cotton had run a campaign to prevent Dimbleby's appointment.

Now this! Grade had got everything he wanted: the job of running the television service, a big budget and his choice for the controllers. He had made a terrible stink over the appointments board that had given the jobs to Powell and Yentob. He had promptly disappeared to run a rival TV channel without telling anyone.

Cotton arrived from a Chinese meal with Grade to report there was no chance of his changing his mind. Hussey might rant and rave, but the mess was inevitable. Grade had tried to find a way of working with Birt but it was impossible. There was enormous confusion over Birt's role in the BBC which, for some reason, Checkland had not been able to clear up.

It was important that a strong candidate for Managing Director was found quickly, and that meant Birt was not to interfere in the process. Ideally Birt should pull back from his involvement in the channels altogether and concentrate on his own area of news and current affairs.

Cotton thought Checkland was at least as much to blame. The Director General was trying to be all things to all men and would not stand up to Birt. And the real cause of this and other difficulties was Hussey. 'Dukey', he decided, was the organ-grinder. Checkland and Birt were the two monkeys whom he would play off against each other when it suited him.

A bland press statement was prepared to cover up the fear and loathing being heaped on Grade inside Broadcasting House. Checkland was quoted as saying: 'I am very sad he has gone. It is a tremendous blow and a shock.' Hussey described Grade to the press as 'an outstanding but itinerant talent' and also said he was sorry to see him go.

Grade's target at Channel Four would be to get the audience share up to ten per cent. This, in itself, would hurt the BBC. With Grade now batting for the opposition, it fell to Jonathan Powell to defend the ratings success Grade had started to deliver.

His first week as controller was not auspicious, and immediately brought him into conflict with Birt and Neil over the place of news in the schedule.

Powell was told the Six O'Clock News would be going live to follow the signing of the Intermediate Nuclear Forces treaty by President Gorbachev in Moscow. This was an important event which, as much as anything, signalled the official end of the Cold War. Ron Neil, the manager of the directorate, was very excited about it. But for Powell it was a real pain: dull footage of men in overcoats signing a piece of paper in the middle of the early evening schedule when he was trying to hook people in for the rest of the night.

The signing session was due to happen at about 7.15 pm, leaving fifteen minutes to fill before the next 'junction' with BBC 2 at 7.30 pm. This was an awkward block of time: too long to be collapsed into trailers, and too short to show a programme of any sort. Powell went to see Neil, telling him not to leave an odd bit of air time between 7.15 and 7.30. 'I don't care what you do,' Powell said, 'get a couple of politicians talking in the studio if you must. Anything you like. But whatever you do, don't leave the network empty.' Neil agreed.

The broadcast was as dull as Powell had feared. But there was worse to come. He was watching out of the corner of his eye in his office when the live coverage abruptly stopped and the channel started showing old cartoons. Powell was appalled. In front of the prime time audience tuning in for *EastEnders*, BBC 1 had gone from a momentous world event to Donald Duck. The test card would have been better. He flew out of his office and along the corridor and collided with Neil just by the swing doors. Powell grabbed Neil's lapels and screamed incoherently into his face: 'You arsehole! Donald Duck!'

Powell started kicking the swing door off their hinges in frustration. Why had they left presentation to fill in for eight minutes? All they had to do was get some bloody general to sit around and rabbit on. They were perfectly capable of that. Did they know anything at all about television? Were they trying to destroy the whole operation?

Neil retreated, urging calm and mumbling apologies. But when Birt heard about the punch-up he ordered Bill Cotton to tell Powell to apologise to Neil. Cotton threw the memo in the bin. Powell might have been wrong to fly off the handle, but it was entirely understandable. The new controller did apologise to Neil, explaining that the tension between the television service and the news directorate was getting to him.

Powell, like others running the network, feared Birt would try and take over the schedules without consulting the controllers, and the Donald Duck horror seemed to prove it. There was even hope that Birt would now realise that his attempts to extend his power were leading to problems. He might be more cautious in future.

This was not to be. Within a few days Birt was again to

clash with Cotton and the channel controllers, this time over the thorny question of giving *Newsnight* a fixed starting time on BBC 2. Birt had always seen *Newsnight* as one of the BBC's most important programmes. It had a small audience but, as a televisual version of a broadsheet newspaper, was avidly watched by 'opinion formers', as Howell James liked to call them. They tended to miss the early evening news because they were working late at the office forming opinions. Irritatingly for these people, the BBC had never been able to give *Newsnight* a fixed start time.

Cotton had looked at the *Newsnight* scheduling problem many times, and decided against a fixed starting time. The reasons were highly technical, and a complete mystery to all but the small band of professional television schedulers. The problem flowed from the need to co-ordinate BBC 1 and BBC 2 as a series of viewing choices throughout the evening. BBC 2 had to offer a half-hour alternative to BBC 1's Nine O'Clock News. When the news was over BBC 2 could start running a movie, allowing the News viewers to tune in. Movies ran for 90 minutes, or sometimes more, meaning that most nights the earliest time free for *Newsnight* was 11 pm, and sometimes later.

If *Newsnight* was locked in at 10.30 pm, as Birt wanted, the option of showing an 'adult' feature film on BBC 2 to compete with ITV would disappear. The arguments between Birt and Cotton got more and more heated, until it became clear that Checkland was going to back Birt.

Finally Cotton held up his hands and told Checkland they would have to agree to differ. But, he insisted, if he was going to push this he should take it to the Board of Governors before any final decision was made. They could argue it out there. Checkland agreed.

A few days later Cotton wandered into a press conference at Television Centre called to announce a new campaign of BBC 'openness'. The Managing Director stood at the back of the studio behind the journalists and listened with mild bewilderment to Checkland's talk about new dawns of accountability and responsiveness. Cotton was about to wander out again when, to his astonishment, Checkland announced *Newsnight* would in future have a fixed starting time of 10.30 'for an experimental period'.

All eyes turned to Cotton. As managing director of the television service he was supposed to be in complete charge of all scheduling decisions, as well as having nominal control over news and current affairs. Some of the hacks began to work out that the announcement, and the way it had been made, was an insult of stratospheric proportions to Cotton. The slight was even greater because the Broadcasting House 'suits' had made the announcement at Television Centre, Cotton's territory.

He turned on his heels and slipped quietly back to his office before the hacks could start asking him about it. Later that day Cotton tried to contact Checkland to find out what had happened, and why he had changed his mind about taking the issue to the Board. But the Director General was unavailable.

The idea of resigning flashed through Cotton's mind, but he decided against it. He had been provoked at various points in his career, but had never resigned over anything. He was not going to start now. It was obvious that Birt and Checkland had not bothered to consult him because he was due to leave soon, which, he thought, was pretty rotten of them. Resigning would only play into their hands.

Instead he disappeared to his flat in Deal where he would be free from the clutches of Fleet Street. It was left to other BBC executives to tell the papers, off the record, that Cotton was furious about the decision. For once BBC TV's sure-footed programme publicity chief, Keith Samuel, was thrown. He told the *Daily Telegraph* that privately he was 'gobs-macked' by Checkland's unilateral decision to give *Newsnight* a fixed slot.

The papers started to run the story big. But it was Checkland, and not Birt, who had to explain the row. 'I deeply regret', he said, 'that Bill Cotton, who has been my colleague and friend for many years, was upset by the manner of the announcement regarding the fixed schedule for *Newsnight.*'

Cotton said nothing in public until Checkland started telling the papers that Alan Yentob had advocated the 10.30 fixed slot at his interview. In fact Yentob, who had not been told about the decision either, had only said he would consider 10.45, and not 10.30, as a possible fixed time. This, at least, would give him enough time to show a short movie.

Cotton denounced Checkland not for making this error, which was bad enough, but for revealing what had been said during a confidential appointments panel. After Birt's talk about leaking, the decision to reveal what Yentob had supposedly said was unforgivable.

Finally Checkland resorted to saying that scheduling decisions were indeed Cotton's responsibility, but on this occasion he had intervened in his capacity as editor-in-chief. Birt's agreement with the decision was purely coincidental, Checkland claimed. Few people believed this.

The row over the fixed time for *Newsnight* rumbled on inside the BBC through the early months of 1988 to the bafflement of the general public, who had no idea of its real significance. Checkland tried to repair his personal relationship with Cotton, the man who had done so much to ease his rise up the BBC, but it was no good. At their first meeting after the fateful press conference, Checkland began to offer a shamefaced explanation. But Cotton could not bear to listen.

'Please don't do the apologising act,' Cotton said. 'You are going to have to live with this. It's a bloody silly decision and you know it. One day someone will get promoted for having the sense to change it.'

Cotton received a personal letter from Hussey about the *Newsnight* affair. 'This was a decision for which I take responsibility,' the Chairman wrote, 'as, ultimately, I do for all decisions taken in the BBC. I know it upsets you and I am very sorry about that. We must meet very soon and I will explain it more fully.'

Cotton did not bother to follow up the invitation. The letter showed Hussey had obviously misunderstood the traditional role of successful BBC chairmen. The post carried enormous formal powers which had to be used sparingly. Unlike the chairman of a commercial company, he could not be sacked by the shareholders; only the Queen could do that. A wiser man would realise how heavy the responsibility was and would steer the whole organisation with a light touch.

But Hussey was different. He had used his power in the most brutal way to get rid of Milne and, as Checkland had admitted, had leaned heavily and repeatedly on the Director General to do his bidding. Instead of keeping his distance Hussey was involved in the day-to-day management, right down to the scheduling of particular programmes.

In his own mind Cotton's suspicions that Checkland had 'given the shop away' to Hussey and Birt were confirmed.

# 10

## *Call Me 'Dukey'*

The idea of getting the BBC to stage a televisual version of a private sector Annual General Meeting was not new. It was one of several publicity suggestions brought to the Corporation by Tim Bell, the politically connected PR man.

The AGM concept had been developed into *See For Yourself*, a three-hour 'telethon' designed to show that the BBC was no longer run by the fuddy-duddy establishment types of public imagination, but was safely in the hands of modern media professionals with the desires of ordinary, decent folk at heart. Stuart Young, BBC Chairman at the time it was decided to go ahead with the project, would have been the ideal man to front the show.

Young was every inch the modern, go-ahead businessman, from his unflappable manner to his immaculately tailored suits. He was to have been joined by Alasdair Milne, who could be a bit dour, but knew all the tricks of the trade. But Young had died and Milne had been sacked before the first annual edition was ready for transmission.

Their places had been taken by Marmaduke Hussey and Michael Checkland. Neither was exactly drawn from the ranks of nature's born television performers. Hussey was a huge man, far too big for the screen, who lumbered about braying at people in patrician tones more suited to the Bath and West Show, where he was President. His style was to crash into rooms, slap his subalterns on the back and overwhelm people with bumbling charm.

He encouraged people to call him 'Dukey' and played up to the image of a crusty and slightly eccentric aristocrat. One habit was to bang on the bonnet of his official car with his stick and call out for his driver. At committee meetings he always appeared to be in a complete muddle, constantly shuffling his papers as he hunted for this or that piece of information.

This was the perfect demeanour for his London club, Brooks's, where he could regale sympathetic members of the establishment with the latest rambling anecdote about 'those bloody people at the BBC'. His other party piece was name-dropping on an heroic scale, which could only be moderated by his wife, Lady Susan, who would shout: 'Oh, for God's sake, Dukey, do shut up.'

The idea of scrapping *See For Yourself* had surfaced momentarily in some people's minds, but by now the project had a head of steam behind it. And Hussey was very keen on the idea. It was quite right, he thought, that people should be able to take a look at the chaps in charge.

Most of the show, when it went out, took the form of a pre-recorded film with a clear message: the politicians and the press had got it wrong, the BBC was now a highly cost-effective organisation and the statistics were there to prove it. The Corporation's managers could account for every penny, right down to the last of the 7,000 bacon rolls consumed on the set of *Bergerac*.

A blizzard of factoids highlighted the cost of running the BBC's New Delhi office; and how much it cost to make different types of programmes by the hour. BBC Enterprises, the nation was told, had milked £577,000 out of the temporary yuppie craze for *Flowerpot Men* videos.

*See For Yourself* was much less illuminating on more sensitive matters. The recent internal history of the BBC was rewritten in best Stalinist fashion. Milne's sacking was dealt with by showing a clip from BBC News that said he had resigned for 'personal reasons'. There was nothing about Michael Grade's sudden defection to Channel Four or the continuing agonies in news and current affairs.

When the filmed sequence was over viewers were returned to the studio for Hussey and Checkland's contribution, which took the form of answering unscripted questions from the public. Alarmingly for the production team, this part of the show was live. So it was anyone's guess where Hussey's verbal perambulations might lead.

The worst thing that could happen was that Hussey would take off his artificial leg and plonk it on the table in front of him. He had once done this at a meeting with union officials during *The Times* strike. This was reckoned to have been a form of intimidation, rather than absent-mindedness, and so the threat was not very great. Checkland, the *Daily Mail's* 'Mr Nobody', was just seen as a man wildly deficient in the sort of charisma needed for good television.

The great danger was that the show would turn into 'negative PR' confirming the public's prejudice that the Corporation was stuffed with upper-class twits and faceless bureaucrats.

Eyes rolled when the Chairman started by instructing viewers to call him 'Dukey', and to address the Director General as 'Mike'. This had come straight off the top of his head, without thought to the public relations consequences, as did his confession that he had not 'actually had time to watch all the programmes' he was supposed to be discussing.

This observation triggered an unfathomable line of thought in Hussey's head which ended up, apropos nothing, with some gobbledygook about seeing a moorhen on the lawn of his country house in the Mendips that morning. BBC veterans watched with dismay. Only another few minutes of this nonsense to go. Next time, if there was a next time, somebody had better make sure the old buffer was pre-recorded and edited.

Checkland's performance was also true to form. He delivered well-rehearsed platitudes like 'the market place cannot provide the only judgement of value', and 'the truth is, you can't let things stand still', with Brummie sobriety.

Everyone in the media business derided *See For Yourself* as 'The Mike and Dukey Show' and weak jokes comparing it to double acts like Laurel and Hardy or Jeeves and Wooster, with Checkland playing the role of Dukey's butler, began to circulate. Nobody in the BBC was very keen to be involved with future editions, which were planned to take place every January.

(Subsequent *See For Yourself* shows were enlivened by Dukey spluttering that he 'had not understood a single word' of Dennis Potter's play *Blackeyes*. And when a woman in the audience asked him why there were no fat female news readers he caused great hilarity by turning to Sue Lawley and whispering 'What's she going on about?' Working on the programme replaced having to do a spell on *Top Gear* in Pebble Mill as the BBC producer's idea of being sent to Siberia.)

The *See For Yourself* programmes were supported by other viewer-friendly initiatives, most of which seemed ill-starred. A new range of TV licence gift tokens, doubling up as Christmas cards, was advertised in *The Listener* eight days before Christmas with a warning to 'allow fourteen days for delivery'. A Howell James-style brochure was issued containing an article by Birt on news and current affairs. The headline said BBC journalism should always 'sparkle and crackle'. Unfortunately it was printed in large type next to a picture of the Piper Alpha oil rig disaster.

Apart from his contribution to the *See For Yourself* brochure, Birt had steered clear of the project. But this did not mean he was not involved in the process of lobbying the Government. His mission to sort out news and current affairs was being accomplished in record time and he was now operating broadly across the whole Corporation. His job now was to make sure that the BBC stayed out of the firing line while the Government drew up its White Paper on the future of broadcasting. This would be published at the end of 1988, laying the foundations for a Broadcasting Bill the next year.

Ever since his presence at the Downing Street 'Last Bastion' seminar Birt had been discreetly courting politicians, becoming a fixture on the Whitehall lunching circuit, where he was in his element. People who had worked closely with Birt at LWT had noticed how he was obsessed with getting to know powerful and famous people. It was said that when Birt walked into a meeting or conference he would target the person who held the real power like a heat-seeking missile. He would then make sure that he sat next to them and spent as much time as possible impressing and flattering them.

Going to any sort of social event with Birt could be a deeply embarrassing experience. The story was told of how he had once been at a dinner where Michael Green, the multi-millionaire owner of Carlton Communications, and a man believed to have the Prime Minister's ear, was present. Birt was stranded at the other end of the table. When he realised he would not get a chance to ingratiate himself with Green, Birt began shaking with frustration.

At another party, given by his former mentor David Frost, Birt was in a huddle with some old pals from LWT, having a relaxed chat. Then Geoffrey Howe suddenly appeared. Birt suspended his conversation in mid-sentence and rushed over to talk to a member of Howe's entourage. Minutes later the introduction was made and Birt was talking earnestly to the Foreign Secretary.

Some said this behaviour was a compulsion, a sort of disease that Birt had picked up during his rapid ascent at LWT. It was said his main professional characteristic was an ability to appeal and make himself useful to the person above him in any sort of pecking order. People who were no longer of any use to him could be abandoned without warning, just as his friendship with Michael Grade was sacrificed the instant it got in his way.

Birt had the BBC's new Policy and Planning Unit, with its 500 staff drawn from areas like broadcasting research and the central secretariat, to help him in his lobbying activities. The Unit was headed by Patricia Hodgson, a fastidious and ambitious former Conservative parliamentary candidate once described as looking like she was sculpted from deep frozen Oil of Ulay.

Birt had formed an important strategic alliance with Hodgson and increasingly used the Policy Unit as a power base and private think-tank for the endless audience research and strategy documents he was lobbing into the Whitehall machine. With all the Eastern European comparisons coming out of events like Leatherhead and the Studio D showdown over current affairs, it was inevitably nicknamed 'the politburo'.

The Deputy Director General had already established a close relationship with David Mellor, the Home Office minister in charge of broadcasting. Birt, as the 'heat-seeking missile', had found Mellor to be a soft target. The Putney MP's detractors said he was a pompous and vain man who responded easily to flattery. He was an opera buff and Radio Three fan, and did not care who knew it. Birt was able to put this to good use over the lunch table.

The Deputy Director General would put a lot of effort into preparing for lunches with important people like Mellor, planning an agenda he needed to work through. Time would be spent anticipating questions that might be asked, and answers would be fully rehearsed. The whole thing had to be organised with military precision because Birt was a weak off-the-cuff speaker and could freeze on the spot if asked an awkward question.

With all this preparation Birt could make a tremendously positive impression by simply echoing whatever it was that the selected VIPs were interested in, answering their questions with precision and to their absolute satisfaction. The number of important people who found Birt was 'on their wavelength' was remarkable and ranged across such fundamentally different personalities as Marmaduke Hussey, David Mellor and Greg Dyke. Meeting him was always an enjoyable experience, a real tonic for the ego, 'inspirational' for some. This was supplemented by Birt's munificent use of BBC perks ranging from free tickets to Ascot and Wimbledon to dinner parties with stars like Stephen Fry and Harry Enfield.

After a couple of sessions with Birt, Mellor and his advisers were won over. They decided the Deputy Director General was a clear-sighted man who, to a remarkable extent, shared their opinions on just about everything. He was talking about taking the BBC to the market and increasing choice for the consumer. They sympathised with Birt's lack of control on the financial side, but were prepared to be patient. They decided that Birt would not 'go native' and would one day replace Checkland as Director General. He deserved their support.

There was now no doubt Birt was desperate to impress Hussey and use him as his route to power. Mellor's support would be useful. With Grade gone the only figure on the programme-making side of the BBC who might block his way was Paul Fox, the heavyweight former BBC 1 controller who had just returned to Television Centre as Managing Director. Fox filled the vacancy left by Bill Cotton's retirement and the sudden departure of Grade.

Hussey and Joel Barnett, the BBC Vice Chairman, had thought about appointing Ian Hargreaves, whom Birt had brought in to the news and current affairs directorate as managing editor. Hargreaves was a classic Birt appointment, and part of a network of people centred on John Lloyd, the ex-hippie *Financial Times* journalist much admired by Birt.

Hargreaves was an earnest man who wore John Lennon glasses and looked a bit like Lofty, the resident 'wally' in *EastEnders*. He was given to writing long tracts in favour of 'Birtism', a phrase he used without irony, which would appear in *Ariel*, the in-house BBC newspaper nicknamed *Pravda*. Barnett met Hargreaves and encouraged him to apply for the Managing Director's job, but he declined for the simple and sensible reason that he knew next to nothing about television.

Checkland turned instead to Paul Fox, who had expressed interest in the Director Generalship, but had demanded to be offered the job instead of applying. This time the BBC made the approach in the way Fox wanted. The first contact came during a party to mark the relaunch of *The Listener* as a joint BBC-ITV publication. A meeting was arranged in a discreet hotel near Box Hill in Surrey and the deal was fixed in half an hour. Checkland offered him the Managing Director's job. Fox accepted on the strict condition he would not be interviewed by the Board of Governors.

Fox then met Hussey. The Chairman confirmed Checkland's offer, but said he would have to be interviewed by the Board. Fox at first refused, but then agreed to a compromise. He would meet the Governors for an informal chat over tea and sandwiches at Claridge's, but he would not come to Broadcasting House for a formal interview. The tea party happened in due course, with Fox trying to make it as unlike an interview as possible, and the Governors doing the exact opposite.

Birt's critics inside the BBC could not believe their luck. Many had hankered after Fox's return for years. At the age of 62 he was getting on a bit, but was still a formidable figure, very much the elder statesman of the industry. With Powell and Yentob running the channels backed by such a strong figure, Birtism in all its forms might now be stopped in its tracks. The optimism soon wilted.

Instead of the stirring statements of intent people had hoped for, the Managing Director's first memos were about things like the need to economise on biscuits served to visitors. Fox at once gave up the nominal control over news and current affairs enjoyed by previous Managing Directors and, crucially, agreed not to challenge the decision over the fixed time for *Newsnight*.

Some in the television service had hoped that Fox would use his weight to overturn the 'stupid decision', as Cotton had called it, of giving *Newsnight* a fixed start at 10.30. They were to be disappointed for the very good, but entirely unknown, reason that Fox had suggested it to Birt in the first place. After advising Checkland to appoint Birt, Fox had taken the new Deputy Director General to lunch to discuss the future. Birt asked Fox how he should go about the job. The old sage's main advice was to introduce the fixed slot for *Newsnight* as a priority.

Disappointment at Fox's laid-back style led to rumours that he shut himself in his office for hours every day. With Birt disappearing off into the bowels of Whitehall, and Fox apparently treading water, Checkland was beginning to look like an increasingly isolated figure in the BBC's internal politics. His power had always been based on mastery of the accounting system he had largely created, and which only he really understood.

One reason why Cotton had found Checkland so useful was the way he could suddenly conjure up badly needed finance for the schedules from reserves prudently set aside for the purpose. He was able to move blocks of money around the system, creating the legend of 'Michael Chequebook: the great facilitator'.

For more than a decade Checkland had carefully salted away reserves of cash to prepare the Corporation for the rainy day of an especially bad licence-fee settlement. Now a monsoon had arrived. The Government had pegged the licence fee to the rate of inflation when money was needed for independent production. Douglas Hurd, the Home Secretary, said he had 'applied a double squeeze' on the BBC's finances because costs were rising faster in the broadcasting industry than inflation in general. Eventually the squeeze was made even tighter by linking the licence fee to the retail price index, minus three per cent.

Checkland had started to draw on some of the reserves he had built up over the years, estimated by insiders to be about £200 million. This enabled him to find the cash for the independents and promised extra in-house programmes like *The Late Show* without having to suddenly announce enormous redundancies. But, in the summer of 1989, Checkland was blown off course by union demands for big salary increases.

Rates of pay at the BBC had always been far lower than in ITV. Previous Director Generals were able to explain this away, saying working for the BBC was special. It was more of a vocation than a job. During the Studio D meeting at Lime Grove, where Birt had introduced the new régime to the rank and file, Ron Neil had given a similar line. 'On wages,' he had said with absolute conviction, 'we are not going to be able to match the independent sector.'

Neil had since been forced to eat his words, as he had on many things, especially after Birt had brought in new recruits from LWT on their old and much higher salaries. Peter Sissons, the latest Birt signing, was reportedly paid £500,000 to lure him away from Channel Four, with another £200,000 compensation to his former employers. At the same time it was discovered that 140 'top executives' at the BBC were being given a ten per cent bonus as well as perks including company cars worth £10,000, plus free health insurance.

Checkland and Birt had received 30 per cent pay increases, taking their salaries to almost £100,000 a year. And one of the first questions during the *See For Yourself* extravaganza asked why the BBC was paying £350,000 to Terry Wogan. Checkland said it was because he 'now had to pay the market rate' for talent.

Union negotiators representing most of the BBC's 25,000 employees said this was fair enough. But now it was their turn. They asked for an immediate 16 per cent pay rise leading to a new pay structure that would mirror the much higher salaries in the private sector. If the BBC was moving into the contract culture, they said, then it would have to pay the commercial rate, just as it did for Wogan and Sissons.

Soon the public found their viewing interrupted by a series of selective strikes. This put the BBC back on the political agenda in a way that was deeply embarrassing for Hussey and the Board, who were presenting the BBC as a case study in the way a public sector body could successfully embrace the market. The message was passed down the management line to hold firm. But as the strikes continued, Checkland began to weaken and make conciliatory noises. Senior managers were left in a delicate position and Hussey was furious.

The new tension between Hussey and Checkland rarely spilled out in public. But during the strike the Chairman attended a dinner with some senior BBC staff in Glasgow and, after a few drinks, growled: 'If Checkland doesn't do something about this strike soon, I'll have to deal with him.' Pat Chalmers, the controller of BBC Scotland, observed: 'These things are not that simple.' Referring to the disastrous strike during Hussey's reign at *The Times*, Chalmers gamely added: 'You may remember your dispute; and you didn't handle that very well, did you?' Hussey straightened himself and barked: 'Don't you *dare* speak to me like that.' The row blew over.

After Checkland's vacillation, the strike was settled with an 8.8 per cent pay increase, costing an extra £75 million a year. To help him find the money Checkland set up a committee called Funding the Future with a brief to 'recommend ways of releasing additional resources'. It was to be chaired not by himself, but by Ian Phillips, the new director of finance recently recruited from British Rail.

Checkland had always gone to great lengths to make sure his lieutenants followed him up the promotion ladder, keeping his own team of loyalists in place. But Hussey and Barnett were very keen to appoint a fellow outsider to the key post of finance director. Phillips had found the Corporation inefficient in some ways, and years behind British Rail which was already being prepared for privatisation.

The system of reporting financial information, Phillips thought, was a bit rickety and hard to understand. But there was no evidence of the huge waste for which the BBC was always being pilloried by the papers. The main problem was the move to independent production which, eventually, would entail shedding a lot of staff to make way for the 25 per cent quota. The timetable for this was being dictated by the Government and the cuts in the BBC's own staff would inevitably come more slowly.

Phillips thought Checkland had made a good start, but detected impatience on the part of Hussey and Birt who thought the BBC needed to move much faster if they wanted to keep the Government on their side.

The White Paper on Broadcasting had recently confirmed the BBC's position as 'the cornerstone of British broadcasting'. But the ghost of Peacock had not entirely been laid to rest, and the signals from Whitehall were clear enough: the BBC had to lose a lot more staff and become 'lean and efficient', otherwise it might not get such an easy ride when the White Paper became the law as the Broadcasting Act.

# 11

## *Out to Lunch*

In May 1989 Margaret Thatcher celebrated the tenth anniversary of her premiership. It was time to reflect on the 'revolution' she had wrought in British society. The Labour Party had been seen off, perhaps for good, in the 1987 election. Most of the industries nationalised since World War Two had been returned to the private sector.

Rupert Murdoch's News International was a shining example of the new age of enterprise Mrs Thatcher had ushered in. It was union-free, dedicated to giving the punters what they wanted and hugely profitable. Murdoch's papers had cheered on the Prime Minister all the way and savaged her critics, including the BBC. Murdoch had always been one of the Prime Minister's favourite businessmen and now the publisher, who had become a naturalised US citizen four years earlier, flew across the pond on Concorde to join the Prime Minister for a select anniversary dinner at Chequers.

As they raised their glasses they had plenty to thank each other for. The previous three years had seen an unprecedented consumer boom with house prices quadrupling in some parts of the country. It had all been done on the back of a tidal wave of cheap credit, boosting the sales of Murdoch papers, bringing in a flood of profitable advertising, and preparing the market for the next consumer fad: satellite television.

But the toast they drank was as much to the future as the past. Ronald Reagan may have bowed out as President in the United States, but their own special relationship was going from strength to strength. The Soviet 'Evil Empire' in Eastern Europe was starting to fall apart under Gorbachev, opening up huge potential markets for Western companies. Leading the way would be the media, and especially satellite TV.

The first dishes were already beginning to sprout on the walls of Prague, Budapest and Warsaw. They relayed MTV, *Dallas*, *Dynasty* and most exciting of all, Western consumer advertising. After years when the shops were full of state-produced semolina pudding and shabby Bulgarian suits, Western advertising was drooled over like a form of exotic pornography. Yet, despite these momentous changes around the world, the shape of the British television industry was still essentially the same as it had been at the start of the Thatcher revolution.

Three months before the Thatcher anniversary Murdoch had launched Sky Television as a direct broadcast operation. It was greeted with universal sneering by what Murdoch and Andrew Neil liked to call the Television Establishment. John Naughton, the *Observer's* television critic, commented on the advent of what he called 'tabloid television' by quoting a BBC technician who calculated sending a signal from Sky's headquarters via the satellite to a house in London involved a journey of 71,546 kilometres, 'which could make Murdoch-vision the longest garbage run in history'.

Sky was based in the unglamorous setting of a 'crinkly tin' industrial estate in the wilderness of Osterley, near Heathrow airport. But unlike the citizens of Bucharest and Bratislava, the people of Bolton and Basildon had shown a marked lack of interest in the venture. Murdoch had already spent

£350 million getting Sky off the ground and the station was losing at least £2 million a week as the dishes piled up in warehouses.

Sky was carefully targeted at working-class males, defined as social groups C and D by market research. Unless they were unemployed, these people were the winners in the Thatcher revolution. They had bought their houses and were now heavily into home entertainment. They had a brilliant track record of buying electronic gadgets of all sorts as soon as they appeared in the shops.

Unfortunately for Sky these people were amongst the heaviest users of ITV and also watched a lot of the more popular BBC programmes like *EastEnders* and *That's Life*. Sky found that it was having to compete on the quality of its programmes, which was difficult. The 'cosy duopoly', as Murdoch called it, of BBC and ITV was proving to be an impossibly strong competitor.

The White Paper on Broadcasting drawn up after the 'Last Bastion' seminar in Downing Street was good news for Sky. The proposed auction of ITV franchises would load the network with the cost of bidding for franchises previously awarded on merit. The White Paper had set no upper limit for the size of bids and they might therefore be ruinous, leaving very little money to buy the expensive mix of British drama, Hollywood blockbuster movies and live, exclusive sport that was providing such strong competition for Sky.

The White Paper was now going through the 18-month process of being turned into a Broadcasting Act, and all concerned were furiously lobbying for changes. The ITV companies had accepted that an auction of some sort would take place, but were trying to limit the damage by persuading the Home Office to include a 'quality threshold'. Companies would have to meet this before the size of their cash bid was considered.

The ITV lobby was called the Campaign for Quality Television. Its message was supported by press adverts taken out by TVS, the ITV franchise-holder for the south coast,

warning that the new satellite channels would end up showing low-budget porn, and an impoverished ITV might end up
doing the same in order to compete. The adverts were
illustrated with a fetching picture of a housewife performing
a striptease: allegedly one of the most popular shows on
Italian TV after deregulation.

Sky wheeled out Rupert Murdoch to rubbish the whole idea
of Quality Television. In August 1989, midway through
Whitehall's consultation period on the White Paper, Murdoch
delivered the keynote MacTaggart lecture at the annual
Edinburgh TV festival. He had been invited by Janet Street-
Porter, who was taking her turn organising the conference.
This was a sign of her growing importance in tellyland and a
great boost to her ego. Delivering Murdoch was a feather in
her cap, described as a 'coup'.

Murdoch was already a bogeyman for many people in the
British television industry. He had recently been portrayed
as the ruthless, power-mad newspaper proprietor in a play
called *Pravda* at the National Theatre. The actor chosen for
the role was Anthony Hopkins. (When Hopkins followed this
by playing a homicidal, cannibalistic lunatic in *Silence of the
Lambs*, Murdoch quipped the actor was in danger of being
typecast.)

He was in another status league to the programme-makers
gathered in Edinburgh and there was a buzz of excitement
about his presence. People said Street-Porter looked as if she
was 'on heat' at the prospect of sitting next to him on the
platform. Another ex-LWT fashion victim, the Yoof TV chief
was sporting an amazing creation described to friends as one
of her 'result' dresses.

When Murdoch took the stand he seemed nervous, and
drawled haltingly from a script. He looked very tired and
grouchy. This was assumed to be the result of the continuous
jetting between the London, New York and Sydney headquarters of his empire that had left his body clock perma-
nently registering 3 am. He drowsily urged the Government
to deregulate the television industry as extensively as poss-

ible in the interests not of himself, but of 'freedom in broadcasting', the title of his speech.

Murdoch cast himself in his favourite role of Joe Public, the ordinary multi-millionaire on the Clapham Omnibus, castigating a mysterious 'establishment' of 'top people' for denying his fellow ordinary Joes the right to watch what they wanted to watch, when they wanted it.

'Much of what passes for quality on British television really is no more than a reflection of the values of the narrow élite which controls it,' he said, adding: 'what I have in mind is best illustrated by many of the up-market costume soap operas which the British system produces, in which strangulated English accents dominate dramas which are played out in rigid, class-structured settings.'

The speech owed a lot to Andrew Neil, who was always banging on about how British television was 'obsessed' with the class divisions in British society. He had used some of the same lines in a less well publicised talk to a Canadian television conference a few weeks earlier. 'In a market-led TV system there is still room for a public service element,' Murdoch continued. 'What I am arguing for is a move from the current system of public broadcasting, in which market considerations are marginal, to a market system in which public broadcasting would be part of the market mix, but in no way dominate the output in the way it does at present.'

Murdoch finished and was granted cool applause. Despite the downbeat performance Janet Street-Porter's excitement was infectious and added to a sense that something momentous was happening. She gravely called on John Birt to reply: the perfect opportunity for him to make a momentous 'I have a dream' rebuttal of the free-market attacks on the BBC.

Instead he stood up awkwardly, adjusted his glasses and mumbled about the side issue of 'the pornography which lies at the bottom of deregulated markets'. Birt dared to contradict Murdoch on one point. The presence on the BBC of Alexei Sayle, the world's leading would-be Albanian Marxist-

Leninist funnyman, showed the BBC was not locked into the past.

The real debate took place in the bar afterwards. BBC chiefs, including Alan Yentob, milled about sheepishly, hugely embarrassed by their boss's dismal performance. Everyone agreed Birt had 'blown it'. Murdoch was far more impressive. At least he had a coherent argument, even if they did not agree with it. There was much angst as people decided Birt had 'a hidden agenda'.

The Deputy Director General was already working to reposition the BBC as the 'public service element' in the 'multichannel environment' Murdoch had described. So, in terms of its overall thrust, there was little in the speech with which Birt could disagree. At the same time Murdoch had evidently softened his line on the Corporation. In his last major speech about British broadcasting he had called for the privatisation of BBC1 and the transformation of BBC2 into a charitable trust paid for by private donations. Now he was happy for it to continue in the public sector.

People worked out that the continued existence of the Corporation was essential to the politics of his attack on ITV; the perfect answer to the argument that worthy material would disappear from the system if ITV did not get the 'quality threshold'.

After Birt's lugubrious performance at Edinburgh, it was left to Paul Fox to reply to Murdoch in more vigorous terms. *The Times* granted him half a page. Fox began by saying satellite TV was starting to become a reality, but would take longer than Murdoch thought to build up a large audience. He said Murdoch was brave to make his speech in front of such a hostile audience. But he did not really understand British television and probably did not watch much of it.

Murdoch's jibe about quality TV drama being nothing more than 'up-market costume soap operas' was entirely wrong, and Fox listed a variety of BBC and ITV programmes including *EastEnders*, *Brookside* and *Minder* to prove it.

Murdoch's critique would be 'risible', Fox said, if it had come from a less distinguished source.

Apart from this criticism from Fox, the BBC's senior management was keeping its head down and saying little about the Government's proposals for dealing with ITV. This struck some as terribly craven.

'It's not too good staying silent in your cell when you know the person in the cell next door is having his toenails pulled out,' complained Roy Fitzwalter, one of Granada TV's most senior current affairs people. But Birt was not about to lead the riot in cell block H so long as he was slinking around Whitehall and knocking on the doors of powerful people.

A new threat to the BBC did emerge at the last moment as the Broadcasting Bill was going through the House of Lords. Lord Wyatt of Weeford, a personal friend of both Rupert Murdoch and Margaret Thatcher, and otherwise known as Woodrow Wyatt, the 'Voice of Reason' columnist in the *News of the World*, was still working on the pre-Birt agenda that the BBC was left-wing. Lord Wyatt had proposed an amendment to the Bill that would require all broadcasters to be politically impartial, backed by the force of law.

Despite Birt's clean-up of news and current affairs, sniping about left-wing bias had continued from the Tory backbenches. In 1990 the BBC's coverage of South Africa had become a bone of contention. Both Bernard Ingham and Norman Tebbit had complained that the BBC, and especially Radio Four's *Today* programme, was running a 'campaign' against apartheid and in favour of Nelson Mandela.

Hussey had already written to the Home Office expressing 'concern' about Wyatt's idea. The Chairman argued that the BBC had done a lot to reform itself politically. New rules would only serve to make life difficult. For once there was some solidarity between the rival broadcasters, except Sky. Liz Forgan, Channel Four's programme director, said Wyatt's proposals were 'a recipe for insipid broadcasting' that would 'cut off bold polemic at the knees'. Impartiality rules would 'nobble difficult journalism' and 'encourage a nice, harmless mush of blandness' and had to be resisted at all costs.

After establishing his strategic alliance with Mellor, Birt still had to make sure the BBC did not upset the Conservative Party too much during the renewed debate on impartiality. Mellor was on the liberal wing of the party and Birt would have to help him fend off pressure from the right. It was important that backbenchers were not sent into a frenzy by an investigative programme like *Maggie's Militant Tendency*. Birt was not too worried. With his referral procedure in place he would be in a position to prevent or tone down anything too provocative before it reached the screen.

Just such a programme came bubbling up through the system in the autumn of 1990. *Panorama* had obtained some very interesting material about the Conservative Party's finances. An edition entitled *Who Pays For The Party* was scheduled for October, to mark the annual Conservative Party conference. Unfortunately, it coincided with the Lords' debate on the Broadcasting Bill, and its impartiality clause.

The programme was based on a five-month investigation triggered by rumours that the Conservative Party had large sums of money in off-shore bank accounts. This part of the story was difficult to prove, but during research other information came to light. For the first time the *Panorama* team started to investigate some of the thousands of donations to the Tory Party from private companies and individuals. They discovered that directors of large public companies, who would have had to declare donations, were channelling the money through small private companies on the quiet.

This pattern of secret donations, *Panorama* thought, was a good story in its own right. But then they had a breakthrough. Producer Mark Killick found out that Ernest Saunders, the man convicted of insider dealing during the Guinness takeover, was approached by senior Conservatives offering help with the takeover if his company started donating money to the party. After weeks of persuasion Killick coaxed Saunders to go on the record.

Killick and the programme's reporter, Gavin Hewitt, were
elated. The programme was already very strong, but Saunders' material was dynamite. Saunders could offer no forensic
proof for his claim, but there was a lot of circumstantial
evidence, so the interview would have to be handled carefully. Saunders was about to become a convicted felon who, it
was established, had lied in court. The programme would
have to 'package' the interview carefully, making it very
clear the Saunders' allegations were unproven and had to be
treated with great scepticism.

*Who Pays For The Party* went through the referral procedure at all stages, with Samir Shah asking to see research
material and demanding extra interviews, rechecks and
changes to the script. The first version of the finished programme was shown to Ron Neil, who thought the journalism
was solid enough, but thought Birt ought to see it. Birt was
not happy. Using one of his key phrases he announced the
programme was 'not ready yet' and would need more work.

The final referral meeting for *Who Pays For The Party* took
place in the Council Chamber at Broadcasting House. Killick
and Hewitt were summoned before Shah and Neil; John
Wilson, head of editorial policy; numerous lawyers, assistants
and various secretaries. These people sat in conclave with
copies of the programme's revised and 'caveated' script in
front of them. Killick had rarely seen so many suits. Checkland, whose role as editor-in-chief was now a thing of distant
memory, was not present.

Birt marched in at a brisk clip, sat down and called the
meeting to order. 'Let me make it clear from the start,' he
said, 'that the interview with Ernest Saunders will not be
run.' There was a slight pause to allow this to sink in. 'Now,
with that out of the way, let's address ourselves to the rest of
the film.'

Birt went through the script, leading a process of editing
by committee, the ultimate editorial nightmare. Finally they
emerged with a script covered in changes and a gigantic hole
in the middle where the Saunders interview had been. Where

payments were being juxtaposed against changes in government policy, with the viewers left to draw their own conclusions, Birt wanted phrases like 'of course all political parties do this sort of thing' and 'there is no proof there's anything untoward in any of this' inserted.

By now the production team on the programme was suffering from a bad case of 'referral fatigue', the demoralisation that sprang from having to take the scissors to a perfectly decent script. The morale problem was made worse by the gloating of the Conservative PR people, especially Brendan Bruce, the Director of Communications. The team needed him to help set up a long interview with Norman Tebbit, who was Party chairman for most of the period dealt with by the programme.

The interview with Tebbit was a grisly affair. Although Mellor and others were now taking a softer line towards the BBC, the former Tory chairman had, if anything, become more wildly antagonistic than ever. Naturally he regarded Hussey and Birt as a great improvement on Milne, and said so in his autobiography. But his return to the backbenches had released him from all constraints of statesmanship. Earlier in the year he had described the BBC as being in the grip of an 'insufferable, smug, sanctimonious, naive, guilt-ridden, wet, pink orthodoxy' and of being a home for the 'third-rate minds of that third-rate decade, the 'sixties.'

Tebbit gave Killick and Hewitt the interview, strongly denying any irregularity in Tory finances. He said companies gave money to the Conservatives because they wanted to see the economy run properly. When he had finished Tebbit eyeballed Killick and said, with real menace, 'This all sounds like another *Maggie's Militant Tendency* to me. And you know what happened to that.'

The programme went out on the eve of the Tory Party conference and was slammed by the reviewers. The *Guardian* and *Observer* lambasted it as timorous, weak and unprofessional; and the Tory papers were just as unkind, even detecting anti-Conservative bias in the way *Panorama* had chosen to highlight the subject and had then provided virtually nothing of substance on the screen.

Some editorial executives sympathised with Killick, telling him there was 'more at stake' in Birt's thinking than simple editorial judgements. He had been worried that a political row over the programme would have breathed new life into Lord Wyatt's attempts to strengthen the impartiality clause in the Broadcasting Bill. This, at least, explained why no executive had objected to the programme until it reached Birt's desk.

Despite all the fuss, *Panorama* was still scathingly attacked from the platform at the Conservative conference. Kenneth Baker, the new chairman, urged everyone present, and all Conservatives in the country, to bombard the BBC with complaints. The conference debate on broadcasting, carefully orchestrated by the platform, allowed the Tory activists to vent their spleen.

One delegate described the BBC as the 'Bolshevik Broadcasting Corporation'. A delegate from Northern Ireland said it was little more than a vehicle for IRA propaganda, paid for by public money. Yet another said it was a wholly socialist institution, not an animal of the market place. 'There is only one solution,' he said to thunderous applause: 'scrap the licence fee and put the BBC into the private sector.'

David Mellor had an uncomfortable time replying to the accusations. 'A lot of people do not think the BBC is biased,' he said to the odd gasp of horror. 'The job of the Government is to recognise those views and not to get carried away with the oratorical heat of the party conference. We must keep a sense of proportion. Every opinion poll indicates that the public does not share our view of what we see on television.' Mellor was doing his bit to protect John Birt. The ravings from the conference floor did not matter much, and things would soon become a lot easier for the Birt-Mellor alliance.

A month after the party conference Margaret Thatcher stood down as Prime Minister. Television played its part in her downfall. She had long opposed the introduction of television cameras into the Commons and her change of mind was to prove fateful. The live broadcast of Geoffrey Howe's speech denouncing her European policies played a crucial part in her demise, and the opportune way John Sergeant, the BBC political reporter, shoved a microphone under her nose after the first ballot in the leadership challenge proved fatal, according to pundits. Instead of staying quiet, which might have saved her, she arrogantly proclaimed that she would carry on. The BBC provided the rope, and she hanged herself.

The arrival of John Major as Prime Minister removed a raft of people from Whitehall and the Conservative Party who had been pushing a hard anti-BBC line for most of the decade. Brian Griffiths, the Prime Minister's policy adviser who had become, according to people who knew him at the time, 'obsessed' with breaking up the BBC, disappeared overnight; and there were changes all the way down the line in the Home Office and those parts of the Treasury and DTI that dealt with broadcasting.

The changes gave Mellor more freedom to shape broadcasting policy in cahoots with Birt. The Broadcasting Act had now gone on to the statute book. Mellor had done what he could to soften the franchise auction. He managed to get the quality threshold condition attached. Wyatt's impartiality clause was dumped. But the Broadcasting Act still ended up as a classic Whitehall fudge. It was Thatcherite in origin, but toned down by lobbying and the new pragmatism that had swept Margaret Thatcher out of office. It ended up pleasing nobody.

Mellor felt scarred by the experience of the Broadcasting Act. He was determined not to repeat the experience. The next legislative challenge would be the Green Paper dealing specifically with BBC. And, after that, the debate over the renewal of the BBC's charter. For the first time in almost a decade the BBC might be able to count on the support of the Government. But only at a price.

# PART THREE

# 12

## Ceauşescu's Palace

In the early months of 1990 BBC 1's ratings began to crumble. By June the channel's audience share was down to 37.1 per cent: a loss of two points in a year. The slide was leading to a six-year low, returning BBC 1 to where it had been before the arrival of *EastEnders*, *Wogan* and Michael Grade.

At the time of the *Newsnight* scheduling row in January 1988 advertising analysts had predicted that BBC 1 would end up with a 35 per cent share within two years. That prediction was proving to be alarmingly accurate.

The underlying position of BBC 1 was even weaker than the figures indicated. *EastEnders* was still enormously popular, and would often be the number one programme in the top ten. But the *EastEnders* figure was pulling up the average for the whole schedule. *Neighbours*, an Ozzie teen sensation bought on the off chance, had become a surprise hit and *Birds of a Feather*, a new independently produced sitcom, was also doing well. But apart from this, the schedule was looking dangerously weak.

Paul Fox thought the ratings slide was due to ITV's heavy spending on home-made soaps and drama series. The old rival was able to do this because the consumer boom of the mid-80s had brought it a lot of extra advertising revenue, at a time when the BBC was having to cope with a frozen licence fee and rising costs. These included the extra £75 million wage bill negotiated by Checkland.

'There's no point in me whingeing and wringing my hands about lack of funds,' Fox said, but the Corporation somehow had to face up to the problem. Otherwise the slide would continue and put the licence fee at risk, no matter how friendly Birt was with David Mellor.

Politicians might criticise the BBC, Fox thought, but they were realistic. So long as the ratings were good they could not do anything too drastic. Wining and dining politicians was all very well, in its place. But the way to protect the licence fee was to make programmes people wanted to watch. If the BBC did not do that, all the strategy documents, seminars and junkets in the world would not save them.

Fox summed up his position at a June 1990 meeting of the Director General's Liaison Meeting, a regular think-tank for senior executives. 'As we move into the 1990s,' he said, 'I believe that BBC TV will be the most important factor in the licence fee debate, and it's the well-being of BBC1 that will help decide the issue.'

Marmaduke Hussey seemed to take exactly the opposite line, telling the papers the BBC was not 'paranoid' about ratings because it now had a 'broader agenda'. Dismissing the old duopoly philosophy, he claimed ITV wanted 'audiences for advertisers, whereas we want programmes for audiences.' The important thing was to show the politicians that the BBC was using the licence fee to provide 'quality, diversity, talent and greater depth'. Direct competition with ITV was off Hussey's agenda, in line with the new shape of the television market implied by the Broadcasting Act.

These mixed messages were making life difficult for Jonathan Powell, the BBC1 controller. Fox's argument was the more familiar. It had always been the BBC's job to compete head-on with ITV. But Fox had never taken on Birt, and was due to retire from the BBC in a few months. So was he supposed to conform to the new game of producing 'quality and diversity', whatever that meant, and take a more relaxed view of the ratings war?

Powell found it difficult to get a straight answer from Birt about the problem. The Deputy Director General was a master of the fine bureaucratic art of speaking at length, and sounding very important, without saying much. He tended to use clever-sounding phrases like 'rigorous and vigorous'; 'programmes of quality and distinction' and 'multichannel future'. Birtspeak, as it was known, was often devoid of meaning, and sometimes flatly contradictory. This was fine for use on politicians, but no good at all for running a television channel.

One thing seemed certain. There could be no repetition of the old trick of buying in cheap audience pullers like *The Thorn Birds* or *Neighbours*. That would mean Birt would have to deal with the eternal and politically tricky question: 'Is this what we are paying the licence fee for?'

Powell started to think about what the Deputy Director General might want. He often seemed more interested in the programmes of 'distinction' being served up by Alan Yentob on BBC 2, like *The Late Show*, a nightly 'culture' programme set up as a unit in its own right with lavish funds (ratings: 0.5 million). Another Yentob innovation was the recruitment of Janet Street-Porter, a Birt scion from LWT, with a wide brief to cater for young people. Youth was an LWT specialism and the station had pioneered various forms of late 'nite' televisual trendiness over the years, based around a mixture of eyeball-perforating graphics, wobbly cameras, pop music and institutionalised rebellion.

But Janet Street-Porter's non-stop 'in yer face' rave party was not much of a guide for Powell. Finally he resorted to running through a list of old shows, trying to work out what sort of programmes Birt might like. Searching for the bottom line he asked Birt what he thought about running something like *Miss Marple*, the 'knitting and nostalgia' detective drama.

The show was a classic and regarded throughout the industry as the definitive example of what BBC entertainment should be all about. *Miss Marple*, Birt said, would be 'at the limits of acceptability'. Powell was horrified. The answer should have been: 'We should be so lucky'.

Powell's confusion was soon reflected in his public statements. After the liaison meeting, where Fox had issued his warnings about the threat to the licence fee, Powell said: 'It is absolutely vital that BBC1 remains competitive, and becomes an increasingly popular network,' then added the muddled rider 'but it must also remain distinctive.'

Underlying Powell's problem was the growing cash problem identified by Fox. There were new programmes in the pipeline, but money was tight and there was no room for error. At the same time ITV was pouring extra millions into programmes for its autumn season. Checkland was looking for more programme money, paid for by cuts across the board as part of his Funding the Future investigation set up after the 1989 strike. But Powell still thought he did not have enough to compete.

The Funding the Future committee reported to a special Board of Governors meeting in January 1991. Ian Phillips, the 'outsider' financial director who had led the committee, recommended cuts of about £75 million from current budgets and much bigger cuts in capital plans. The main casualty was the proposed joint radio and television news and current affairs centre. Birt wanted to add the centre to the BBC's new hi-tech corporate headquarters next to Television Centre in White City. Cancellation of the project saved £300 million. But the centre was a Birt pet project and he complained bitterly at the meeting that Checkland had promised it to him on the day he was appointed. He had announced the centre's construction during the Leatherhead conference and had promised it to the staff at the Lime Grove Studio D meeting. Cancellation would make it look as though he had changed his mind.

The news and current affairs centre was to have been housed in Phase Two of an enormous building project Checkland had offered to the Governors as part of his application for the Director General's job three years earlier. The idea was to replace the BBC's *ad hoc* collection of buildings, possibly including Broadcasting House itself.

The plan looked brilliant on paper and made a lot of sense. Selling off the old property would pay for it all, and the Corporation would save a fortune by moving out of rented property. At the same time the BBC would be rehoused in wonderful modern buildings, more in keeping with the image of Checkland's 'billion-pound business'.

Phase One had already been completed. The six-storey status symbol had half a million square feet of open-plan offices organised around a central courtyard, designed to accommodate thousands of office workers. It was a bodged designer 'statement' from the silver-grey aluminium cladding and triple-glazed smoked-glass windows of the exterior to the vast atrium, infra-red controlled air-conditioning and indoor trees next to the computerised visitors' book in the reception.

People working at Television Centre next door had watched the rise of Phase One with mounting anxiety. To some it was like one of the pods in *Invasion of the Body Snatchers*, being lovingly prepared to receive the body of the BBC and transform it into a hideous Birtist monster while the rest of the organisation withered and died. It was even more spooky when the building remained strangely under-occupied.

Some Board of Management people thought the transfer of staff from central London to White City would never work. They correctly predicted that various arms of the bureaucracy would resist the move from the West End, to the netherworld of White City, which was next to a motorway junction and a tube-train shunting yard. The provision of a special pillion-rider motorcycle taxi service designed to ease communications with central London did not prove much of an incentive.

Birt persuaded Patricia Hodgson's Policy and Planning Unit to go there; and some of the Birtised specialist programme units joined her. There was also a collection of operations like the legal department and the burgeoning training, accountancy, equal opportunities and Corporate Affairs-related departments as well as weekly current affairs shows like *Panorama*.

Broadcasting House always had a forbidding air about it. George Orwell had used it as the model for the Ministry of Truth in his novel *1984*. As a programme-maker Jonathan Powell had followed suit, using its endless winding, darkened corridors and anonymously numbered rooms as the headquarters of MI6 in *Tinker, Tailor, Soldier, Spy*. The Phase One White City building was much more light and airy but, as the physical headquarters of Birtism, it was dubbed Ceauşescu's Palace.

Phase Two was due to be completed by 1995. It was designed to house all of the BBC's journalists who, as part of the plan, would be trained to be 'bi-media', meaning that radio reporters would contribute filmed reports for television and vice versa.

The centre would have three TV studios, five main radio studios, a central news information area and 'multi-purpose lecture threatre' that would replace the collection of old sheds at Lime Grove. The architect's plan was the definitive Birtist statement: an exciting five-storey V-shaped affair crowned by a central tower with all the superstructure on the outside like the Lloyd's Building in the City.

Birt had strong and typically fashionable views on architecture. He had visited the Lloyd's Building when it opened a few years earlier and his praise for the place knew no bounds. It was a 'bold post-modernist vision,' he gushed, 'that puts the guts of the building on open but orderly display, and offers dizzying vistas.' The inside of the building was even better, a yuppie Shangri-La of coffee-house desks and table-top computers' populated with 'young, sharp-suited, Jonathan Ross lookalikes: the new Britons of a new Britain.' He asked: 'Will this enterprise and confidence spread? And northward?'

Birt had tried to spread it westward to White City but the dizzying, bold, post-modernist Jonathan Ross vision of the future had to be put on ice because of Phillips' economies. Phase One of White City soon began to fill up with staff but the Phase Two news and current affairs centre was eventually turned into a car park.

Birt, a neatness fanatic, would therefore have to cope with a split site; his empire and minions dotted about around several buildings in London. The resolve to move most of the BBC there dribbled away. Instead of saving money, Checkland had burdened the Corporation with an extra and underused building. The way the move was handled was added to the growing list of complaints Hussey and Birt were able to level against Checkland.

If cuts were needed, Birt thought, they should have been made elsewhere, especially out in the regions where, although he did not yet have the facts, he suspected there was massive duplication of resources. He would sometimes complain quietly to his friends about Checkland's money management, ranging from his habit of placing too much importance on the regions, to smaller matters like company cars and entertainment budgets.

Birt, who had a puritanical streak, was horrified to find that all managers above a certain level were provided with well-stocked drinks cabinets, and he attempted to abolish this practice. In 1988 the *News of the World* had dubbed the BBC the 'British Boozing Corporation', claiming bottles of spirits were distributed around Television Centre and Broadcasting House on trollies. 'My first memory of the BBC was a man wheeling a trolley full of booze. People were snatching bottles as he went by,' one curiously anonymous BBC 'worker' was quoted as saying. Tabloid hyperbole apart, a certain amount of drinking had always oiled the creative wheels at the BBC, as it did in many media organisations.

Although Birt thought himself entitled to an expensive Range Rover, he was unhappy that more junior people had been given similar status machines and thought the use of cars was profligate. It was normal for all members of the Board of Management to have a company car as well as being provided with another chauffeur-driven car for attending meetings. The drivers had little to do and used to sit around in the garage playing cards. Birt was soon telling old cronies in ITV that the position was so bad that the man who ran the car-hire company used by the BBC had become a million-aire on the proceeds.

Birt's frustration with the way Checkland was running the show would sometimes burst through his normally calm demeanour, especially after the setback over the White City news and current affairs building. There was internal opposition to bi-media working because it cut across the existing territory of both the television and radio empires. The managing directors of radio and television would lose power as a result. Fortunately for Birt, neither Paul Fox nor David Hatch, the radio chief, was opposing him. But there was still a lot of submerged aggro further down the line.

Ian Hargreaves, the assistant Birt had hired from the *Financial Times* to help him create the News and Current Affairs Directorate, was amazed by the scale of opposition and real hatred Birt generated. Hargreaves had thought the *Newsnight* scheduling row had been like a debate over compulsory castration for all twelve-year-olds. He had seen people shaking with emotion about the decision. One person had told him it would 'destroy the BBC'.

Opposition had gone underground where, he was convinced, there was a guerilla campaign of foot dragging. People had gone quiet, but some of the *Panorama* producers would 'die in the last ditch' before admitting they should have anything to do with the news. There were some people in radio, Hargreaves thought, who would rather have their right hand cut off than be associated with TV news. He was convinced those opposed to the merger were out to wreck the new directorate and were praying for Birt to trip up in some way.

Sometimes the hostility would get to Birt and he would look exhausted, depressed and descend into a deep, dark mood. Ian Phillips had an odd encounter with him when he was in one of these states. The two men were going home after a difficult meeting and Phillips, noticing that Birt looked more wound up than usual, told him to try and relax a bit. He should realise, Phillips said, that change was difficult, but it was amazing what could be achieved when three or four people at the top of an organisation worked together on a common agenda.

Birt, absolutely grim, replied: 'Forget it, Ian. I am not in the business of making deals.' Birt got into his Range Rover, slammed the door and sped off. Phillips was astonished. He was only trying to cheer him up, but Birt had thought he wanted something in return for his support. Phillips began to feel sorry for him. Here was a deeply insecure and lonely man who thought everyone in the organisation was plotting either with him or against him.

After the cancellation of the news and current affairs centre Birt was determined to take control of the review of resources Checkland had been conducting since 1985, and push it much further. His argument was that he had given up a lot with the postponement of the White City development and ought to be allowed to see if money could be saved. To general amazement on the Board of Management, Checkland agreed to Birt's request, allowing him to pick up from where Phillips' Funding the Future Committee had left off, but restricting him to a review of network television resources.

Network television was the guts of the BBC, claiming up to 80 per cent of the licence fee. Birt had already made himself the BBC's editor-in-chief for all practical purposes. He had also taken the lead in the Corporation's negotiations with Whitehall. Now he was moving into the core area of Checkland's power.

Birt's investigation was to take the form of the Network Television Resources Committee. He would be the chairman, acting with the authority of the Director General. Its brief would be to look at all the facilities used by BBC TV in the regions as well as Television Centre in London.

There were to be two distinct sets of people on the committee, reflecting the growing split between Checkland and Birt. Will Wyatt, soon to replace Paul Fox as Managing Director of Television, and Keith Anderson, the Controller of Planning and the man so far responsible for working out what resources the network needed, were chosen by Checkland. They were joined by the Controller and Assistant Controller of Regional Broadcasting, Keith Clement, and Dick Bates, who Checkland also put on the committee.

The Director General was convinced this professional group, who had more than seventy years of experience in programme-making and senior management at the BBC between them, would deliver a sensible report and might even teach Birt a lesson or two about the reality of how the BBC worked. He confided in them, saying he put Birt in charge of the committee to give him something to do. Since the reorganisation of news and current affairs, Checkland said, Birt had become 'a loose cannon'. He was spending far too much time courting politicians and governors.

'I want this committee to be a success,' Checkland told them. 'I want you to keep it going. I want John out of my hair for a while.' The reason was that Checkland's contract as Director General would come up next year and he wanted a free hand to negotiate an extension.

The other half of the committee was mainly appointed by Birt: outside consultants and financial advisers attached to the Policy Unit. These included the BBC's Chief Accountant, John Smith, and Mark Oliver, a recent Policy Unit recruit who specialised in forecasting the way the finances of the television industry were changing. Like Birt himself, this group saw themselves very much as 'outsiders'.

Birt threw himself into the work of the Network Resources Committee with characteristic zeal. As was the case with anything to do with Birt, the committee at once started to generate a mountain of paperwork. Documents would be delivered by motorcycle courier to the homes of committee members who were expected to read them overnight for discussion the next day.

Members came to dread the Sunday evening bang on the door, which signalled the arrival of a despatch rider and another great pile of Birtspeak, a lot of it highly abstruse, with what colleagues regarded as figures shown because they supported the decision he hoped the committee would make. Some committee members found they were up until three or four in the morning trying to read it all. Others just flicked through, tried to master the bits that dealt with their immediate area, or just gave up. It was a great technique for preventing proper debate or criticism.

The meetings themselves were run like clockwork. Birt was a punctilious chairman, introducing each report in turn, listening to a short presentation by the consultants and then closing discussion when the allotted time was up. If others raised objections or queried anything, Birt would listen in silence, and thank them courteously for making an interesting point, saying it would be investigated and reported back on at the next meeting. But it rarely was. Objections were not usually recorded in the minutes and would disappear from the agenda.

Eventually the Checkland faction focused on one important question: why was Birt so keen to use the material that he got from the outside consultants, rather than the information prepared by the BBC's own departments? Birt's papers looked impressive, and often had glossy covers, but to BBC veterans they sometimes seemed deeply inaccurate or, at least, based on different accounting conventions than those used to actually run the BBC.

One report showed that BBC programmes were more expensive per person employed than those made by the ITV companies. But existing research, conducted by Checkland himself, showed just the opposite. 'Why are we now saying this?' the in-house people kept asking, complaining that even a rough calculation showed that ITV spent more money on its network to produce far fewer hours of programming than the BBC.

'Where are you getting your information from?' Mark Oliver said the information came from handbooks and discussions with people 'in the industry'. Birt weighed in on Oliver's side. His report made an important point, Birt said; the BBC was less efficient than ITV. That was the report's purpose.

The committee then set off on a lightning tour of the BBC's English regions, visiting every major production centre. The visits always took the same form. The committee would arrive at nine in the morning and be given a tour. They would then sit down with the centre's management and discuss the ways in which facilities were used. After this the local managers would be dismissed for Birt to deliver his verdict.

In Manchester he started off by saying: 'Right, we've had the tour. It is quite clear to me this is not a place the BBC should be in the 1990s. It is old-fashioned, dirty. A total waste of time. My recommendation is that we should move to close it down.'

Birt was asked why he had bothered to visit the Manchester centre at all. He did not seem interested in real productivity issues or the relative cost of making programmes there compared with London and other centres. He seemed to be basing his decision on pure prejudice and the state of the decor. £8 million had just been spent refurbishing and extending the centre's main studio. It had not even been reopened yet, and yet he wanted to close it down. That would make them all look a bit silly.

Apart from the studio there were other production facilities. He had seen them with his own eyes that morning. Now he wanted to replace the separate regional TV studio, ump-teen radio and sound studios and the expensively and acoust-ically built concert hall used by the BBC Philharmonic Orchestra. It did not make sense. 'You must stop thinking in these negative terms,' Birt replied. 'We should think posi-tively and close this building down.'

The Checkland-appointed people on the committee won-dered if Birt was being serious. He wanted to close down all the regional studios, getting rid of 'craft' production workers like scenery makers and cameramen. Regional centres would become office blocks for programme-makers and accountants who would work together to buy studio and other facilities on the open market.

Complaints that buying services might work out more expensive than using the existing facilities were brushed aside. The important thing was to reduce the number of people on the BBC's payroll quickly.

The BBC's South and East region at Elstree, just outside London, received similar treatment. The studio complex had been built in the 1920s as a back lot for the British film industry and had expanded and contracted into a ramshackle collection of shabby buildings. There was nothing neat about it, or the range of programmes it made, although they were some of the most popular and efficiently produced in the whole network.

The people who worked there told Birt that the mixture of programmes, which ranged from quiz shows like *Mastermind* to documentaries like *Timewatch* for Yentob's BBC 2, added a touch of creative chaos to Elstree. The shabby look of the place did not bother them, they said, though it could use a lick of paint. Birt looked at them as though they were mad.

Birt asked Ian Kennedy, the head of the centre, what he planned to do with 'his' studios. Kennedy, astonished, explained that they did not belong to Elstree but were an extension of Television Centre which owned and operated them. He had put all this in a briefing paper sent to Birt before the visit. Kennedy realised Birt had not read it.

After the regional visits Checkland called a member of the committee and asked him what was going on. 'Birt is not telling me anything,' he complained, anxiously. 'What's he up to?' When the Birt plan for divorcing production from editorial work was described, Checkland became even more worried: 'This is far too radical,' he said. 'Birt is going over the top. Can't you keep him under control?' But there was no stopping him.

The Checkland faction finally decided to have it out with Birt. They were prepared to accept that the committee's recommendations would be different from their own, but only if they were satisfied he had listened to dissenting views, understood them and thought all the issues through: 'but you are not listening and that is wrong,' they said.

Birt replied gravely: 'You must remember I have a goal. You have got to have a goal. I know exactly where I want the BBC to be. You cannot change your goal once it has been decided. That is the first rule of effective management. You must not change the vision.'

# 13

## *Sex, Drugs and Sand Pits*

Things were settling down in his news and current affairs power base as John Birt went off on his tour of the BBC's regional centres. While he was recommending swingeing cuts for the regions, the Directorate's empire-builders continued to thrive.

In August 1990 Ian Hargreaves, the Director of News and Current Affairs, bowed out, having seen through the merger and the introduction of specialist journalism. He was replaced by Tony Hall, the Editor of Television News and Current Affairs. Hargreaves admitted that in the early days of the merger there were 'moments of confusion, tension and frustration', but these had passed and the BBC's journalism had become 'harder edged and more authoritative'.

This was important, he said, because ITN and Channel Four were still following a different formula: 'The Hollywood-Fleet Street tabloid brew of sex, drugs, rock 'n' roll and violence.' *Panorama*, in contrast, was dealing with a news agenda of serious concern. He was very proud of a recent edition featuring Polly Toynbee, the newly appointed BBC social affairs specialist, discussing the problems faced by the elderly.

Was this Birtism? he asked himself. 'Well, yes it is,' he replied, claiming: 'the thrust of the Birt-Jay thesis was simple enough. It beseeched television journalists not to become so entranced by pictures and the sensational that they failed to detect the important.' With that Hargreaves returned to the sex, drugs, violence and, virtually, picture-free zone of the *Financial Times* with a promotion to deputy editor.

Hargreaves knew Birt was angling to become Director General and had been fighting a strategic battle to land the job ever since he had arrived as Checkland's deputy. Birt was making good progress. So far he had satisfied the Government there would be no more 'moments of tension' over the content of BBC programmes. But avoiding criticism was a negative sort of success. What Birt needed was a stunning editorial triumph to back his claim to be a potentially great Director General.

The opportunity presented itself in the autumn and winter of 1990 and 1991 in the form of the Gulf War: the first major international conflict since Birt's arrival at the BBC. The war should have been meat and drink to the 'Birt-Jay thesis' Hargreaves had praised. Here was a war brimming with all kinds of diplomatic, economic and historical subtleties. The opportunities for analysis seemed enormous.

In his original 'bias against understanding' articles Birt had complained that television journalism had so far failed to tackle the subjects of the 'Middle East or Oil'. Now Birt was in charge of the mighty BBC news machine and would finally get the chance to put his theories into practice.

Rule Number One of Birtism was that television should never suggest there is only one cause of any problem, or only one answer: 'Trying to get to grips with the often bewildering complexity of modern problems is a formidable task,' he had written, 'even without trying to put the result on television; and the failure rate is high.'

But during the war the BBC's news agenda was no different to anyone else's. The cause of the war boiled down to the
truism that Saddam Hussein was 'mad' and 'evil'. There was
a lot of analysis, in the form of endless studio discussions, of
just how mad and evil he was; but the basic and monolithic
premise was maintained throughout.

In his writings Birt had argued that one of the main
sources of the 'bias against understanding' was the use of
studio panel discussions. 'Rarely has a technique been so
abused,' he claimed, adding: 'they encourage interviewees to
abandon any attempt to discuss issues in a fresh and sophisticated manner and are little more than an entertaining way
of feeding the viewer's already existing prejudices.' But the
BBC filled up its Gulf news programmes by encouraging
retired generals and 'experts' to debate the sorts of military
equipment being employed, or to harmlessly speculate on the
military tactics being used by both sides. They were assisted
by Peter Snow, the *Newsnight* presenter, who explained
strategy with the help of what was described as a sandpit
and lots of toy tanks. (After the conflict the sandpit was given
to a thirteen-year-old boy from Warwickshire who had written in to ask if he could have it.)

Radio Four's FM wavelength was turned over to non-stop
studio discussion between scheduled news and current affairs
programmes. But with very little happening other than a
continuous American bombing campaign, the main subject
for discussion was when the Iraqis would lob one of their
Scud missiles at Saudi Arabia or Israel. Radio Four debated
this subject at such length that it was nicknamed 'Scud FM'.
This was, of course, news; and people were very anxious
about it. But it was hard to see how all this Scud-spotting
was furthering the Birtist mission to 'get to grips with the
bewildering complexity' of the causes of the war.

Ian Hargreaves had summed up Birtism as a warning
against picture-led journalism. The reality of the BBC's Gulf
effort, like any other major television news organisation, was
a technical operation organised around beaming satellite

pictures back to London, with access carefully controlled by the military. Bulletins were organised around Pentagon pictures of precision bombing, which the BBC showed as eagerly as everyone else. It was only after the war was over that most people woke up to the fact that the pictures were essentially propaganda.

Pentagon material was supplemented by reliance, to a remarkable extent, on the American Cable News Network. CNN's coverage featured the 'Scud Studs': hunky correspondents in places like Tel Aviv and Riyadh who would come on the screen when the air-raid sirens sounded, gabble hysterically and then disappear heroically into the bunkers clutching their helmets. As the same story continued to run, the Scud Studs livened things up by dramatically reading their reports while wearing gas masks. The game was given away by technicians who would sometimes wander into view smoking cigarettes, wearing nothing more protective than a T-shirt.

A lot of people in the business thought this was great television. The BBC's own teams were pleased they had secured prime positions to film Scud explosions and the vapour trails of American Patriot missiles. They were right to be proud: it was impressive footage, bravely gathered. But Birtism it was not. Journalistic purists point out that reporters on the spot sometimes knew less than anchormen in the studio.

Current affairs offered a chance to apply a spot of rigour and vigour to the war's causes, including the way that the UK had helped Saddam Hussein to power and then sold him weapons. Following impeccable Birtist principles, *Panorama* set off to examine this aspect of the conflict. The team discovered that British scientists and companies had helped the Iraqis build a means of firing gigantic artillery shells, possibly tipped with chemical, biological or even nuclear warheads: the supergun.

Reporter Jane Corbin and Mark Killick, the producer who had worked on the neutered *Panorama* about Conservative Party funds, researched the programme for six months, using the title *Project Babylon*, the code name for the supergun itself. The key to the story was an interview with Chris Cowley, one of the British engineers who had worked on the supergun and attended test firings in the presence, he believed, of British intelligence agents.

The film had gone through the referral system and was ready for screening on January 14, by which time the allied ultimatum to Saddam Hussein had passed and war was inevitable. *Panorama's* editor, Mark Thompson, replaced supergun show with a studio discussion with contributors from different parts of the globe linked by satellite. The supergun programme would not lose much by being held over for a week, Corbin and Killick thought. But when the edition was again delayed the following week the producers became angry and worried.

Thompson told Corbin and Killick there was a problem. He had been informed by Samir Shah, the executive in charge of weekly programmes, that the film could not go out as promised. Killick was by now exasperated. He confronted Shah, who was at first unwilling to talk, but finally admitted: 'It's not my decision, but it can't run.' Killick found this bizarre. There was no criticism of what it said, or Birt-style demands for caveats or extra research. He kept asking what was wrong with the programme, but Shah could only say a decision had been taken at a senior level. It had been decided the programme was 'out of line with the mood of the country'.

Cowley, the programme's key interviewee, was as alarmed as the journalists. He had promised them an exclusive provided the programme was shown in January. He was shortly to appear in court and needed to go public with his side of the story to help his case. He had accepted the original reason for the delay, but now became angry. The BBC had let him down so he gave part of his story to the *Daily Mirror*. The *Panorama* journalists thought that now that most of the information was out in the open there could be no possible objection to running the film and filling in the rest of the picture.

Worse still, *Panorama's* ITV rival, Thames' *This Week*,

was talking to Cowley and promising him the publicity he wanted if he would deal with them instead of, or as well as, the BBC. Shah made an emergency call to Cowley, begging him not to talk to *This Week*. He explained how the *Panorama* team had invested a lot of time and money in the programme and how everyone was very proud of it. Cowley wanted to know why, then, it wasn't on the air. Shah said it would be transmitted that week. But he still had to get Birt's permission and Birt would not budge.

By now the *Panorama* team were bewildered. Everyone in town was doing supergun stories expect them, and there was no collapse of troop morale, mass desertions or mutinies. *Panorama* was supposed to be the flagship of the entire current affairs effort. They had the definitive account of a matter of enormous public interest, but they were being forced to sit on it for reasons that nobody could explain.

Cowley had started to become impatient and Corbin discovered that *This Week* had an appointment to interview him. There seemed no doubt that Cowley's message would be broadcast. It was now down to direct competition between the BBC and ITV for the same story. Surely Birt would not allow his flagship to be scooped by *This Week*, the show Birt had written off as 'a sad little programme' at Leatherhead.

The production team demanded Shah get in touch with Birt at once. They were being made to look like complete idiots. Why had Birt not even asked to see a video of the programme? He would then realise it was perfectly sound. But Birt did not seem interested in even discussing the issue. *This Week's* reporters meanwhile interviewed Cowley and produced a version of the story in five days flat. It was shown to the station's programme controller, David Elstein, who approved it. Elstein then called Birt, a former ITV colleague, to let him know what was happening. Birt told him the Board of Governors could not risk being accused of demoralising troops on the eve of battle.

The BBC was so paranoid that it had taken *'Allo 'Allo* off the air. Feature films with military or morbid themes, including *The Naked and the Dead*, were proscribed. BBC disc jockeys found that a list of 67 pop songs ranging from Elton John's 'Saturday Night's Alright for Fighting' to Lulu's 'Boom-banga-Bang' and even Desmond Dekker's 'The Israelites' were banned for the duration.

Some current affairs people thought Birt's interference in programmes like *Project Babylon* fitted a pattern. He was happy to back them on certain programmes, and had even been prepared to take on Robert Maxwell, a formidable litigant, over a *Panorama* investigation that exposed the massive scale of the publisher's corruption. But when it came to an issue that might embarrass the Conservative Party, or otherwise damage the core interests of the political establishment, he would back down.

The Gulf War ended as a ratings triumph for the BBC. Audiences for the Nine O'Clock News increased by 20 per cent. The coverage owed little to theoretical 'Birtism', which many people inside the BBC now saw more as a self-serving argument for changing the personnel in news and current affairs rather than a philosophical commitment on the part of the Deputy Director General. The success was based on old-fashioned professionalism and a lot of hard work by journalists who, for once, had been given the resources they needed to do a good job.

For John Birt personally, with his political agenda, the crowning glory came when the BBC's coverage was praised in Parliament by the Prime Minister. Instead of the ritual denunciations of BBC reporting during the Falklands War and the Libyan bombing, John Major was effusive. 'I believe what the BBC is doing,' he said, 'in what has already been some remarkable reporting, is trying to keep proper balance in reporting.' The official endorsement was proudly printed in huge type across the cover of *Ariel*, the BBC staff magazine.

The position was less clear on what had always been the other aspect of government concern: the structure and finances of the BBC. Checkland had been working on this, in one way and another, for more than a decade. Nobody doubted he wanted greater productivity, 'a leaner, fitter BBC', and until recently he was seen as the only man who could bring this about. But now there was a new model for rapid and brutal change. ITV was going through its 'big bang', with companies turning their production departments and studios into self-contained businesses that had to sell their services on the open market. The result was a sudden and dramatic reduction in the payroll. The pace was, as usual, being set by LWT, now being run by Greg Dyke, who was a legend in the industry for his frank talk and lack of sentimentality.

Dyke made his name in the early 1980s by transforming the fortunes of TV-am, introducing *Roland Rat* and *Batman* repeats to replace Peter Jay's original 'mission to explain'. He had applied the same commercial drive to LWT, securing its place as one of the most profitable companies in the network.

Now Dyke was invited to give the keynote 'outsider's perspective' speech at the annual governors' and managers' get-together at the Lucknam Park Hotel, near Bath. His overall message was that Checkland's financial reforms were a step in the right direction, but far too cautious. 'No matter how well you think you've done in the past few years,' he said, 'we in ITV have done much better. You are falling behind. The gap is widening, not closing.'

Dyke advised the Governors not to cut, but to 'hack' at staff numbers 'and then go back and hack again'. The problem, he believed, was that the BBC had a 'strong internal culture that was hard to break'. Perhaps only outsiders could do that. Ultimately, he suggested, the BBC might abandon programme-making altogether and become a publisher-broadcaster like Channel Four, screening material made by independents. But whatever its future form, Dyke warned, the BBC would not survive into the next century unless it shed a lot of staff, and shed them quickly.

Birt, Hussey, Barnett and most of the Governors applauded

enthusiastically. But Checkland looked aghast. Large parts of the speech had come over as a direct, personal attack on the pace of the changes he was making, all the more significant because Birt was leading his review of BBC resources at the time.

Dyke was an enormous admirer of the Deputy Director General, telling people Birt's leadership at LWT had been 'inspirational'. The two men had stayed in close contact since Birt's move to the BBC and both joined in regular Friday LWT football matches. Dyke knew his old friend was running a campaign to become Director General.

There was immediate suspicion Dyke had been put up to the speech by Birt. The LWT chief denied this, saying he had been invited by Patricia Hodgson and the Policy Unit and had not discussed what he was going to say with anyone at the BBC. But Checkland was the Director General and had the authority to invite or veto speakers at events like Lucknam Park. He could have guessed what Dyke would say. Now it looked as if he had even ceded this last minor power to the Birtist Policy Unit.

# 14

## *Dukey*
## *Rides*
## *Again*

Before the arrival of Marmaduke Hussey, chairmen of the BBC had tended to see themselves as remote figureheads, gently steering the Governors and leaving the day-to-day running of the BBC firmly in the hands of the Corporation's professional management team. But Hussey was different. He saw the Chairmanship as a full-time executive job.

People said Dukey acted as though he owned the BBC. His role models were newspaper proprietors like Rothermere and Murdoch, whom he had worked with in the past. Unlike previous chairmen he worked full time from his office in Broadcasting House and travelled around like an emperor, making all kinds of political promises about what the BBC would, and would not, do.

Hussey made full use of his chauffeur-driven car, and a large international travel and entertainment budget. He felt entitled to a good salary and all the dignities and perks of ownership. His remuneration was set by the Top Salaries Review Body. Since arriving a 25 per cent pay increase had taken his BBC earnings to £60,000.

Hussey's power had also been increased by changes in the

composition of the Governors. Membership of the Board had always been a matter of political patronage. But before the arrival of the Thatcher administration no government had stayed in power long enough to see through a virtually complete cycle of appointments.

By the spring of 1991 the Government had been able to influence the shape of the Governors to an unprecedented extent. Independently minded governors like Curtis Keeble found their appointments were not renewed. They were steadily replaced by solid Hussey supporters like the crime writer P. D. James.

Some Governors, like Lord Nicholas Gordon Lennox, were old friends of Hussey's, whom he had been able to introduce to the wonderful chauffeur-driven world of the BBC, with its endless round of lunches and dinners with all kinds of interesting and important people. During their five-year-term, Governors could reasonably look forward to sixty-five free 'black tie' dinners and were paid £12,000 a year to attend one or two meetings a month.

Collectively the Governors were a crusty bunch, with diverse talents. P. D. James was able to help out by correcting the grammar in a BBC press release issued by Howell James' Corporate Affairs department. Cultural diversity was supplied by Shahwar Sadeque, a member of the Commission for Racial Equality.

But the Asian Governor was a Conservative stalwart with conventional 'middle England' tastes. Her hobbies included collecting thimbles and perfume bottles. Bill Jordan, the engineering union leader, was the only Governor likely to be hostile to Hussey. But he was in such a minority that he often did not turn up to meetings.

By now Hussey was used to getting his own way with the Board, and tended to boss them about. It was thought he would have been even more overbearing if not for the diplomatic skills of John McCormick, the long-suffering BBC secretary. It was his job to smooth relations between the Chairman's office and the Boards of Governors and Management. McCormick was one of the few people who could make Hussey laugh and a rich source of pithy observations. 'You won't get your way if you ask for it directly,' he would tell the chairman, 'but if you take the scenic route you'll get there in the end.'

The main brake on Hussey's power was the fact that his own tenure as Chairman was due to end in the autumn of 1991. He was 68 years old and in constant pain from his war wound. It was very unlikely he would get a second term. But the political lobbying surrounding the succession had already begun. Paul Fox was one of the first to go public.

Fox had been brought in as Managing Director of the TV service to keep things steady after the traumatic departures of Alasdair Milne and Michael Grade. Now, in February 1991, the three years he had given himself in the job were up. He handed over to the less weighty Will Wyatt, his Birt-backed successor, and bowed out gracefully with the customary retirement lunch given by the Board of Governors.

In his farewell speech Fox talked about the need for continuity at the BBC, so the process of healing he had started could continue. Reminding people about the arrival of Hussey and the sudden departure of Milne, he said changes in future should be made more gently, so that people could again begin to plan for the future with confidence. It would be a good idea, Fox said, if the Home Office made up its mind about a successor soon.

When Fox finished his speech Clive Whitmore, the permanent secretary at the Home Office, stood up. 'Paul has spoken so clearly about this,' Whitmore said, 'that I must go back to the Home Office and sort something out. I see no reason why there should not be an announcement this evening.' But there was no announcement that evening.

Fox left the BBC and was beginning to forget about its problems when, in April 1991, he read in the paper that Hussey had been reappointed for another five-year term. Fox was amazed. A second term would take Hussey through to 1996, the year when the BBC's charter came up for renewal, when he would be 73. As he puzzled over the decision, Fox concluded that Kenneth Baker, the markedly anti-BBC Home Secretary, must have been nervous. With the gathering recession and the fall of Mrs Thatcher, the Conservatives were in disarray and a general election was on the cards for the autumn of 1991. All over Whitehall ministers were locking politically correct appointees into quangos in case Labour won the election.

The reappointment put new wind into Hussey's sails. Members of the Board of Management noted with dismay how the decision was an incredible ego boost and an aphrodisiac that made him and Barnett feel invulnerable. Hussey issued a statement saying he would use his second term to 'complete the job of changing and developing the BBC which Joel Barnett and I started in 1986.' Significantly there was no mention of Michael Checkland, whose five-year contract as Director General was due to come to an end in 1992. He had asked for an extension to his contract.

In July 1991 Hussey and the Governors met in secret to consider Checkland's request. The Governors staggered their arrival through the evening in an attempt to put reporters off the scent. The paranoia was such that Hussey dismissed the waitresses and shut the doors when they had served supper on the Corporation's best silverware. It was to be a tricky meeting.

According to tradition, Director Generals could usually expect a second term unless they had managed to badly upset the Governors, as Milne had done. But Checkland had done nothing wrong and had started the process of producing the more slimline and politically acceptable BBC most of them wanted to see. The problem was what to do about John Birt.

The Deputy Director General wanted to take over from Checkland when he left, and many believed Hussey had at least hinted this would happen when the two men had met at the Howard Hotel to confirm Birt's appointment in 1987. The media meteorite had already served as Checkland's deputy for four years and was unlikely to be happy playing second fiddle to Checkland for another six.

At the same time the franchise round in ITV had vastly increased salaries and perks like 'golden handcuff' contracts available to people with Birt's experience. He had already been linked in press speculation to the plum job of ITV network controller. He was therefore in a position to deliver an ultimatum: either he became Checkland's designated successor as Director General at once, or he would return to the lusher pastures of commercial television.

The Governors were split down the middle, drawn in different ways by the lobbying of Checkland's supporters on the Board of Management, including James Arnold-Baker and John Tusa, and loyalty to Hussey and Birt. Checkland won the first vote 7–6 but the meeting went on into the early hours. The decision was reversed after Hussey persuaded John Parry, the Welsh Governor, to switch his vote.

With Birt appointed as Director General (designate), there remained the problem of what to do about Checkland. Instead of facing up to the consequences of their decision, the Board came up with the muddled idea of giving Checkland a one-year extension instead of the three years he was asking for. It seemed likely Checkland would refuse. In that case he might solve the problem for all of them by resigning. The Governors disappeared to their beds.

The next morning Hussey called Checkland into his office, gave him the bad news and asked him if he was prepared to continue. Checkland remained calm. In similar circumstances Milne had risen to the bait and written out his resignation on the spot. The story was later told of how he took a walk around the block. On his return Checkland called the Chairman's bluff and said he would stay.

After the decision Checkland loyally tried to make as much sense of the situation as he could, presenting it as business as usual at a press conference. There was no question of being a 'lame duck' as some of the hacks suggested in their questions. 'As the man who brought John Birt into the BBC,' he added, 'I am delighted that there will be a continuity of the policies which we have both worked to achieve, to set the BBC's place in the changing broadcasting market and its course for charter renewal.' Birt said Checkland had done an excellent job, that they had enjoyed a 'fruitful partnership' and he had learned a lot from him.

Later that day the pundits were in full flood. Ian McIntyre, a former controller of Radio Three, told journalists: 'Michael Checkland has been discarded in slow motion. He is now not merely a lame duck, but a quadriplegic.' Others noted Birt had been appointed to the Director Generalship without being subjected to competitive interview, either when he became Deputy Director General, or Director General. His BBC career had been created by Hussey alone.

Paul Fox denounced the method of Birt's appointment. Writing in the *Daily Mail*, he said it probably broke the law on equal opportunities and was 'certainly muddle-headed and unfair to Checkland and to Birt, let alone John Tusa, the managing director of the World Service, who certainly deserved consideration for the Director Generalship.'

Privately Fox was even more outspoken. He thought the way Birt was appointed was 'an outrage'. It was 'monstrous' that Tusa had not been interviewed and that applications were not sought from others. Tusa complained directly to Hussey, saying he should have been interviewed. The Chairman replied: 'You wouldn't have got it, even if you had applied.' Tusa felt slighted. He was happy to continue as head of the World Service, but his relationship with Hussey deteriorated.

Inside the BBC the decision to go for 'dual control' caused enormous confusion. Checkland was greatly weakened, but Birt was not in full charge either, and could not reveal what his plans were. He was scrupulous, as ever, and always deferred to Checkland in public. He never pushed his position or disagreed with his formal superior. The two men remained civil, but Birt's supporters were quietly spreading the line that Checkland had been a great choice for Director General in the mid-80s, but had now gone soft. He had presented the Governors with a brilliant blueprint, and got things moving, but was not dynamic enough to see it through. They could all see what had happened with the BBC's buildings plan: a great idea, but abandoned halfway through with a weak compromise.

At Board of Governors' meetings Checkland was being cast as the reactionary who would never grasp the nettle, always trying to catch up with what Birt was proposing. Things began to come badly unstuck at Governors' meetings in the Autumn of 1991. Led by Hussey, the Governors would line up to lay into Checkland on the question of staff numbers.

They were now four years into Checkland's five-year plan and less than 5,000 of the BBC's original 25,000 staff had been shown the door. Hussey complained he had to face awkward questions from journalists at press conferences. They wanted to know when the promised redundancies would actually happen. Checkland floundered. It was not that simple, he said, there were bound to be lags during the transfer to independent production. Hasty action could destroy the BBC's production base and they would never be able to put it back together again. At meetings like this Birt would give his own report: typically a crisp account of discussions aimed at closing whole production centres with dramatic staff reductions. He would sit in dignified silence as the Governors resumed their onslaught. Another source of friction was the way Checkland had managed the BBC pension fund. Like a lot of companies in the 1980s the BBC was paying too much into its pension fund. Ian Phillips reported that there was enough money in the fund to meet pension obligations until the year 2000 and the BBC could afford to stop making contributions for several years, diverting the money into other activities.

To be completely safe he proposed that contributions should continue, but be reduced to three per cent of the payroll. This figure was agreed with the actuaries who safeguarded the fund. Checkland and Phillips might have expected praise for this neat piece of financial footwork, which would help tide the BBC over during the transition to the 25 per cent quota. Instead Phillips was attacked by Barnett, who said he and Checkland were again trying to avoid making the immediate staff cuts the Board wanted.

The roasting went on through lunch. Afterwards Checkland, his voice full of sarcasm, asked a member of the Board of Management: 'And where was the Deputy DG during all that?' When his pension proposal was rejected, even Checkland's supporters on the Board of Management thought that he and Phillips should have resigned. Control of the fund was a purely technical aspect of the day-to-day management of the BBC, way beyond the competence of the Governors to decide, and well beyond their brief to steer the BBC on matters of grand strategy.

While making all the running on the internal reform of the BBC, Birt plunged himself into the next external lobbying target: the planned Green Paper on the BBC due to be published in November 1992. This would point the way to the renewal of the BBC's charter in 1996. The Corporate Affairs chief Howell James had kicked things off by setting up 15 'taskforce' committees, each looking at a different area of the BBC's activities. The idea was that they would review the entire range of BBC activities, 'thinking the unthinkable', so that the Corporation would be ready for any questions the Government might throw at it.

The taskforce exercise was massively bureaucratic and involved almost 200 BBC producers and executives, with a bias towards Birtist recruits and placemen. Each had to work to a 'mission statement' set out in excruciating American-style management speak. The Arts taskforce was given the pompous title of 'BBC as Cultural Patron' and its 'mission' was to 'identify the most appropriate economically sustainable range of cultural commitments that the BBC should make.' Another taskforce, featuring Janet Street-Porter, dealt with news and had the title 'The BBC, The Information Provider'. It was asked 'to evaluate whether the BBC should provide news and information, and if so in what ways and to whom.'

One of the most important was called 'The BBC: The Standard Setter'. This taskforce ranged right across the BBC and dealt with the concept of 'positioning' in the 'multi-channel future'. Its brief contained such nostrums as 'institutionalising ethical targets'; 'promoting standards that must derive from clarity of vision which carries conviction in its application' and 'enabling individuals to share common experiences, so promoting a sense of community in an increasingly complex world' (previously known as 'watching television').

Critics of the taskforces, drowning in a sea of paperwork, committee minutes and doublespeak, noted that when the Crawford Committee was set up to look at the future of broadcasting in 1925, it received a single three-page memo from a one-man taskforce called John Reith.

Overall, what the taskforces were suggesting would push the BBC's centre of gravity even further towards news and current affairs at the expense of more popular areas like sport and light entertainment. The light entertainment and sport taskforce, 'BBC – The Entertainer', apologetically said 'the distinctive nature of BBC programming has been diluted by our own sins of omission and commission.' It advocated the adoption of a 'High Ground' policy that would 'express the BBC's commitment to quality above all other considerations,' and would 'reduce the opportunity for compromise with the BBC's chosen brand image'. BBC TV, it said, needed to 'concentrate on what it does best rather than matching in all cases what the competition does best', which was seen as threatening an end to all-out competition with ITV.

The entertainment taskforce vaguely called for 'more investment' in drama, where this fitted in with the sort of quality criteria outlined by the separate arts and culture taskforce. There was no enthusiasm for light entertainment. The taskforce wanted 'greater use of the independent sector' and 'a more fluid structure making greater use of freelance and independent producers'. Sport was praised as the 'cheapest form of indigenous production' but the taskforce wanted to slim down coverage: 'the BBC should not go into the next century as the purveyor of sixty sports,' it said. Previously this was one of the Corporation's proudest boasts.

The taskforce reports made gloomy reading for Jonathan Powell, still struggling to hold up the ratings against well-financed opposition from ITV. Powell felt excluded from the process. He went through the names of the 200 people selected to serve on the committees and worked out that only five came from entertainment and drama. Membership was vastly weighted towards news, current affairs, high culture and factual programmes and was full of 'obscure Radio Four people who lived in cupboards', as he thought of them.

Powell complained about a stitch up, but was told the names were taken from the BBC staff list. Entertainment and drama were not under-represented. It was just that a lot of programmes in these areas were being contracted out to independents or made by freelancers.

Running alongside the taskforces was Birt's investigation of network television resources, which was now complete. The original idea of closing down the studios in regional centres and turning them into purely editorial operations had now been dropped. This was partly because of the Governors' insistence that the BBC should maintain a strong regional presence for political reasons.

Birt had instead come up with the idea of turning regional TV facilities into 'centres of excellence'. The plan would save overheads, he believed, and allow particular types of programme-makers to work together. This was standard Business School thinking about the way production processes were best handled in any industry. Manchester was to become the centre for the BBC's religious programmes and for Janet Street-Porter's 'yoof' empire. Birmingham's Pebble Mill was to become the centre for daytime television, drama and leisure programmes.

Keith Clement, a member of Birt's network resources

committee, had opposed the rationalisation, saying that it would only get rid of 250 people, which was not much of a saving when set against the disadvantages. The untidy ragbag of programmes in places like Manchester was all part of the BBC's creativity. Elstree, where Clement had been Head of Broadcasting, provided the network with game shows, cookery, anthropology and history as well as being the site for *EastEnders* and *Grange Hill*. It might look like chaos to Birt, but it provided a creative atmosphere and it worked. Creativity could not be planned into a flow chart. Good programmes got made, Clement said, because producers passionately wanted to make them and the facilities were there to let them get on with it. The idea that 'excellence' would be created just because someone had their office in Birmingham instead of Norwich was silly.

Birt's final report on network resources was delivered to the Board in November 1991. Insiders estimated that consultants' fees alone had cost £2 million. The report that Birt and the consultants presented included the 'centres of excellence' idea and detailed the movement of several London-based programme units out to the regions. This, he said, showed that his strategy was not anti-regional. But having received this new business, the core production units in Manchester, Birmingham and elsewhere were to be cut by 40 per cent by the start of 1993.

Some London units, including video editing and camera crews, were to be cut by half and the BBC film studios at Ealing were to be closed altogether. The existing four English BBC regions were to be reduced to three by closing the network centre at Elstree and placing the old BBC South and South East region under the control of Bristol.

Birt had wanted to close Elstree entirely, but was talked out of it mainly because of the cost of rebuilding the set of *EastEnders*. At first Birt had blithely said he would rebuild the set, probably at the drama 'centre of excellence' in Birmingham. This was easier said than done. Dismantling a perfectly good set and moving it brick by brick 100 miles up the M1 and then getting the actors to commute from London would cost millions. Then there was the insurmountable problem of the skyline which formed the background. This included blocks of flats surrounding the studio site, which would be impossible to move.

Elstree was saved as a location site for *EastEnders*. The Television Centre studios located there were kept open and used to produce *Top of the Pops* and *'Allo 'Allo*. But the Elstree department making programmes for the network was to be closed. The centre's head of network programmes, John Slater, later met one of the consultants advising the Birt committee and asked him why it had happened. The consultant said he was sorry but, for the life of him, he just could not remember.

After the closure of Elstree the fear and loathing that was felt after Birt's arrival in news and current affairs began to spread to the whole organisation. Few of those still working for the Corporation were prepared to speak out; but those who had already left, or had been disposed of, had no such inhibitions.

In January 1992, a few weeks after the first leaks of the taskforce proposals, Alasdair Milne popped up in the *Guardian* to ruminate at length on how things had gone since his execution five years earlier. 'BBC television has somewhere lost its way,' he said, 'BBC 1 is oddly planned and frequently quite unappealing; BBC 2 is increasingly charted like a private arts channel, heavily metropolitan-based.'

As a result BBC 1's percentage of the audience slipped to the low 30s; BBC 1 and 2 combined were 'struggling' to reach 40 per cent: the audience share the BBC had always believed it needed to justify the licence fee.

The situation was not yet an emergency, Milne said, and he was not blaming the programme-makers. But the Governors were getting it wrong, and their behaviour had damaged the BBC: 'The Governors have forced out one Director General, handed down a contemptuous offer of a year's extension to another, and appointed a third without advertisement, competition or even formal interview. They appear to exalt administration and management above creative leadership. It is time they drew back and again thought hard about their role.'

Hussey, Milne noted, had been praised for bringing in Birt to sort out news and current affairs, but at the cost of what he said people in the BBC were calling 'Sovietisation' of the management structure. The reappointment of Hussey for a second term of office had 'demonstrated either a wildly eccentric view of his achievements or, more likely, a pathetic poverty of imagination about a new appointment.' It was time, he said, for the Governors to 'speak up for the BBC' instead of criticising it, as Hussey tended to do: 'Two critical points should be made: a reaffirmation of the nature of public service broadcasting and an unequivocal support of the licence fee as the best means of funding the BBC.'

This was especially important, Milne said, in an election year. 'Which party will hold the reins of power after the forthcoming general election is a matter of great importance for the BBC,' he said. A Labour government would be an unknown quantity. But if the Conservatives were returned there would, he warned, be 'voices like that of Kenneth Baker at a recent Royal Television Society symposium, sharpening the Corporation's wits by reminding it that everything is up for grabs, no stone to be left unturned. Perhaps he did it partly to tease; who knows?'

Milne was referring to a new threat to the licence fee Baker had put on the agenda, the old idea of setting up an 'Arts Council of the Air'. Instead of the BBC getting the licence fee, the money would be doled out to any channel that could show it needed the money to make particular 'public service' programmes. The idea dated back to the Peacock Report, but had remained on the shelf until Andrew Neil breathed life back into it during a speech at the Edinburgh festival the previous year. The *Sunday Times* editor was given a rough ride, and was even accused of wanting to create a job for himself as head of the council.

Neil wrote in the *Sunday Times* how he was so appalled by the rudeness shown by television's 'smug bunch' that he had vowed never to return to the festival. The only person he had any time for was John Birt, one of the few people at the festival prepared to give him a decent hearing. 'The Director General designate rose to say it was vital to reconsider the sort of programming the BBC should provide in the new television environment,' Neil gloated. 'I smiled. Clearly the new boss of the BBC is not impressed by the posturing of the self-serving.'

After this the *Sunday Times* campaigned for the Arts Council idea. Jonathan Miller, the paper's media correspondent, was soon jeering at the BBC again, calling it 'a monolithic provider of public broadcasting services; its imperial mission financed by a compulsory poll tax.' Its control of all public funds for broadcasting was out of date. 'Britain does not operate a monolithic education system, under the control of a single entity. The universities and polytechnics are independent, and properly so. Yet monolithic bureaucracy has somehow become accepted as the only way of operating public broadcasting.'

Miller, who had also worked as the head of public relations for Murdoch's Sky TV during the lobbying over the Broadcasting Bill, felt moved to declare a possible conflict of interest. 'This is not a pitch for handing cash to Sky News,' he wrote, and then flatly contradicted himself: 'If Sky News found itself commercially unfeasible, there should be no reason why it could not reorganise itself as an independent non-profit company, and make a plea for finance.'

Miller's job as media correspondent on Murdoch's biggest selling broadsheet had given him one of the hottest seats in British journalism. People did not tend to stay in the job for long. But Miller, like Neil, was a true believer in the multichannel future. People who worked with Miller saw him as 'a bit of a nerd'. But they developed a soft spot for him because he was so charmingly guileless about combining the role of propagandist and journalist.

Miller was always claiming to be very chummy with Murdoch and his favourite line in any conversation was: 'Y'know Rupert told me the other day . . .' One former colleague remembered going with him to interview Murdoch about Sky in his office at Wapping. Reversing the normal roles of journalist and interviewee, Miller spent most of the session saying things like: 'Well, Rupert, what we should say is this . . .'

Progress towards the Arts Council of the Air, and the other legislation Wapping wanted to see, depended on keeping the Conservatives in power, which, in early 1992, was still in some doubt. The extreme unpopularity of the Government the previous year was countered by jettisoning Mrs Thatcher, and John Major's performance during the Gulf War had gained him a lot of credit. But with the recession beginning to bite it looked as if Labour might be in with a chance.

The Conservatives kicked off the 1992 election campaign with a tax-cutting budget. *Panorama* marked the event with an analytical programme about the economy, fronted by Peter Jay. The core of the film was Nigel Lawson's assertion that the Cabinet was wrong not to have joined the Exchange Rate Mechanism of the European Monetary System in 1985. The result was low interest rates, growing inflation and a boom that had got out of hand.

The programme had already been billed in the TV listings guides when Samir Shah rang Jonathan Powell to warn him there might have to be a change to the BBC 1 schedule. Shah explained he was worried about the political slant of the programme and he was having a lot of trouble persuading Peter Jay to cut it. Powell was not very interested in the details, and could not see what the problem was. When it came to economics Jay knew what he was talking about. In line with the Birt specialist strategy, he was supposed to be the country's greatest expert on the subject.

Powell listened impatiently as Shah described the programme. It sounded as if it was saying politicians tend to screw things up, which was not very remarkable. In any case

Shah had a whole week to add balance and caveats if he wanted to. Samir was just flapping, he decided. Powell replaced the phone and returned to more urgent matters.

On the Sunday night before the programme was due to go out Shah called in Gerry Baker, the producer, and *Panorama's* acting editor David Jordan. Shah said the *Panorama* team had done an excellent job, and provided a scoop. The problem was that he had not asked for this. He wanted what he described as a piece of 'bog standard economic analysis'. Instead they had made a film that showed the Conservatives had wrecked the economy. 'You know we just can't have that,' he said. The programme was pulled.

Five years of 'old guard' frustration boiled over all at once. John Ware, the veteran *Panorama* reporter, led the charge. People overheard a stand-up row between the two men in Shah's office. 'Either you go; or I go,' was Ware's general line. After this Shah agreed to meet the whole of the *Panorama* staff to explain his decision. The head of weekly programmes looked drained and nervous, as he often did on these occasions. After five years in this job Shah was still telling people he did not understand the old Lime Grove approach to film-making.

Shah said he had pulled Jay's programme because it was not fair to those involved, and did not 'test the issues'. This brought howls of protest. There was plenty of time to insert the usual disclaimers. But this time there was nothing to disclaim. Did he expect Lawson to be re-interviewed and call himself a liar? According to those at the meeting Shah floundered and was slaughtered with questions accusing him of 'being afraid of his own shadow' when it came to political stories.

The atmosphere turned even nastier when Baker let it slip that Shah had told him that the programme could not go out because the BBC could not afford to be accused of telling 'half the story' during an election campaign. Armed with this information all the senior *Panorama* people signed a letter addressed to Tony Hall, the head of the directorate, demand-

ing a meeting at which they would propose a vote of no
confidence in Shah.

When it came to the crunch the Birtists changed their
tune. One of them was overheard saying: 'Samir Shah is my
friend. I will deny everything.' He said Shah was being
persecuted and he would say anything to protect him. The
letter was redrafted. It was pointless if the people who had
all the evidence were not going to join in the protest.

The old guard thought this was typical of the cabalistic,
semi-masonic way the Birtists operated. The protests fizzled
out, but the question of whether Birt had ordered the programme to be pulled remained unanswered in some minds.

Birt said the decision was made entirely by Shah. Jay
blamed Shah as well. The decision to pull the programme
was, he later said, a 'disastrous mistake made by one person,
for reasons I do not understand and which are barmy.' Jay
'did not know how anyone could be so dumb.' It was a fit of
'temporary madness' and 'a brainstorm'. The decision was
'just nuts.'

But others doubted it. Jonathan Powell thought it 'inconceivable' that Shah would have changed the published schedule of BBC 1 without getting permission from Birt first. The
decision was above Shah's level of authority, and he could
have been sacked for making it without the designated
Director General's support.

Days later there was more bad news for the *Panorama* old
guard. Glenwyn Benson, the editor of *On the Record*, the
Birt-inspired weekly 'talking heads' politics programme, was
promoted to become *Panorama*'s new editor. Her appointment
caused much gloom. After Birt had established his complete
control over the operation, it was quietly admitted that there
was merit in the old Lime Grove ways and *Panorama* was
starting to do 'story-based' journalism, the Birt speak phrase
for ordinary professional reporting, again.

But Benson was a hard-line Birtist, a former deputy editor
of *Weekend World* and a keen member of the taskforce on

news and current affairs that had advocated even more 'vigour and rigour'.

To illustrate a point Benson unwisely announced she did not care if only five people were watching, so long as the BBC could not be accused of bias or sensationalism. The remark was hurled back at her as 'The Drive For Five': a crusade to actually lose viewers.

After watching an early and especially dismal Benson programme about housing policy, Paul Woolwich, who had previously failed to land the *Panorama* editor's job, noted in the *Guardian* how the two ITV current affairs shows *World in Action* and *This Week* were attracting more viewers than Birt's four specialist current shows and the Birtised *Panorama* put together.

'However it may have played in Whitehall,' Woolwich wrote, 'Birtism has been a disaster at the box office.'

# 15

## *A Very Improper Answer*

The eighteenth-century Lucknam Park Hotel is one of the country's most expensive conference centres. Set in 300 acres near Bath, it promises patrons 'unabashed luxury in plush and stately surroundings'. Rooms cost up to £310 a night. Every executive need is catered for, from tennis courts and 'whirlpool baths' to a Michelin-rated restaurant and a private rose garden.

In May 1992 the joint BBC Boards of Governors and Management met there for an annual think-in on the BBC's future. Inside Marmaduke Hussey was presiding, welcoming each chauffeur-driven guest with a cheery wave of his walking stick, directing the arriving grandees towards tea that was being served on the lawn.

Outside, at the gate, there was a trade-union picket. The militants sweating under the early summer sun belonged to BECTU, the union representing most of the BBC's staff. They were protesting against a limit of 3.7 per cent for the annual pay increase and the threat of thousands of redundancies mentioned in the leaked 'BBC – Providing our Services' taskforce report. In keeping with the civilised tone of the proceedings, even the pickets, who soon mingled with a bigger crowd of journalists, were served chilled glasses of beer from time to time.

The hacks soon discovered that Hussey was booked into the hotel's exclusive Camellia Suite, equipped with an antique four-poster bed, and provided with hand-made chocolates and a courtesy bowl of fruit. The menu for that evening was offering gâteaux of foie gras, truffles, baked breast of teal served on a potato galette with Madeira sauce, and similar gourmet delights.

The Corporation's PR men desperately pointed out that the place was being hired at the mid-week budget rate, and the Governors were not allowed to dine *à la carte*.

It was vital they got away from London, it was said, so that they could concentrate on their agenda and look at all the issues in comfortable surroundings. They were making a start on an entirely new blueprint for the BBC that would be published to coincide with the Government's Green Paper later in the year. It was probably the most important meeting the BBC had ever staged, and things needed to be done properly.

'But why this place?' the hacks kept demanding. The answers got feebler and feebler until a beleaguered press officer unwisely suggested: 'Well, it's got all the right number of electrical sockets; and that's important for a conference of this kind.' Another great BARMY BEEB story was born, with instant back-of-an-envelope calculations about just how many old-age pensioners had to pay their licence fee to foot the bill.

Apart from this, the main journalistic interest revolved around the visit of David Mellor, who had just joined the Cabinet as Heritage Secretary following the Conservatives' fourth consecutive election victory. It would be his job to write the promised Green Paper on the future of the BBC. A first draft of the document had already been prepared by Kenneth Baker, his more hawkish predecessor. Mellor had thrown Baker's effort in the bin and started again. John Birt, he thought, was already pushing the BBC in the direction he wanted and deserved much more support than Baker was willing to give. 'Better for them to reform themselves, than for us to get involved,' Mellor told his staff. 'We don't want another poll tax with this. If it ain't broke; don't fix it.'

Mellor's official car swept past the pickets and hacks. 'Hello, Dukey!' he boomed at the Chairman. Hussey asked him what he wanted to do first and Mellor said: 'Well, why don't we have a cup of tea together, you and I, now that I've come all this way to see you.' The two men disappeared into a drawing-room where people overheard occasional raucous guffaws.

Later that day Mellor gave a speech. It was full of praise for the way the BBC was changing, but he warned the Governors they would have to do more. 'You must sort out your role for the twenty-first century,' he said, 'you must prepare a vigorous, intellectual, well-argued case for the BBC; and you must, if you want to carry on being publicly funded, demonstrate that you deliver value for money.' With that the 'Minister of Fun' disappeared back up the M4.

The rest of the conference was devoted to discussion and clarification of 'programme objectives', or 'market repositioning', the key concept in the 'intellectual case for the BBC' that Mellor and Birt had already discussed several times. When the jargon was stripped away this boiled down to the old Whitehall complaint that the BBC should spend its money on quality programmes, defined in various ways, and leave the private sector to provide the rest. A start was being made with the Birt-inspired taskforces. But these appeared to be essentially an internal public relations job in that they had thrown up so many ideas that Birt would be able to go in any direction he liked and still say: 'We did this together; it is your strategy as much as mine.'

With Mellor's speech out of the way, the BBC hierarchy got down to discussing what sort of material should be provided by BBC radio and television. Curiously, the two men directly responsible for putting programmes on the screen, the channel controllers Jonathan Powell and Alan Yentob, were not booked in to Lucknam Park. As part of this they were asked to attend a brief session and describe their scheduling strategy.

Jonathan Powell had strong opinions of his own on 'programme objectives', the subject under discussion. His objective was to get programmes that would stand up to the ratings blitz about to be unleashed by ITV. As part of this Checkland had primed Powell to raise the thorny side-issue of when to show *Songs of Praise*, the Sunday evening service.

ITV, now officially instructed to worship Mammon by the Broadcasting Act, was preparing to dump the traditional Sunday evening God slot, replacing it with blockbuster feature films. The BBC had to follow suit or lose a lot of viewers, Powell explained. The number of people watching at that time of the evening was not great, but if they switched to ITV and stayed tuned for the rest of the night, this would hit BBC 1's ratings, which were already getting to be diabolical. But discussion was inconclusive. The Governors were unhappy about the proposed change. Birt was put out because he had not been consulted and Powell realised that his trip was a complete waste of time.

Peter Menneer, the head of BBC audience research, was just as dissatisfied with the proceedings. As part of the repositioning strategy, Birt wanted to 'test' the case for keeping Radios One and Two, harking back to the Peacock Committee's proposal that they should be privatised.

It was hard to prove there was anything distinctive about them; similar services were being provided by commercial stations like London's Capital Radio and planned new networks like Richard Branson's Virgin station. This might be a reason for getting rid of them. The problem was the stations were most heavily used by the sort of people who watched far less news, current affairs and 'distinctive' material: which was where licence money was increasingly being spent. Without Radio Two, and especially Radio One, the audience for the BBC's output would be heavily skewed towards the elderly and the middle classes, making the licence fee that much more difficult to justify.

Menneer put the statistical case against axing the stations, helped by a planted question lobbed at him by David Hatch, the Managing Director of BBC Radio. Hatch asked how many people would be left listening to BBC radio if Radios One and Two were abandoned. Maneer said audience share would drop to 20 per cent, leaving the BBC as a rump broadcaster. Menneer's warning about the threat to the licence fee made a big impact with the Governors, few of whom ever bothered to tune in to Radio One or any FM pop station. The fact that Radio One was listened to by more than 16 million people appeared to be news to them.

When the session was over Hussey took Menneer to one side and complained: 'that was a very improper answer you gave in there.' He replied that he was sorry; but the facts were the facts. Menneer, who believed in objective research, was later sacked by Patricia Hodgson, head of the Policy Unit. He decided that his face no longer fitted and that he was not 'One of Us'.

Menneer's departure coincided with the announcement that the BBC would go ahead with a continuous news service on Radio Four's long-wave frequency, leaving Radio Four available only on the BBC's FM waveband. The decision was argued over for months, and had its roots in the Corporation's coverage of the Gulf War, Birt's finest hour, when Radio Four had been commandeered for the continuous 'Scud FM' service. Birt had wanted to carry on with non-stop news, but he had been overruled by Checkland who had David Hatch and most other people in BBC radio breathing down his neck. And Peter Menneer had told policymakers there was no real evidence to show that licence payers wanted an all-news radio network.

The problem was Radio Four's loyal and articulate listeners. They were used to the rock-solid reception they got on long wave. They were outraged that they might lose their beloved station to the new-fangled FM band, which did not even feature on some of the older and much loved wireless sets still in circulation.

Worrying stories, dismissed as untrue, began to circulate about FM reception. It was said to be unreliable and prone to invasion by pirate radio stations. The last thing the Radio Four audience wanted was sudden blasts of ragga-reggae and adverts for minicabs and all-night Ecstasy rave parties interrupting *A Book At Bedtime*. In 1988, an 84-year-old lady Radio Four fan was arrested in the foyer of Broadcasting House after shooting a commissionaire with an air pistol because reception, even on long wave, was not good enough.

A more nonviolent middle-class revolt was now set in motion, led by a Winchester maths teacher who persuaded the nation's letter-writers to bombard Broadcasting House with complaints. As Menneer knew to his cost, BBC research backed up what they were saying: rolling news on Radio Four was a deeply unpopular idea.

Checkland had appeared on the January 1991 *See For Yourself* to fudge the issue. He said the service would come into being by the mid-1990s if he could be convinced there was enough news to fill it. 'We don't want it to be more speculation and not enough news. That irritates people enormously,' he said. At a recent public meeting, Checkland said, only three people in an audience of 350 had put up their hands when asked if they wanted a rolling news service. But Birt had pressed ahead regardless, and rolling news was a nagging undercurrent in the discussion of radio at Lucknam Park.

There was no communiqué at the end of the conference. Instead Checkland and Hussey, annoyed at reports of money being wasted on four-poster beds and plug sockets, presided at a press conference. The BBC hierarchy wanted to talk about the new role for the Governors and other grandiose aspects of Mellor's 'vigorous intellectual case for the twenty-first century'. As far as the hacks were concerned the millennium could wait. They had deadlines and started asking more hard-edged questions. Checkland was tackled about leaks from the BBC's finance departments that showed the Corporation was heading for a deficit of £100 million in the following year, and that BBC Television had 'mislaid' up to £60 million over two years.

The saga known as 'the missing millions' began when the BBC started putting out programmes to independent producers to meet the 25 per cent quota placed upon it by the Government. For every programme they bought from an independent there was supposed to be an equivalent cut in the BBC's own programme-making budgets. But this had not always happened. As a result there had been double spending in parts of the system. Matters were made worse when a new Education Directorate was set up to make programmes that had previously been made by the television service as a whole. Nobody told the television accountants that the new directorate was, in effect, spending some of their money. The result was another double spend.

None of this was revealed until Ian Phillips, the director of finance for the whole of the BBC, drew up the end-of-year accounts in April 1992. Phillips reported the problem to the Board, brought in outsiders to look at it and made what he described as 'changes within the management of the TV service'.

At the press conference Checkland blandly explained it all away, saying the BBC would rebalance its budget over time. 'We will live within our licence income as we have always done,' he said. 'We will continue to run the BBC in that responsible way.'

The hacks were not very impressed by this, and opened up a second front of hostile questioning, this time about the deal the BBC had done with Sky to share screening rights to Premier League football. Jane Thynne, the *Daily Telegraph's* media correspondent, wanted to know if Hussey and Murdoch had worked together on the deal and, if so, what was agreed. Hussey turned bright red at the impudence of the question. He banged his walking stick on the table, declared the press conference over and was bundled out of the room. Thynne and the others realised they had touched a sensitive nerve.

Negotiations for league football screening rights were one of the big set-piece battles between television networks. The arrival of Sky TV had opened up new possibilities for the football authorities. Murdoch had taken a strategic decision that he had to have live Premier League football for Sky – the perfect marketing tool needed to sell dishes to his target audience.

Sky had made a very careful pitch to the chairmen of selected Premier League clubs, enticing them away from the familiar territory of BBC and ITV towards the uncharted waters of satellite. In the past the duopoly had given preference to a cartel of the 'big five' clubs, namely Manchester United, Arsenal, Liverpool, Tottenham and Everton, in the screening of games, which was valuable to them in terms of sponsorship and promotion. The big five had all the power within the League and were to vote in favour of selling rights to live Premier League games to ITV, with the BBC coming in as a subsidiary partner with rights to show edited highlights.

But Murdoch had shrewdly organised a revolt of the smaller clubs like Crystal Palace and Chelsea, playing on their resentment about the way previous deals were stitched up. The smaller clubs were much more interested in getting a share of the subscription money available from Sky, and cared far less about the problem of over-exposure, which troubled the big clubs.

Selected club chairmen were flown to Sky's pay-per-view subscription centre in Scotland and its impressive new technology. 'Everyone who needed to be stroked was stroked. There was a lot of shmoozing going on; it was megashmooze,' one of the Sky people later revealed.

The Murdoch camp went as far as blocking the takeover of Tottenham Hotspur by Robert Maxwell, who wanted to play a role in the rights negotiations. Murdoch's rival was certain to either charge Sky a fortune, or help deliver the rights to

ITV. Murdoch called his business partner Alan Sugar, who made the dishes for Sky, and told him to put in a counterbid for Tottenham with the words: 'Don't let that fat c**t Maxwell get Tottenham.'

These elaborate preparations showed how important football was to Murdoch, but it was still by no means certain a majority of clubs would vote for a deal with Sky, regardless of how much money he offered, if it meant disappearing from the television screens of the 80 per cent of the population who still did not have access to satellite.

The problem was solved in the final week of the negotiations when the BBC pulled out of its joint offer with ITV and, to general amazement, joined forces with Sky to offer £304 million for 60 live games a year, edited highlights and exclusive rights to live FA Cup and England games. The satellite channel was to pay most of the money and would show the live games in an expensive subscription service. The BBC secured the return of the *Match of the Day* Saturday night highlights, and the two networks shared the FA Cup and internationals.

Greg Dyke, head of ITV sport, was apoplectic. He thought he had a joint deal with the BBC, but they had changed sides without warning in a way that would take live football off most of the nation's screens.

Dyke also said the affair showed that Hussey's talk about the BBC defending the rights of the public and extending choice was 'bullshit'. The public had lost the right to see live football, previously provided by the BBC–ITV duopoly, and might now start to complain about paying the licence fee when they had to stump up an extra £70 a year, at least, to watch it on Sky.

The theory was that a tripartite future for British television was beginning to emerge. Sky would provide the premium subscription services, like live sport, which would only be profitable if it disappeared from the BBC. Football was the perfect example of this. The BBC would slim down to its 'public service' core, showing unpopular material that

Sky was not interested in broadcasting anyway; and ITV would be left as a cheap and cheerful 'service of last resort' for people who did not fancy Peter Jay's nonstop mission to explain on the BBC, or could not afford Sky subscriptions.

The football deal was a turning point for the BBC, Sky and the future of broadcasting in the UK. Jonathan Miller, the one-time Sky public relations chief and *Sunday Times* media correspondent, was soon telling people that when the history of Sky's impending triumph was written it would start by saying: 'In May 1992 satellite television got the rights to Premier League football for a trifling sum.'

The deal with Sky over the football, and what it seemed to mean for the future, merged with the various problems crowding in on the BBC to provide plenty of material for the annual summertime 'whither the BBC' season, building up to the Edinburgh Television Festival at the end of August. The rows over the pulling of *Panorama's* 'sliding into slump' during the election still rankled, as did the possible privatisation of Radios One and Two; the confusion over rolling news on Radio Four; Birt's controversial appointment as DG (designate); the cash and ratings crisis and the 'missing millions'.

In August David Attenborough added to the sense of crisis by delivering an unprecedentedly critical speech at the British Association Science Festival. He said the accountants had taken over at the Corporation; the morale of the BBC's staff was being 'gravely eroded' and 'the very things that gave the BBC its unique stature and strength are being destroyed.'

Two weeks later, at the Edinburgh Festival itself, Attenborough's message was taken up and pushed much further by a much more commercially aggressive figure: Michael Grade, the chief executive of Channel Four.

Six years earlier at Edinburgh Grade and Birt had played the light-hearted Ratings Game, and were the greatest of pals. Now The Great Scheduler was about to deliver a withering attack on his former friend, and all his works.

# 16

## A Bourbon in Red Braces

The news that Michael Grade was to deliver the keynote speech at the Edinburgh Television Festival caused a ripple of excitement in TV-land. The Channel Four chief always looked forward to the event. He was in his element at the conference, flattered by the wheedling of an army of independent programme-makers trying to get into his good books, and the admiring phalanx of BBC people who still thought he ought to be Director General.

Grade was a great showman who, according to legend, had once enlivened a dull programming conference at LWT by wearing an electrified revolving bow tie 'for a laugh'. On his best form he could be hilarious, working the audience and, more often than not, delivering a bombshell of some sort. The occasion was circled in red ink in many a Filofax.

Grade spent much of August shut up in his Hampstead house writing his speech. Secretaries at Channel Four were told to wind down his diary so that he could concentrate on polishing the text, uninterrupted by the business of running the channel. In the week before Edinburgh the TV industry was buzzing with talk about how Grade's speech would pull no punches; and that it would be a wholesale demolition job on the Hussey régime.

In the George Hotel, the place to be seen at Edinburgh, there was only one topic of conversation: would Michael have the courage to denounce Hussey and Birt's rule at the BBC and speak up for the thousands of suffering BBC employees? Journalists were given copies of Grade's speech in advance. The word began to spread. What he had to say was 'dynamite'.

Howell James, the BBC's Corporate Affairs chief, looked worried. Dealing with the fall-out from Grade's speech was to be his last major jobs for the BBC. Having seen through the taskforce reports he had decided to resume his working partnership with Lord Young, now running Cable and Wireless. 'Thank God I'm going,' he murmured to journalists when copies of the Grade speech began to circulate.

Grade arrived in Edinburgh and spent the afternoon rehearsing his lines. He arrived in the George to change out of his gunslinger waistcoat and into a grey business suit for the evening. Grade bantered with the media correspondents. 'Is it a good speech?' he beamed mischievously. 'Do you think it's worth a line or two?' The hacks rushed off to talk to their newsdesks, telling them to clear a lot of space.

Grade mounted the podium to warm applause. This time there were no jokes or gimmicks. The speech was delivered straight. It was heartfelt and received in stunned silence, except for the occasional gasp of approval as he took Hussey and Birt apart.

'The latest jargon inside the BBC speaks of "downsizing", "delayering" and "out-sourcing": that's closure, redundancies and dark studios to you and me,' he said. The BBC, Grade said, was 'in terminal decline', and Birt and Hussey had done what the Government wanted using 'pseudo-Leninist' management methods. They were planning a new and much reduced future for the BBC in their 'all-too-frequent and debilitating negotiations with Downing Street.' The taskforce reports showed Birt's 'arrogance' about the BBC's future role, and were full of meaningless 'designer slogans' designed to placate the Government. But Birt could not save the BBC by retreating to the 'high ground' of programming as the Government seemed to want. This was an 'Alice-in-Wonderland policy which will only deprive viewers and threaten the licence fee'.

The Governors had followed a policy of 'political appeasement' and continually interfered with programmes. But appeasement would only weaken the bedrock of public support and make it easier for the Government to give it an even smaller role. 'This great institution would become marginalised and all the human misery resulting from all the cuts become sacrifices in vain,' he said, adding: 'This must not be allowed to happen.'

There was 'a massive revolution' taking place, carried out 'with brutal zeal', Grade continued, 'by an army of accountants.' Checkland had set this in motion and Grade attacked him just as scathingly. The BBC had 'abandoned its heritage' the moment Checkland had described it as a billion-pound business, he said: 'The BBC was never meant to be a business. It was set up to be a centre of excellence.'

Now Checkland was being denied the extension to his contract and Birt had been appointed Director General designate over 'port and cigars' in secret. That decision left the Corporation with 'virtually two chief executives for eighteen months: one a lame duck; the other a Trappist monk, unable to speak publicly.' Nobody else was speaking out, Grade said, because the BBC had become a 'secretive and forbidding place to work,' it was 'an airtight fortress from which no stray opinion is permitted to escape. The staff are afraid to speak publicly unless every word has been cleared with the BBC's own thought police. The silence is eerie, ominous.'

'But wait a minute,' Grade said, pausing before half-whispering a knock-out punch: 'She's gone.' The reference to Mrs Thatcher hit the mark. The BBC was starting to bring in consultants and privatise everything in sight, just when the country was beginning to wonder if this was the right thing to do.

Howell James gave the first official reply in a statement to journalists. 'Michael Grade caricatures some of the ideas that have been discussed without properly considering the arguments behind them,' James said. 'He seemingly offers only that the BBC should respond to change by staying the same.' (Meanwhile Norman Tebbit popped up with a counter-attack; denouncing Grade for producing 'dirt, smut and rubbish' on Channel Four.)

The first journalist to contact Marmaduke Hussey for his reaction was Jonathan Miller of the *Sunday Times*, who called the Chairman at home. Hussey gave Miller an exclusive and vitriolic response. The BBC Chairamn described the former controller as 'a Bourbon in red braces' who was making 'wild accusations that did not stand up'. He then added that the BBC could not afford Grade's salary (put at £480,000 by the *Sunday Times*) or his policies. 'Michael Grade hasn't learnt anything,' Hussey continued, 'he is making an emotional and nostalgic pitch for the BBC in the 1980s.' Grade's claim about dictatorial management was 'total rubbish'. Never before had the BBC consulted its staff so frequently and thoroughly: 'I do this myself. I have lunch in the canteen and ask them,' he claimed.

A lot of people in the BBC thought it was pitiful that Hussey could only find his trips to the canteen as an answer to the serious criticisms Grade was making. Reverting to military style, Hussey liked to mingle ostentatiously with the 'lower ranks' as he called them, figuratively inspecting kit, wiping the dust from the tops of doors and ordering the repainting of lavatories.

The people he spoke to during the canteen ritual were mostly quite junior, and would be fully briefed by their superiors before they were allowed to pick up a fork. Phillipa Giles, the producer of BBC 2's *Oranges Are Not The Only Fruit*, immediately challenged Hussey's point about consulting the staff. She had attended one of Hussey's canteen lunches. 'I must have been sitting on his deaf side because he ignored virtually everything I had to say,' she told colleagues.

And there was anger that Hussey had given an interview to Murdoch's *Sunday Times*, but had refused to talk to the BBC's own reporters. This was later explained as force of circumstance. Hussey, it was claimed, was caught off guard by Miller. It was his birthday and he had a house full of relatives. After that he reverted to the standard policy of saying nothing to anyone.

Grade himself thought the interview Hussey had given to the *Sunday Times*, the heaviest hitter in the Wapping stable, was outrageous. The next time he met Andrew Knight, the chief executive of News International, Murdoch's senior manager in the UK, he complained: 'I have been kicked to death by your lot for ten years: first at the BBC and now at Channel Four. When are you going to stop?'

It was interesting, Grade said, how the Wapping line had softened after the deal between Sky TV and the BBC over Premier League football. And now they were defending the BBC and its Chairman against the criticisms he had made at Edinburgh. 'From "break up the BBC" to praising it is a bit of a U-turn, isn't it?'

Birt was on holiday in Santa Fe, USA, during Grade's Edinburgh speech and Miller was again on the trail, reporting his reaction. 'Michael Grade simply doesn't understand what is happening,' Birt said. 'His description of the current BBC reads to me like a wild fantasy. It is grossly inaccurate.' Privately Birt told people Grade's speech was 'venomous', an unjustified exercise in rabble rousing. He had done it out of sour grapes and an infantile desire for revenge after the row over their respective roles in the BBC.

If Birt did not recognise the picture Grade had painted at Edinburgh there was a huge number of BBC employees who did. Grade received hundreds of letters. Some were from household names, others were from more humble figures. They all contained the same message. One way or another the BBC was killing itself from within. Other senior BBC people agreed with Grade's message but thought it lacked credibility because The Great Scheduler had deserted the place in its hour of need.

Grade wondered if Checkland would now take the chance to make his own criticisms of the way Hussey and Birt were running the BBC. Instead the Director General went on Radio Four's *Today* programme and said: 'I'm not limping, I'm not lame, I'm sprinting for the tape.'

Birt and Checkland managed to maintain a façade of unity in public, even after Grade's speech. The previous year, when Hussey had been reappointed, the Director General had loyally issued a statement saying he enjoyed working with him and was 'delighted' by the decision. Now, out of the public gaze, things were very different. In the months after Grade's Edinburgh speech Checkland received increasingly harsh treatment at the hands of the Governors.

In the autumn of 1992, after receiving another roasting at a Board meeting, he asked a colleague: 'Do they want me to go now? Because if they go on like this, I will.' He then angrily referred to the Board's admiration for Birt. 'I don't know why they all think he's so bloody clever,' Checkland grumbled; 'he's only got a third-class degree in engineering.'

The Director General finally vented some of his frustration at a meeting of the Royal Television Society, an up-market version of the Edinburgh conference for senior television managers, at the end of October. Unlike Birt, Checkland was an effective public speaker and presented the standard BBC line in a highly competent, if slightly predictable, way. But in the question-and-answer session that followed something seemed to snap in his head.

A question about the way the BBC was being run led to a remarkable outburst. It was wrong, he said, for the BBC to have the same Chairman for ten years. And it was 'bizarre' that the job was held by someone like Hussey who would be 73 when the BBC's Charter came up for renewal in 1996. 'You need a younger kind of leadership at certain points in the BBC's future,' he continued. 'When you talk to the

Governors about FM you want to be talking about frequency modulation and not fuzzy monsters.'

Bill Cotton, sitting in the front row of the audience, eyed the tumbler of clear liquid the Director General was gulping from time of time. He turned to his neighbour and said: 'I don't know what's in that glass, but it's certainly starting to work.' There was more. Hussey, Checkland said, had placed him in 'an absurd position' by announcing Birt as his successor almost two years before he was due to stand down. This, he said, was a 'ludicrous way to operate'. Checkland castigated the rest of the Governors, describing them as 'a very elderly group of people' who were out of touch with the reality of broadcasting.

With that Checkland flew off to a Commonwealth Broadcasting Conference in Gaborone, Botswana, chased by Jonathan Miller of the *Sunday Times*. Licking his lips at this latest luscious example of Fat Cat activity, Miller described how Checkland was on safari followed by cocktails at the poolside buffet in the five-star Gaborone Sheraton Hotel. All at a cost of £10,000 to the licence-payers.

Hussey responded to the Fuzzy Monsters attack by sending a letter to *The Times*, jointly signed by Barnett and claiming to represent the views of all the Governors. It ignored the accusation that he was too old, and that his reappointment had given him too much power. Hussey merely said Birt was 'the man for the future' and that Birt and Checkland stood 'foursquare together behind the BBC's editorial vision, its resource policies and all other aspects of the BBC's case.' This vision was taking its final form as *Extending Choice*: the BBC's blueprint for the future, due to be published within days of the Government's Green Paper.

Hussey had replied in advance to the Green Paper with another *Times* article. 'We in the BBC are the inheritors of a great institution,' he said, 'but all institutions have to adapt to changing circumstances in which they live, or they become fossilised relics.' Some thought the reference to fossils was unwise in the circumstances.

Hussey's claim to have inherited the BBC was also alarming. But the Chairman continued, setting out the definitive version of the 'market repositioning' concept: 'We accept that in due course the market will come to provide a fully adequate supply of certain kinds of programming,' he wrote. 'In television it will provide general entertainment channels and channels with specialist appeal.' The BBC would fill in the gaps and provide 'programmes of quality and distinction'.

The Green Paper and *Extending Choice* were, on most points, more or less identical. The main difference was the inclusion of the old 'Arts Council of the Air' idea. David Mellor had jettisoned the proposal the previous summer, calling it 'potty', but Peter Brooke, his recent replacement as Heritage Secretary, had revived it as a sop to the ideological anti-BBC lobby on the Tory backbenches. Even so, this resurrection did not seem all that threatening.

Brooke was not a powerful figure in Whitehall. He had arrived from the Northern Ireland office under a cloud after tactlessly singing 'Oh my Darling Clementine' on Irish television the same day as an IRA bomb killed seven building workers. Now was he grappling with the internal difficulties of the Heritage Department which covered activities as diverse as the restoration of ancient monuments and football hooliganism. It was derided as the Ministry of Fun (and, under Mellor, the Ministry of Free Tickets) and was as near as Whitehall had ever got to the Monty Python idea of a Ministry of Silly Walks.

Like Hussey, Brooke came over as a likeable Ealing comedy upper-class gent. His critics found it difficult to be too harsh with him; but did suggest he ought to be preserved in a museum somewhere as part of the heritage he was supposed to protect.

Brooke put the Arts Council of the Air back into the Green Paper as an option. But he was not very enthusiastic about it, as he was to demonstrate during an extraordinary 'debate' organised by the BBC's *Late Show* to mark its publication.

The Secretary of State kicked off *The Late Show* on The Future of the BBC by woodenly reading an autocue straight to camera in the style of a Prime Ministerial broadcast from the 1950s. 'The BBC makes and commissions programmes at the moment, as well as transmitting them,' he observed helpfully, his voice quickening to indicate surprise and excitement. 'But how many of these functions need to be carried out by those employed by the BBC?' he asked, inconclusively.

A studio discussion was kicked off by Sarah Dunant, *The Late Show* presenter. Her guests were David Attenborough, Melvyn Bragg, Gus MacDonald of ITV, and Ray Snoddy, the media correspondent of the *Financial Times*. The panel pronounced itself happy with the Green Paper, which 'very supportive of the BBC'. Snoddy thought it was pleasantly 'littered with questions, refreshingly open in its approach and remarkably undogmatic.' He concluded: 'Reading between the lines, this is a status quo document.' It was a shame, they all said, the 1990 Broadcasting Act which dealt with ITV had not been as sensible. Brooke beamed indulgently. The others smirked back at him. They all knew it was because Mrs Thatcher, the loopy old bat, had nothing to do with it.

Attenborough asked the minister about the Arts Council of the Air. How could anyone decide which programmes contained a public service element, and which ones did not? Surely 'public service broadcasting' was a system of channels like the BBC, and not a reference to particular programmes that might need financial support. The Secretary of State was good-natured but evasive. Attenborough pressed him, asking for the Government's definition of public service. Brooke said nobody really knew what it was, but everyone could recognise it when they saw it, adding oddly: 'It's like an elephant.'

Dunant tried to zip things up a bit by saying: 'There comes a point when efficiency can't be gained without cutting back,' and she emphasised her words with a series of karate chops.

Gus MacDonald wearily said: 'Mike Checkland and John Birt have had a bad press, but they have done a good job anticipating this Green Paper. The BBC, despite the unpleasantness for the people who work in it, and it must be terribly unsettling . . .' Attenborough began to roll his eyes, but Dunant butted in before things strayed into 'Pseudo-Leninist', 'Alice in Wonderland' and geriatric 'Fuzzy Monsters' territory. 'And we should say that the BBC will be launching its own paper on Thursday,' she remarked, helpfully.

The discussion was wrapped up by Snoddy who again praised the Green Paper and added: 'Dramatic changes are coming. Cable and satellite are happening; but not as quickly as people think. It is important not to destroy an important institution by taking action before it is needed.'

The BBC launched *Extending Choice*, its reply to the Green Paper, a few days later at an all-singing, all-dancing press conference at Television Centre. Birt took the lead, surprising the hacks with his fluency and new confidence as he emerged from Trappist monk mode. He was flanked by Hussey and Checkland, also looking relaxed and happy. Things got under way with a promotional video offering a guide to the 'best of the BBC'. Clips showed walking national institutions like John Peel, the venerable and 'distinctive' Radio One DJ, mixed with extracts from much loved BBC shows.

The hacks were suitably impressed, but like David Attenborough on *The Late Show* they wanted somebody to nail down exactly what was meant by 'distinctive' programmes. This was the only point of interest about *Extending Choice* as far as most of their readers, the ordinary TV viewers, were concerned. Was *Neighbours* 'distinctive'? Or was it for the chop as 'imitative, derivative or formulaic' material, which *Extending Choice* said was no longer allowed. Hard-edged questions like this were smothered in a welter of doublespeak. But Birt was categorical about one thing. The BBC, he said, could expect to have only 30 per cent of the 'multichannel' audience by the year 2000 AD.

The *Extending Choice* report itself was a 90-page glossy document, bristling with slogans, pie-charts and impressive-looking graphics. It was not so much written as compiled by Patricia Hodgson and Matthew Bannister, being lined up as the new Birtist controller of Radio One, with the help of Howell James, whose Corporate Affairs department published the document.

*Extending Choice* started with the sweeping and debatable assertion that 'almost everything about the broadcasting world has changed since the BBC's current Charter was issued in 1981.' Satellite and cable were starting to get a foothold, but apart from the launch of Channel Four, surprisingly little had changed. The rest of the document was full of similar material and littered with Maoist-sounding slogans, tautologies and statements of the obvious: THE BROADCASTING INDUSTRY HAS BEGUN TO MOVE TOWARDS A NEW STRUCTURAL MODEL was one, printed in large type. THE BBC WILL FOCUS ON PERFORMING A SET OF CLEARLY DEFINED ROLES was another.

The document said little about the BBC's achievements, and endlessly repeated the fact that there would be more channels in the future, emphasising the defeatism of Birt's prediction that the BBC would be a minority broadcaster within ten years.

More literate people read the document with real dismay. It was full of ugly, obscure writing. It talked about 'complex networks of interlocking relationships between fragmented social groups', 'segmentation of the broadcasting market', 'concentrated effort to sustain a viable long-term future', and the need to 'liberate resources from unproductive use'. On and on it went. It was inconceivable to some that the BBC, which had once employed or broadcast the likes of George Orwell, and A. J. P. Taylor, could put out so much literal nonsense in its name.

*Extending Choice* summed up its message by saying 'the Old World in which the BBC's traditional role and services were developed has passed into history.' Having buried the past in this way, the rest of the document promised the BBC would in future display such admirable things as 'high-quality programmes', 'impartial news and information', 'programmes that innovate, challenge and entertain', 'value for money' and that it would 'bring credit to the UK', as though the BBC had not been trying, with varying degrees of success, to do all these things since it was set up.

People might have expected something like *Extending Choice* from Hussey, who had never liked the BBC and was still, even now, referring to most of its staff as 'them'. And it bore the mark of John Birt. He had declared Year Zero for BBC news and current affairs when he had first arrived, rubbishing much of what had gone before. Now the Corporation as a whole was in danger of getting the Pol Pot treatment.

Most people who worked closely with Birt found him to be privately amusing, cultured and even generous; at least if they were at the same status level as him. At the same time even his admirers, thought he was oddly, even irrationally, obdurate. Some said he was like a First World War general: he had a plan, was convinced of its rightness and nothing, despite the mounting losses, could persuade him it was wrong.

But there was real anger that Checkland had put his name to *Extending Choice* and the 'libelling of the past' some thought it entailed. Most of the heavyweights who had left the BBC, including Grade, Cotton and more middle-ranking people in the financial and administrative departments, had not sympathised when Checkland complained about the way Hussey had treated him. They saw him as a terribly weak man who had not opposed Birt or spoken out when he had the chance to do something about it.

As long ago as 1987 Cotton had begun to worry that Checkland was prepared to give in to Hussey and Birt too easily: 'giving the shop away' as he put it. The events of the intervening six years had not changed his mind. There was little sympathy when Checkland bowed out in the week before *Extending Choice* was published. He would leave at Christmas, three months before his contract came up.

Birt took over at a meeting of the Director General's liaison group. He made a short speech, saying a lot of the credit for the Green Paper and *Extending Choice* should go to Checkland who had been 'a most distinguished Director General'.

When Checkland had taken over, Birt reminded people, there was 'widespread hostility to what was seen as the 'arrogance' of the BBC.' He then moved on to the out-going Director General's most politically useful characteristic: 'Mike Checkland never had any problem about admitting when the BBC was wrong.'

# 17

## *The Paperclip Problem*

With Checkland out of the way, Birt was able to speed up the pace of the internal reforms he was advocating. Top of his agenda was producer choice, the internal market system Checkland had started three years earlier as a small experiment in the film department. Birt wanted to push the idea much further, taking in almost every aspect of the BBC's operations.

Producer choice involved turning programme-makers into business units, allowing them to buy what they needed from other business units inside the BBC or on the open market. Birt claimed his enthusiasm for the scheme proved he was not a 'pseudo-Leninist' centraliser, but quite the reverse. 'Producer choice involves a profound decentralisation,' he told *Ariel*. 'I'm a decentraliser, not a centraliser.' The BBC would, he said, 'be a much happier place to work' as a result.

'If you're in a self-contained unit with your purposes clear and you have infinitely more freedom to determine how you spend your money on resources and support services, it will unleash enormous creativity and enterprise within the organisation,' he enthused, showing once again that for him 'creativity' was a matter of management structure.

Producer choice involved dividing production costs into 'tariff' items to be charged against particular programmes, and 'non-tariff' items including constant overheads like the transmitter network. The expense of having the Governors and the dozens of regional and specialist advisory committees was also 'non-tariff' and, in addition to his own salary, was to be taken straight off the top of the licence fee as the unavoidable cost of being the BBC. All other expenses, right down to heat, light, office space and telephone bills, were 'tariff' and would be charged against particular programmes.

Like many of the things being cooked up by Birt, the idea of creating a separate and tradeable resource base for the BBC was not new. His slogan that 'the BBC must move into the future' and 'respond to rapid change in the broadcasting industry' was repeated with Orwellian intensity; but a lot of things he was proposing involved moving backwards into the past.

Until 1970, for example, the BBC's transmission department had been kept separate, and programmes had to budget for the cost of sending out the signal. But this had led to pressure for the engineers to do everything on the cheap and might have led to the UK having the sort of inferior technical broadcast standards found in the USA, and so the arrangement was abolished and transmission costs were absorbed into general overheads.

All the way down the line, from the transmitters to the costume departments, everything was provided centrally to keep up quality. In the happier times of the 1970s, when quality was the only consideration, nobody at the BBC doubted the system had carried a lot of fat. Checkland had been steadily tightening things up in an undramatic way, but this had not been good enough for Hussey, a manager of the 'big bang' school.

It was feared that breaking up the facilities into separate units would reduce standards as people competed to provide services at the cheapest cost. At the same time producer choice might end up costing more money as economies of scale were lost and the BBC had to buy everything from outsiders at market prices.

Another aspect of the system involved classifying all programmes within 'genres' such as science or comedy. The channel controllers then had to work out the average tariff cost of each genre, then draw up a list of how many hours of each genre they intended to transmit and feed this information into the system. The list would be broken down even further. So if the controllers planned to put out 200 hours a year of light entertainment 'genre' they would reclassify this as, for example, 100 hours of 'star-led sitcom genre'; 50 hours of 'non-star-led sitcom genre' and 50 hours of 'panel game genre'.

The average tariff cost of these sub-genres would then be calculated and, in an additional complication, would be used to help fix the price paid to independents, who had to make 25 per cent of everything. Yet another twist was provided by guidelines on the number of hours that had to be made in regional centres. The system would enable Birt to be able to tell Whitehall just exactly how many hours of every type of programme the BBC was going to put out, and what it all cost down to the last telephone call.

(Showing rare moderation Birt specifically excluded paperclips from the system. After thinking about what had been called the 'paperclip problem' it was decided they would still be provided centrally. 'Hotels have this sort of problem,' he explained, 'they have to work out what they leave free for people to use in their rooms. All of these questions will be addressed sensibly.')

The system had the advantage of giving Birt and his coterie of central assistants complete power over the organisation. Some said this was its only advantage. For everyone else it was a bureaucratic nightmare.

Jonathan Powell immediately fell foul of the system. The first difficulty was deciding which genre programmes fell into. In the past channel controllers could look at the ratings and decide whether they needed more or less of particular types of programmes, and whether they could afford it. If they had blown a lot of money on an expensive drama series they would find something cheap to fill up the rest of the hours and bring the whole channel in on budget.

Under producer choice this crucial element of flexibility was being undermined and replaced with 'programming by prescription'. The budget was cut up into thousands of little bits and locked in for a year, making it more difficult to respond to a tactical scheduling attack by ITV. It also involved gathering endless information to feed Birt's database which, in turn, was supported by what appeared to programme planners to be 'an army' of statisticians.

Powell soon received a stuffy memo asking why he had commissioned half an hour less of science programmes for 1993. He was baffled. As far as he was aware he had simply recommissioned all the science programmes for the same runs and exactly the same times. But after hunting through the schedules for two days Powell discovered one edition of the science show *QED* had been allowed to run for an extra half-hour, because it was thought to be worth it at the time. When the series was recommissioned for its customary half-hour slot, the one-hour special had not been built in, and the computer reported a year-on-year 'cut' in science programmes. After this he lived in dread of a visitation from the statisticians.

Appropriately enough Birt had chosen April 1 1992 as the date for 'full implementation' of producer choice. As people began to gear up for the big day, tales of bizarre arrangements began to circulate. One immediate result was a boom in power lunches and a glut of glossy and expensive brochures aimed at getting the BBC's producers to use the BBC's facilities.

The Bristol studios were among the first in the ring, producing a brochure full of appealing pictures of the studios complete with smiling cameramen. This was supplemented by a celebrity sales video featuring Michael Buerk, praising the facilities and the 'friendly Bristol welcome'.

This activity was copied throughout the BBC, at vast cost. A regional costume department published an eight-page brochure detailing tariff charges down to the last button and zip. When the BBC's music libary started charging a minimum of £8 for a snippet of background music, studio engineers started taping everything they used and building up their own libraries. It was the same story with reference books, which were either stolen or photocopied and kept in a mutating series of private libraries in offices throughout the organisation.

The BBC pronunciation unit was turned into a business unit which radio producers and reporters would have to pay to consult by quoting a programme production number and accepting a minimum charge against their budget. Producers used it far less often as a result, but the cost of providing the service went up because there were fewer transactions.

The internal market often produced bizarre price differences. Staff working at the World Service had to work through the night and, in the past, they had been provided with a utilitarian bed-and-breakfast arrangement at the service's Bush House studios in the Strand. The BBC tariff for this was so high that producers found it cheaper to check people into the Waldorf across the road.

The cost of logging and billing the movement of individual library books, boiled eggs, zips and buttons around the Corporation required the service of a vast new bureaucracy and pushed up prices already inflated by the cost of carrying the BBC's senior management as an overhead.

In addition, a vast new training effort was needed to explain the system. At a network radio conference, one of dozens of internal meetings held to explain the scheme, one producer said: 'I've got an identity crisis. I started off as a production business unit. A couple of months ago I became a resource business unit; and a couple of days ago an orchestral business unit. What does this mean, please?' The reply was a snide dig at Birt: 'just as a tariff is not a price, a genre is not a programme.'

A lot of the training bore the hallmark of the booming American-inspired 'huggy feely' personal therapy and counselling industry and 'role playing' imaginary business negotiations. One technique was an exercise in 'working together', cutting out paper frogs and pretending to sell them to each other. £15 million a year was provided for training activity of this sort, and keener people could pay £15,000 to enrol on a Master's Degree in BBC management. 'You integrate it into your work; it's project orientated. You look at various areas of your activity and learn about managing in a creative environment,' Birt explained at a press conference.

A Management Training Office and Technology Unit was established as a subdivision of the Policy Unit, offering additional training at the rate of £300 a day, charged to programme budgets. Special training opportunities for women included a two-day course on martial arts for self-defence; a three-day course of career development and a five-day course on 'leadership'. Female make-up artists were sent on assertiveness training courses, at £1,000 a head, to teach them how to sell their services to producers.

All producers were given a 62-page glossy booklet explaining how the system worked 'in outline', together with a fifteen-page summary entitled *A Producer's Guide to Producer Choice*. This was immediately superseded by a new set of guidelines. When these went out a covering letter asked for the original to be returned to the Corporate Internal Communications Department 'in the interests of recycling paper'. The new guidelines, the letter said, contained a 'ten-point self-assessment section for you to see if you are ready to handle producer choice.'

Producer-choice literature was supplemented by an avalanche of information including new health and safety manuals, copies of the fifteen taskforce reports, various editions and summaries of *Extending Choice* as well as the leaflets, brochures, videos and vast output from the Equal Opportunities Unit which seemed to exist mainly to produce bumf saying it existed and was producing bumf. There were constant 'update' leaflets, bulletins and loose-leaf supplements to be added to ring-bind folders.

One six-page glossy brochure called 'BBC News and Current Affairs' was sent to all 2,000 people employed by the directorate informing them, amongst other things, of the times when bulletins were broadcast. One producer told the *Daily Telegraph*: 'If I ever forget what time my own programme is transmitted this will be very useful. Other than that it is a complete waste of time and money.'

Most of this literature was written in the same excruciating management-speak as *Extending Choice*, providing light relief as people competed to find the most ludicrous examples. The multiple euphemisms for sacking people provided a rich seam. Producer choice involved getting rid of another 2,000 people on top of the 5,000 Checkland had already targeted, and perhaps many more than that.

Michael Grade had mentioned 'delayering', 'downsizing' and 'out-sourcing' in his Edinburgh speech. These phrases were supplementd by 'liberating resources', which was how sacking people had been described in *Extending Choice*. The phrase was used internally to describe the sacking of that part of BBC middle management which previously booked people into studios and organised camera crews. They were now dispensed with as operators of 'the Soviet-style command economy,' that was being swept away by the free market of producer choice.

Examples of Birtspeak were cut out of *Ariel* and posted anonymously on noticeboards as a silent protest against the new linguistic barbarism. The all-time humdinger Birtspeak phrase was reckoned to be:

> *We need to establish a less prescriptive corporate framework which offers business units greater flexibility within the parameters of common core corporate guidelines.*

But it was soon surpassed in a report by Margaret Salmon, the Director of Personnel. She described how the 'Overheads Review Taskforce' had decided to sack another 1,200 people by . . .

> *focusing on activities rather than departments and*
> *developing a cost-benefit matrix as a tool to help*
> *prioritise the areas in which we would work hardest to*
> *develop savings ideas.*

Having abolished its central supply operation the BBC would have to duplicate it in all 160 units, with a fairly substantial business organisation in every department. Soon producers found that in order to make a studio-based programme at Television Centre they had to negotiate with 11 separate business units and sign contracts with each of them, sometimes involving lawyers.

There was no evidence that really expensive resources like studios were being used more efficiently under the new system. Now that producers had the choice they used it to make life as easy for themselves as possible and were not in a position to plan the overall use of the studios, even if they wanted to.

Soon it was found that the studios had no bookings for the summer months and would lie empty at huge cost. This was because producers liked to do their location filming during the maximum hours of daylight. Before producer choice, studio managers could bully lower-status programme departments like religion and education to use the capacity in summer. Now they were able to compete with the rest, creating huge and equally expensive excess demand in the winter.

Producers soon found BBC production facilities more expensive than the commercial market they were now allowed to use. The pressure mounted to buy in services, threatening the closure of the BBC's own craft base as many had feared.

When producer choice started accountants and marketing managers had been employed to replace the production planners. But within a few months the Corporation started employing people with strange job titles who were, in effect, production planners. The number of administrators began to double in some production areas. What had started out as a cost-cutting exercise was starting to become very expensive.

Birt announced no production facility would close as a result of producer choice. This was good news. But if he was not prepared to allow production units to close if they could not compete in the market, people wondered why he had started producer choice in the first place. A whole new layer of bureaucracy began to steadily grow with the job of making sure that producers not only made a choice, but that they made the right choice.

Ian Hargreaves, the former Birt lieutenant who had returned to the *Financial Times*, observed that it was very difficult to simulate free-market conditions without full-blown privatisation. Like others he believed the market was a jungle.

But producer choice was more like a zoo.

# 18

## *Soft Soap, Flywheels and the Poisoned Chalice*

In January 1993 John Birt assumed the mantle of Lord Reith and officially became the twelfth Director General of the British Broadcasting Corporation. He set out his thinking in a 35-page 'mission statement' called *Turning Promises Into Realities*, unveiled at a press conference. It posed the key question: 'Are we ever prey to clichéd thought, received wisdom or inward-looking perspectives?' Birt unveiled a master plan to merge television and radio journalism into a single 'bi-media' service under central control.

When Hussey and Birt had arrived some six years earlier they had found a profoundly federal organisation, where department heads had made most of the decisions and competed for money and influence. It had always been thought that this was the only way to run such a large organisation without applying the dead hand of uniformity.

Hussey and Birt had changed all this, vastly increasing their own executive power and running the Corporation much more like an ordinary company, led by a single management team. Birt wrote off the old approach, describing it as 'baronialism' which was now a 'dirty word.' At the New

Age BBC 'fudge it and fix it, hostile leaking and secretive and manipulative behaviour become techniques and tactics of the past,' he said.

Apart from this, the main news was a shake-up of personnel at the top of the organisation. Liz Forgan, the woman who was so withering about Checkland's lack of stature, was brought in from Channel Four to take a seat on the Board of Management. Forgan was a popular appointment and, in some ways, a surprising one. Her television career had started late when in 1981, at the age of 36, she moved from editing the *Guardian's* women's page, a bastion of 'feminism with a sense of humour', to become the commissioning editor of Channel Four in charge of factual programmes.

The fact that Birt was now turning to Channel Four for top people was seen as highly significant by some. Birt had applied to become the channel's first Chief Executive back in 1980 when he was still at LWT. He had put an immense amount of work into his application. In many ways Channel Four was Birt's natural home. It had designer headquarters in trendy Soho and its approach to broadcasting was based on the post-1968 thinking Birt admired so much.

Channel Four was essentially the sum of its parts, officially required to cater for a series of minorities with special interest programmes, rather than aiming to provide an evening's entertainment the majority of the population might be interested in. There were specific programmes for women, gays, ethnic minorities and trade unionists which, it was realised, might not have much appeal for anyone else.

This seemed to be the perfect environment for Birt, with his theories about 'audience segmentation' and specialist programming. Birt was known to be a man who was inflexible in his thinking and Birt-watchers often worried that he was trying to apply a version of his Channel Four plan at the BBC, especially after *Extending Choice* had placed so much emphasis on programmes for minority audiences. The greatest fear was that he might be working towards turning the BBC into a publisher-broadcaster, buying in all or most of its programmes, except news and some current affairs, from independents.

The Channel Four board had rejected Birt's masterplan and given the chief executive's job to Jeremy Isaacs instead. Isaacs appointed Forgan as head of factual programmes, a plum job, providing her with an £80 million budget and a blank sheet of paper.

Forgan had her difficulties at first, especially when the channel's first current affairs shows like the *Friday Alternative* were hammered for leftist bias. But she cleverly counter-attacked against the accusations of bias and permissiveness with several shows that were explicitly right-wing, including an anti-homosexual tirade that castigated the local government union NALGO as NALGAY. This was followed by triumphs like the invention of *Right to Reply* with its video box where the great unwashed could wander in off the street and, at the channel's discretion, have their views broadcast.

After deriding her at first, Birt had come to admire Forgan, and the feeling was mutual. In 1987 when Birt was being criticised for 'destroying' Lime Grove, she had organised a 'friends of John Birt' dinner at the White Tower restaurant in Percy Street to cheer him up. After that she had worked alongside Birt providing a sterling defence of TV current affairs against Woodrow Wyatt's unsuccessful campaign to strengthen the impartiality clauses in the 1990 Broadcasting Act. Wyatt had described her as 'a fearsome lady' who was 'unfit to be in charge of any programmes anywhere which have any bearing on matters of political or industrial controversy.'

But her views on the role and management of the BBC were oddly at variance with what Birt and, especially, Hussey wanted. In the run-up to Michael Grade's denunciation of Birt's 'pseudo-Leninist' management style in the summer of 1992, she commandeered a page in *The Times* to warn: 'A poisoned chalice is being held out to the BBC. It contains a witches' brew of free-market jargon, political threat, seductive adspeak and plain poison. One gulp could be fatal,' adding bluntly: 'The BBC is not a business.'

This sort of talk was certain to make her popular with BBC programme-makers. She also had a likeable if some-times overbearing personality. She was described as being like a 'jolly hockey sticks' school games mistress who, while being deadly serious about the programmes she com-missioned, tended to giggle a lot in meetings. Arriving at Broadcasting House, she soon got down to work in typical style, sending a cheery memo to all radio staff: 'I've been listening like crazy for the past few weeks and I am simply knocked out by the treasure house of interest, revelation and pleasure you are putting out,' she gushed, adding: 'please treat my office like Waterloo station. I'll try to see the refreshment facilities are better, but stop in on your way to places and talk to me about what you think.' After all the talk about 'vectoring critical productivity performance paths' unleashed by producer choice, this more chatty approach made a nice change.

Forgan had been tipped as Birt's Deputy Director General ever since Checkland announced he was going. Instead she was given the odd position of Managing Director of Radio. The deputy's job went to Bob Phillis, chief executive of ITN and one of the most respected financial brains in television. This too was thought to be a brilliant move.

The Director General had somehow learned to talk like a hot-shot businessman, and there was a great hunt for the textbook he had got it all from so that people could stay one chapter ahead. But Phillis was a real businessman who could be safely assumed to know what he was talking about. He was the ideal man to take on a Checkland-type role, appro-priately as Number Two to the Director General. There was optimism that he would sort out some of the more baroque aspects of producer choice and attend to the Corporation's mounting financial problems.

Birt explained that under the 'Promises into Reality' strat-egy Phillis would lead a Performance Review to monitor 'implementation' in such areas as equal opportunities and productivity. Forgan would be in charge of a Programme Review alongside Alan Yentob to ensure that all the BBC's output was 'distinctive and original'. These two committees, Birt said, were to act as the 'flywheel that drives the BBC and keeps us all alert and self-questioning about everything we do'. The self-questioning flywheel was to be supplemented by several new cogs in the BBC machine, including a new Board of Management Programme Committee; the Board of Management Commercial and Business Committee and the Board of Management Technical Committee.

When the jargon was stripped away, Forgan's Programme Review boiled down to video-taping everything the BBC broadcast, watching it round the clock, noting what ought to be kept and what should be junked. Attention immediately turned to *Eldorado*, the early evening soap that had replaced *Wogan* six months earlier.

*Eldorado* was the BBC's answer to the aggressively popular schedule ITV was preparing following the introduction of a more loosely regulated system in January 1993. But even before this ITV was making the running with a ratings attack led by David 'Del Boy' Jason, lured from the BBC's *Only Fools and Horses* to star in *The Darling Buds of May*, a ratings hit that peaked with 18.5 million viewers. Other successes included *Inspector Morse*, the *Ruth Rendell Mysteries* and *London's Burning*. This was the sort of well-crafted, middle-brow material that had previously been the BBC's speciality. Greg Dyke, the unofficial head of ITV, claimed his side was winning by 'out-BBC-ing the BBC'.

BBC1 controller Jonathan Powell set himself the target of pushing the ratings back up from 35 to 37 per cent. At the time this seemed to be a reasonable ambition. On Sunday, Tuesday and Thursday, when the BBC had *EastEnders*, there was not much of a problem: the share was a steady 40 per cent. But the overall figure was being dragged down by Monday, Wednesday and Friday, when ITV was way out ahead.

Powell explained all this to a meeting of the Board of Governors, and got straight to the main point. *Wogan* had to go. The show had formed a vital part of Michael Grade's 1985 ratings triumph. But now it looked tired, and ITV was slaughtering BBC1 when it came on. The problem was that *Wogan* cost only £20,000 an edition to produce, compared with up to £80,000 for *EastEnders* and similar long-running drama. A new drama would be even more expensive to begin with, carrying heavy set-up costs like building a set.

The Governors' eyes started to glaze over. When Birt told them that he needed extra money for news and current affairs, they could understand that. It meant more foreign reporters or longer bulletins and extra programmes. It was much harder to convince them extra money was needed for more lightweight material. When it came to light entertainment Powell feared they were thinking: 'Why do we need this stuff in the first place?' Some of them had never got used to *EastEnders* and he knew most of them didn't watch it, like it, or even understand it.

The Board included a lady novelist, a former ambassador, a distinguished Oxford historian and a classical orchestra conductor. This made them a difficult bunch to handle. Powell thought the Governors were in general trying to be helpful. But they sometimes got sidetracked by peculiar bees in their bonnets.

Famously, during a discussion about the need for more popular drama on BBC1, one of the Governors had reputedly asked: 'Why don't you consider televising some amateur dramatic performances?' This, it was suggested, would solve his budget problems and would be in keeping with the BBC's mission to foster worthwhile cultural activities. Powell had to be careful when things like this cropped up. If he was honest and said: 'No. Don't be silly. That's ridiculous' and engaged them in debate he could well end up with an instruction to do it.

Powell persisted. He gave the Governors a carefully drafted report that showed that, excluding the soaps, the BBC had only 89 hours of drama, compared with 220 hours on ITV. This seemed to wake them up. Since the arrival of Birt, the Governors had become addicted to statistical information of all sorts, and did not seem to be able to function without rows of numbers in front of their eyes. Powell got what he wanted. He was given an extra £40 million over two years for drama. *Wogan* could be replaced by at least one new series to fill the weak spot at eight on Monday and Wednesday after *Coronation Street* had finished on ITV.

Powell decided the best bet was to take the successful hospital drama *Casualty* and turn it into a 'quality soap'. It would run twice a week at 8 pm after *Coronation Street*. *EastEnders* would stay, supported by an entirely new soap to replace *Wogan*.

Powell looked at ideas for the new soap from dozens of independent producers, ending up with a shortlist of six. The winner was Tony Holland, a former BBC drama producer who had previously had great success with *Angels*. Holland teamed up with Julia Smith, the producer of *EastEnders*. The final part of the production package was put together by bringing in Verity Lambert, creator of *Minder*, and her independent production company Cinema Verity.

Smith had been impressed by the success of Ozzie soaps like *Neighbours* which she believed were popular partly because they were filmed in sunny locations. The conclusion was obvious enough: produce a soap with similar characters and plot lines to *EastEnders*, but base it on a Spanish beach.

A lot of people thought this radical new departure was high risk, but Julia Smith dismissed their misgivings with breezy references to the 1992 Single European Market and the dawn of European unity. Instead of the sometimes violent and unpleasant portrayal of inner-city life successfully served up by *EastEnders*, the new show, Smith said, would feature John Major's version of a classless society 'at peace with itself'.

The working title was *Little England* and Smith later claimed the idea had come to her when she was on holiday in

Portugal, and had not met a single native. Everything from the supermarket to the bars was run by English expatriates. The series was commissioned in June 1991 as *Eldorado* and work began at once constructing a permanent set on the Spanish coast near Malaga. Cinema Verity's co-producer was JDT Productions, headed by John Todesco, which built and equipped the set. Much hilarity was caused by the title of the company: 'JDT' translated phonetically into Spanish as 'Fuck You'. The on-site receptionist spent her day answering the phone with a cheerful: 'Hello. Fuck You. How can I help?'

The location had a huge bonus for Todesco. For years people in the film and television business had talked about developing a 'EuroHollywood' production complex in Spain, for the same reasons the US movie industry had moved from New York to Los Angeles at the start of the century. Labour costs were much lower, there were no existing union agreements and open-air filming could go on all the year round. The *Eldorado* set would be the first step and, according to plan, would one day double up as a 'production village' for location shooting on American and European films.

As a result the whole operation was to have a pan-European feel, and the original series idea was expanded from a group of English ex-pats to a more multi-national cast of Germans, Spaniards and Swedes. It was thought this might help the BBC recoup some of its investment by selling the series throughout Europe. It would also put the Euro-Hollywood idea on the map. The snag was that the chosen site was in the middle of nowhere. The nearest airport was in Malaga, a hair-raising one hour drive round mountain hair-pin bends. Soon the building project was well over cost and by the time filming started there was very little money left in the budget.

Back at Television Centre Powell was steering the project through the choppy waters of the BBC's internal politics. He had persuaded Wogan to stay on the screen until July 1992, when *Eldorado* was due to start, which was difficult after

Wogan knew he was going to be replaced. The two men came to an arrangement and Powell felt sufficiently secure to fix a press conference to announce the changes. But before this could happen Powell needed to clear the changes at a meeting of Governors, which he regarded as an exercise in rubber stamping.

From Powell's point of view the meeting was not a success. Birt, looking like thunder, wanted to know why he had not been consulted. Together with *Casualty* and *EastEnders*, the arrival of *Eldorado* meant the BBC would be showing three soap operas in peak time. To Powell's horror, Birt wanted the decision to be reversed. Powell and Birt met in private to talk through the problem.

Powell at once realised Birt's ego had been damaged. It looked as if he was going to make the supposed overdoing of soaps a big issue of principle and that it was going to be hard to persuade him to back *Eldorado*. Powell ran through his plans and the ratings logic they were based on and complained that arrangements had already been made. But Birt showed little sympathy, saying Powell had created difficulties by exceeding his authority and not checking with him in the first place.

The two men reached a compromise. Birt said Powell could commission one extra soap, but not two. This left the BBC1 controller with a choice between the plan to run *Casualty* twice a week or proceeding with *Eldorado*. The option of doing both was closed. Powell thought it over. Verity Lambert, whose production company had been commissioned to make *Eldorado*, was an important figure in the world of television drama and he did not want to fall out with her, even if it was legally possible to back out of the deal, which he doubted.

*Eldorado* would go ahead, and *Casualty* would remain as a weekly show. Even after this Powell sensed that Birt was still fuming and that their working relationship, which had never been very happy, was coming to an end. The whole process of replacing *Wogan*, which should have been a simple and obvious scheduling decision, had given him endless grief. Life was getting to be impossible and he decided to leave.

*Eldorado* thus went into production in less than favourable circumstances. The project was already weighed down by its experimental nature. Its £10 million budget was by far the largest independent television project undertaken so far by the BBC, but left no money for getting it wrong. There was no experience of handling independent work on this scale. The scenario for the show had departed from the tried and trusted formula of 'kitchen sink drama' successfully applied since *Z-Cars* and still working with *EastEnders* and *Coronation Street*. Instead it was setting off into the uncharted waters of pan-European appeal.

The new approach was to be tested in the middle of the worst recession since the war and brought to life by what turned out to be a partly amateur cast working in what was, so far, non-existent set miles from the nearest airport. Powell thought the whole thing was a hell of a gamble, and would have needed tight management at the best of times. Instead the BBC would be kept at arm's length because of the geography and the fact that it was an independent production.

*Eldorado* was a disaster waiting to happen and things began to come unstuck almost at once. The cost of building an entire ersatz Spanish village set was soon soaking up most of the budget. The exotic location far from London meant materials had to be bought expensively or brought long distances, and the cost of flying people to and from Britain began to mount up. Things started to be done on the cheap.

Money allocated for transporting and accommodating script-writers on set was raided for other purposes. This was a problem because a lot of the action was to feature people wandering from building to building. Some of the writers had never seen the place and ended up working from the architect's plan (which kept changing) and, eventually, snapshots.

A lot of the cast was hired locally. This was part of the original plan. Julia Smith's success with Anita Dobson, the

Angie character in *EastEnders*, had convinced her anyone with the right attitude could act. Dobson was a bit-part actress who had been cast for *EastEnders* the day before the first episode was filmed. The *Eldorado* cast had a few professionals at its core, but one was a former model, and another was an optician. Dieter, the beach bum character, was recruited by giving out leaflets on the beach asking for good-looking blue-eyed German blonds.

Holland and Smith had endless rows over recruiting policy, which tended to lower the already sinking confidence of the younger, less experienced actors who soon began to wilt under the pressure of the 16-hour shifts needed to get the production ready in time. There were fewer camera crews than would have been ideal, and production schedules were chaotic. Actors would sometimes turn up to find the crew was not available. At least once an actress kicked the production manager's door down in frustration.

Other vital members of a normal production team were likewise thin on the ground. The continuity assistants, the people who make sure the cast are wearing the same thing in scenes that might be filmed days apart, were inexperienced and so the actors would appear to miraculously gain and lose sunglasses as they moved from building to building. Things that would happen as a matter of course in a properly staffed studio in London were left to the actors.

Leslee Udwin, who played the owner of the Eldorado Wine Bar, once served a round of drinks which had to be spat out because the bottles were full of slimy green mould. One of the worst problems was the set itself. Despite extra money that the BBC had supplied to keep the production on schedule, proper sound-recording preparation had proved too expensive and the sound quality was dreadful. The improvised answer was to film as much of the dialogue in the open air, which had its own sound-recording problems, involving the inexperienced actors in a lot of aimless wandering about on camera.

The first episode was rushed on screen during the first

week of July and was panned as El BORE-ADO by the critics. The idea was to surprise ITV by launching *Eldorado* in high summer when a lot of the potential audience were on holiday or enjoying the long summer evenings. When viewers began to switch on again in the autumn, the initial glitches would have been ironed out. That, at any rate, was the plan. But after an initial flutter of viewer interest, ratings slumped as low as 1.6 million. This was worse than *Panorama*. The plan to sell the programme abroad had not come off, though it was a surprise hit in Sweden and, more appropriately, Mauritius, the home of the dodo.

There was soon talk of big changes in the cast, with a rumour that most of them would be killed off in a coach crash during a day trip to Gibraltar. This was an old trick in the science of soapology. When *Coronation Street's* ratings had drooped soon after its launch, the less televisual members of the cast were taken on a charabanc trip to the Lake District and promptly fell off a cliff to meet with a horrible death. Other firmly touted disaster scenarios involved a cholera epidemic and even a thermonuclear attack. But the original cast soldiered on.

A month after the launch Smith disappeared on a six-month holiday, including a couple of weeks spent in New York watching Wagner's *Ring* cycle in its entirety to cheer herself up. Verity Lambert and Powell were flown in to supervise the show on site. They were joined by a psychologist hired to deal with the 'emotional exhaustion' of the cast, restore their confidence and untangle the rows and resentments that had grown up.

There were signs of life after this, with yet more money spent to try and improve the show. But the enthusiastic confidence needed to get any new creative venture off the ground was destroyed by continuous leaks that it would be taken off. Powell was annoyed by the way Birt was prepared to write off the Corporation's £10 million investment without trying to rescue it first.

But Powell left the BBC in December 1992, a few weeks

before Birt officially took over as Director General. His place was taken by Alan Yentob, who moved over from his position as controller of BBC 2. At the same time Yentob was replaced by Michael Jackson, a former media studies student from Macclesfield, who took charge of BBC 2 with a Birtist mission to make it more 'innovative and experimental'.

*Eldorado* limped on through the winter until Yentob finally announced that it would be taken off in July 1993. The demise of *Eldorado* should have been a triumphant moment for the new Director General. The debacle could be blamed on Checkland and Powell. The newspapers could cast Birt in the role of the defender of quality and distinctiveness, a new brush sweeping the rubbish out of the schedules.

Unfortunately for him, the *Eldorado* announcement would do little to offset the more unwelcome personal publicity he was about to get.

# 19

## *Surprise! Surprise!*

At eight o'clock on the morning of Saturday, February 27 1993 there was a knock on the door of the Birt family residence in Wandsworth, South London. The master of the house answered the door, dressed in his customary weekend tracksuit. 'Hello, Mr Birt,' said the bespectacled and prematurely balding figure on the doorstep, 'I'm Chris Blackhurst from the *Independent on Sunday*. I've been trying to get hold of you and, er, I'm on my way to the office and wondered if I could take up five minutes of your time.'

Blackhurst looked more like an innocent boffin than the sort of seedy foot-in-the-door merchant who would bother to stake out the Director General of the BBC. But his innocuous appearance belied his reputation as a sharp business reporter with an instinct for the jugular. He was well known for his tussles with media moguls like *Telegraph* owner Conrad Black and James Gatward, deposed head of TVS. He wanted to talk about John Birt Productions Ltd, the Director General's private company.

Birt was polite but firm. 'I don't talk to journalists at my house,' he said, and began to close the door. Blackhurst leaned forward. The process of 'doorstepping', as it is called in the trade, is an exciting moment for any hack, and one that needs just the right mixture of controlled aggression and quick wits. 'But, Mr Birt,' Blackhurst pleaded, 'you *are* a journalist. You're the Director General of the BBC.'

Birt did not rise to the bait: 'I have told you that I don't talk to journalists at my house,' he repeated with an enigmatic smile. 'I am not going to slam this door,' Birt added in his methodical way, 'I am going to close it.' And so he did. The reporter shuffled off to his office and called Marmaduke Hussey's flat in Chelsea. Lady Susan answered and said Dukey was in the Far East and she didn't have his hotel phone number.

Blackhurst replaced the receiver. It was not surprising that the BBC's hierarchy was proving difficult to pin down. He had been calling the Corporation's press office for days, asking for confirmation of a story he had been sitting on all week: the Director General of the BBC was not on the staff of the Corporation. He was paid as a freelance through John Birt Productions as a way of keeping his distance and avoiding tax.

The information had come from a good source and had been easily checked at Companies House, directly across the road from the *Independent's* offices on the fringes of the City. All he needed now was a decent quote from Birt or Hussey.

With his deadline approaching, Blackhurst phoned Birt at home. Jane, the Director General's American wife, told him John was unavailable. She suggested he ring the BBC press office again. He did so. There was a breakthrough. The press office told him a statement was being prepared, and would he please stop calling the Director General at home.

A few minutes later the fax machine near Blackhurst's desk began churning out the confirmation he needed. The statement said freelance arrangements were commonplace in the television world and John Birt had worked as a freelance for more than 20 years. 'The same contractual arrangements that operated when he was director of programmes at LWT

applied when he joined the BBC as Deputy Director General,'
it said. The story was splashed under the headline: BBC
HELPS ITS CHIEF TO AVOID TAX. It caused immediate
outrage.

Blackhurst was jubilant. He had hit a raw nerve. Many of
the BBC employees who read his story had recently been
forced to accept short-term contracts while being taxed as
full-time employees. But the Director General, the architect
of changes aimed at abolishing still more staff jobs, was
evidently allowed to have it both ways.

Birt had job security, the pay and privileges of being the
Director General and now, it turned out, tax advantages as
well. It was not as though he was 'just helping out' as a
casual employee during a busy period. The story showed he
did not see himself as part of the BBC; and was ammunition
for the growing band who feared he had arrived to hit the
place hard and then move on from the wreckage.

When Birt joined the BBC in 1987 as a freelance, there
were arched eyebrows in the personnel and finance departments, but Birt said there were precedents. Michael Grade
got away with it, and he wanted the same treatment. Checkland agreed and nobody seemed too bothered until Birt was
promoted to Director General. Checkland then tried to persuade Birt to join the staff. He refused.

After all, the former LWT man was an iconoclast, a radical,
a 'man from another world'. He was not going to become
institutionalised like the Corporation's salaried ranks. That
was the BBC's whole problem. It used 'mid-century' employment techniques. He was a child of the freewheeling sixties,
and not a dull accountant in a Marks and Spencer suit who
went home to suburbia every night to a gin and tonic and a
snooze on the sofa in front of *Panorama*.

In less than 48 hours Blackhurst's story accomplished what
Checkland, Hussey and Barnett had failed to achieve in 18
months. John Birt said he would join the BBC staff. Otherwise there was silence while the BBC worked out how much
damage had been done.

The hunt for the whistle-blower began at once. Pamela Taylor, who had replaced Howell James as director of Corporate Affairs, began by innocently asking Birt if he had any enemies at the BBC. Birt could not suppress a wry grin. But only a handful of people knew about his tax arrangements. Hussey and Barnett had negotiated the deal, and Checkland had agreed it. Some in the finance and personnel departments knew about it, but no more than half a dozen people.

The *Sunday Times* fingered Ian Phillips, the finance director who had not seen eye to eye with Birt and, coincidentally, had left the organisation the day before Blackhurst turned up on the Director General's doorstep. The *Sunday Times* got it wrong. The real source was a person still active in BBC journalism. To protect his contact, Blackhurst denied there had been a tip-off. He said the information came from a random browse through the files at Companies House. It was not unusual for financial journalists to trawl through, randomly looking for interesting names.

The mole-hunt quickly ran into the sand. Birt issued a letter on headed paper 'from the Director General' to all BBC staff. 'I very much regret the distress that I know the contractual arrangements that covered my term as Deputy Director General have caused to staff,' the letter began. 'Most of the reporting about my past arrangements has been seriously misleading, as it has failed to appreciate the basis on which my accounts were drawn up.' Birt claimed he was saving only £810 a year.

Hussey and Barnett issued a separate statement the same day: 'When so much of what has been written has been misleading and unjust,' they said, 'we wish to make our position clear, as the Chairman and the Vice Chairman of the Board who brought John Birt to the BBC. John Birt is a man of integrity and conviction, as all who know him recognise.'

It was explained how Birt gave up a valuable share option when he left LWT. Although Hussey did not go into details, the fact was that by leaving LWT Birt had given up about

£400,000 worth of LWT shares which, by now, would have been worth several millions. He had demanded compensation in various ways, including unusual contributions to his own, rather than the BBC's, pension scheme. 'We agreed,' Hussey and Barnett said, adding: 'This was the judgement we made, and we stand by it.' But they had asked Birt to join the staff when he was appointed Director General and they now regretted discussions 'were not concluded more quickly'.

An independent investigation into Birt's accounts, they continued, had proved 'beyond doubt the veracity of his statement and the falsehood of the accusations made against him.' Great stress was placed on the fact that Birt had filed his accounts with the Inland Revenue. This seemed like an odd and obvious point to make. If he had not done so the Director General could have been on his way to jail.

The statement was signed by only Hussey and Barnett. Normally such an important announcement would have gone out in the name of the whole Board of Governors, as collective guardians of the public interest. But, as was soon to become clear, the Board was deeply split over the issue. Apart from the morality of Birt's contract, some were furious they had been kept in the dark and not told the full details about the Director General's terms of employment.

Having given this official version of events, with much muttering in the background about how trivial the affair was compared with the whole future of the BBC, Hussey and Birt hoped it would blow over. This was not to be.

Months earlier the Director General had agreed to be interviewed by Jeremy Isaacs at a conference on the future of the BBC. The talking shop was taking place at the National Film Theatre, on London's South Bank, as part of the feeble 'national debate' supposedly launched by the Green Paper and *Extending Choice*. Birt had been looking forward to this new crowning moment in his ascent to the top. The fact that it would involve Isaacs playing the secondary role of interviewer was especially delicious.

In Birt's mind the interview would settle once and for all

the vital question of who would go down in broadcasting history as the more important figure. He would calmly field Isaacs' questions about the future with the carefully contrived and impressive sounding nostrums of *Extending Choice*. But Isaacs had other ideas. He decided to put Birt through the wringer about the tax affair.

Birt looked edgy as he entered the National Film Theatre, trailed by a BBC television news team. Isaacs at once set about his old rival with relish, wrong-footing Birt by asking if he wanted to repeat his statement of regret about the tax affair. Instead of sounding contrite, Birt attempted to justify the deal. 'I came from another world and that arrangement seemed to me at the time a sensible one. When I say "another world",' he added, realising he had made a gaffe, 'I mean a more commercial world where the arrangement seemed sensible'. The audience could not believe Birt was making such a hash of things.

There was worse to come. Isaacs asked Birt if he would name the unidentified secretary mentioned in the accounts of John Birt Productions. A breakdown of expenses included £15,000 for the secretary, along with amounts for a Volkswagen car, a satellite dish and clothing, believed to include Birt's favoured Armani suits. 'It is not right that I should have to reveal every detail of my personal matters, and I do not intend to do so,' Birt replied, seething at the way Isaacs was attacking him.

Birt left the building in a huff, refusing to stay for the drinks party where the conversation was naturally dominated by his earlier performance. The story circulated about how Birt had rounded on his interrogator the minute they came off stage, accusing him of playing to the crowd, asking loaded questions and ambushing him in front of most of Fleet Street.

BBC Television, after virtually ignoring the story when it surfaced, was at last starting to run extensive coverage. Despite the tight deadline, a full report of Birt's brush with Isaacs was included on the Nine O'Clock News. The pack was in action and the story began to snowball. The *Daily Mail* carried by far the fullest accounts of Birt's inept self-defence of the night before; and the next day the newspaper devoted most of page three to 'a great new *Daily Mail* competition: Can you identify John Birt's tax-deductible secretary?' The paper offered a reward of £500 or an Armani suit to anyone who could name the elusive Miss X.

The prize was claimed at once by Ray Snoddy, the *Financial Times* media correspondent, who faxed a copy of an article he had written naming Birt's wife Jane to the *Mail's* newsdesk. (Snoddy was not in the same style league as Birt and asked for cash. He bought the two most expensive suits he could find in his local Uxbridge branch of Marks and Spencer and got an anorak with the change.)

The news about Birt's wife elevated the tax story to a different league. Paying wives as secretaries was not illegal, but it was very hard to see that it could be justifiable as the Director General had ample secretarial help at Broadcasting House. And as far as anyone could tell, John Birt Productions had not made a single film or television programme since the company started. The question remained: what secretarial help did Jane Birt, an artist by profession, actually provide to justify her pay?

Besides this Birt presented himself as a New Man, very much opposed to sexism, as *Extending Choice* and the proliferating equal opportunities initiatives made clear. After all this, would he really employ his wife as a factotum and paid servant? Once again he seemed to want it both ways.

Birt had claimed early press stories were 'misleading' and had 'failed to appreciate the basis on which my accounts were drawn up.' This was correct; but only because the business of paying his wife had not been reported. Hussey's ringing endorsement of Birt as 'a man of integrity' who had 'established beyond doubt the veracity of his statement', was now looking extremely hollow. His 'repudiation' of the allegation that Birt had been secretive was in tatters.

Events were starting to spin out of Hussey and Birt's

control. Sixty-four Labour MPs put down a parliamentary motion calling for the Director General to resign. The broadcasting unions said Birt must go. The Director General and the Chairman were denounced by the veteran broadcaster Ludovic Kennedy. David Attenborough said 'Lord Reith, Lord Hill, Lord Normanbrook, Charles Curran or Hugh Greene would not have accepted the situation.' At first the only 'outsiders' prepared to speak up for Birt were David Mellor and Roger Gale, the irascible backbench Tory who wanted to privatise Radio One.

Condemnation was spreading as more and more important people were asked if they were for or against Birt. Ray Snoddy, decked out in his new anorak, was working on a tip-off that John Major had told colleagues the Queen was taking a personal interest. The monarch, who had her own tax problems, had allegedly asked Major if Birt's tax status would have been changed if it had not been exposed in the papers: 'Are there not times when honour should take precedence over ability?' she asked.

Birt was already tottering on the edge, and if the *Financial Times* could stand up the rumour, he would definitely have to resign, especially in view of Hussey's connections at the Palace. But the story did not run. Snoddy and his contacts hit a brick wall as the establishment closed ranks. But during the chase, Snoddy had mentioned the potential scoop to Ian Hargreaves, the paper's deputy editor. Hargreaves, who had recently returned to the *Financial Times* after a spell as head of the BBC news and current affairs directorate, asked: 'Are you trying to stage a public execution?' Snoddy said he was only doing his job.

That weekend the Sunday papers were full of calls for Birt's resignation. 'The mood inside the BBC is now mutinous,' said the *Independent on Sunday*. 'Mr Birt's reputation has been badly and probably fatally damaged as Director General. The advice is rarely taken these days in Britain and we offer it sadly, without crocodile tears. Mr Birt and Mr Hussey should resign,' the paper concluded.

By now the affair was turning into a psychological as well as a professional drama for Birt. He was a man who valued order and control over his destiny above all else. The events now engulfing him were way beyond his control. With journalists doorstepping his Wandsworth home and camped outside his Welsh retreat in the Brecon Beacons, Birt ran for cover.

He went into hiding at the West London home of Nick Elliott, a close friend and former LWT colleague. Birt and Elliott went back a long way, to the time when they had shared a flat in Manchester as fledgling programme-makers at Granada. They had the sort of friendship that could withstand the occasional argument, and had once fallen out very briefly, over the very issue of Birt's attitude to the morality of tax avoidance.

The row took place after a boozy LWT executives' night out during the *Prix Italia*, the annual international television awards festival. When the delegation rolled back to their hotel Michael Grade became philosophical and kicked off a starry-eyed discussion about the vital importance of education in the world. Birt joined in and laid into Elliott for sending his kids to private school, while his own went to the local comprehensive.

The exchange became bitter and personal, with Elliott accusing Birt of hypocrisy. By this time Jane Birt and Gillian Elliott were in tears. Grade and Melvyn Bragg attempted to cool things down but the row continued. 'Come off it, John, you even claim your haircuts against tax,' Elliott roared. The next morning the two men were very apologetic for making such fools of themselves the night before. But now the argument was long forgotten and Elliott was happy to do what he could do for his old friend.

The moment Birt went missing lurid stories of his psychological condition began to spread. Rumours ranged from sullen resignation to growing exhaustion, with reports that he had not slept for several days.

Convinced he was finished as Director General of the BBC, and his whole career was in the balance, John Birt had become desperate.

Help was soon at hand.

# 20

## *The Dinner from Hell*

Tim Bell, the BBC's public relations consultant, always had surprisingly strident views about the Corporation. Like Hussey and Birt he had never really warmed to the organisation. He even casually told people its very existence was 'an anomaly' in an age of consumer choice and privatisation.

During the *Real Lives* row Bell had been seen in his office banging his fist on the desk and howling 'fucking BBC terrorists', at the newscaster reading the Six O'Clock News.

Sometimes it was hard to tell when Bell was being serious. But as a consummate professional, paid a reputed £300,000 a year by the BBC, he never let his personal feelings get in the way of his work for a client.

Bell was officially employed to work on the BBC's image. He was the architect of *See For Yourself* and a key player in smoothing relations wtih the public, Whitehall and Downing Street. Now he went in to bat for Birt.

Strictly speaking it did not matter to Bell who the Director General was. He could just as easily find himself publicising the reason for Birt's sacking. But, more than any other Director General since Reith, John Birt was the BBC. Weak jokes about the Birtist Broadcasting Corporation fell flat because, well, that was how a lot of his supporters saw it.

So it was not unnatural for Bell to exceed his BBC brief and go into action on behalf of the beleaguered Director General. There was a lot at stake. Birt had, in his own words, 'only just started' to remodel the BBC for its new role in the multichannel future. The task of demolishing the 'Old BBC' was only half complete, and only John Birt could be relied upon to finish the job.

Chris Blackhurst, the *Independent on Sunday* journalist who broke the tax story in the first place, heard Bell was acting for Birt and called him to find out what was going on. At first Bell denied he was working for the Director General. But when Blackhurst persisted, the PR man revealed he had been very busy in the past 48 hours on Birt's behalf. 'You could say I've been marshalling support,' he said.

Bell set out his argument. Blackhurst was patronisingly praised for breaking a good story. Fair enough. It must have done the struggling *Independent on Sunday*'s circulation a lot of good. And yes, John Birt might have been unwise to have stayed freelance. But so did lots of people in the media these days. The BBC was a media business like any other. What were people getting so excited about? The real story, Bell said, was the way Birt had been 'set up' by the BBC 'Old Guard' who had lost the intellectual debate and were using the tax affair as a way of toppling him. Hard details did not matter to Bell, who was mainly interested in impressions.

Blackhurst interrupted with a practical question. Was there any chance of having a word with John Birt? Bell offered a deal. If the *Independent on Sunday* agreed not to run another editorial calling for Birt's resignation, he would get the interview. Otherwise he would not. And it was no use trying to contact the Governors, Bell said, because they had been put under a three-line whip not to talk to journalists. At this point Bell was interrupted by an urgent call on the other line. It was none other than David Mellor, self-appointed head of the Westminster branch of the John Birt fan club. He told Blackhurst to wait.

Mellor, now relieved of his office after a tabloid monstering over his sex life and alleged acceptance of freebies from PLO sympathisers, had become more enthusiastic about Birt than ever. 'I like and admire John Birt immensely,' Mellor had gushed in the *Guardian* when Birt had officially taken over as Director General six weeks earlier. Praising Birt's 'mission statement' and new 'flywheel' management committee structure, Mellor said: 'Surely it is impossible to deny after his announcement that this is indeed a remarkable man. In a real sense he is the BBC's last great hope.'

Bell completed his business with Mellor and came back on the line to Blackhurst. He explained that the ex-Minister for Fun was 'going tougher' on the Birt story; meaning he was hardening up his support, as were others. Blackhurst was warned that of all the Sunday papers, only the *Independent* and the *Observer* would be taking a line hostile to Birt. prediction proved to be remarkably accurate. The next day the *Sunday Times* led the way with a big feature headlined THE BASHING OF BIRT by Jonathan Miller, the former Sky TV lobbyist. It accused Bell's mysterious 'BBC Old Guard', helped by 'feather-bedded unions', of leaking the original tax story and then stoking up a press campaign against Birt. 'For months, newspapers sympathetic to his foes published increasingly hysterical attacks on Birt,' Miller wrote, quoting an untypically shy backbench politician. 'One Tory MP,' Miller reported, 'compared the daily torrent of stories about Birt to those that preceded last year's demise of the National Heritage Secretary: "Birt's being Mellored".'

Miller later claimed Birt was 'buoyed' by reading his article, and that it helped him get back on his feet and start hitting at the 'reactionaries' who were out to get him. Moral support was also being provided by Lady Elspeth Howe, the wife of the former Chancellor, who promised she would organise public statements of support. Howe was impressed by the way Birt had backed a project called Opportunity 2000 designed to promote equality for women. She thought it was silly that the BBC should lose a pro-feminist Director General because of his tax affairs.

More important was the support of the BBC's own Board of Management. Collectively the Board was reluctant to rock the boat while they were trying to cope with the Green Paper, charter renewal and producer choice. They knew that talk of an 'Old Guard' coup was 'balls', as even one of Birt's strongest supporters put it; a fiction dreamed up by Bell to bamboozle the politicians and punters. Birt had no immediate rivals left. He had outlasted them all. The only vaguely plausible opponent was John Tusa, the former World Service head mentioned to Blackhurst by Bell.

Some had their doubts about Birt, but did not want to see him forced out over what they saw as a sideshow. After the unhappy departures of Milne and Checkland, the Corporation could not afford to lose another Director General and all the internal turmoil that would entail. They agreed that Birt had been unwise to stay freelance, especially after becoming Director General. But there was some truth in what he had said about coming from LWT, the cutting edge of the 'contract culture'.

LWT had paid senior executives through private companies since the 1970s. It was unremarkable that Birt had been paid in this way when he was at LWT. When Birt joined the BBC in 1987 it never occurred to him that he should suddenly join the salaried PAYE ranks. His great friend Michael Grade had been paid via his own private company when he arrived at the BBC and Birt wanted the same treatment. Unlike Birt, Grade said he had joined the staff when he became a member of the BBC Board of Management.

(Grade's arrangements had caused murmuring in the BBC personnel department, but these were dismissed by Bill Cotton. 'That's the way the industry is going, what's wrong with it?' he shrugged. When the head of television's personnel department Glynne Price suggested it showed less than total commitment to the organisation, Cotton was withering. 'Do you mean to say you can't expect loyalty from people like Michael Grade?' Days later Grade disappeared without warning to join Channel Four.)

The Board of Management declared their 'unanimous support' for Birt in a letter to *The Times*. This was an important moment in the affair. With the Governors still wobbly, the support of the Board of Management was to prove crucial.

For the general public there was more interest in another letter sent to *The Times* on the same day and signed by more familiar names including John Simpson, the veteran foreign affairs editor. Other signatories, like Peter Sissons, Polly Toynbee, Robin Oakley and Peter Jay, had been hired to play key roles in Birt's merged news and current affairs directorate. The letter declared:

> Old axes are grinding, old scores are being settled in the attacks on the Director General. John Birt has done nothing unlawful. He has hidden nothing from the Inland Revenue. John Birt's real offence is to be the architect of the plan which is effecting radical change at the BBC. We call on the Governors to keep their heads in the face of such wild press coverage and to offer their full support for John Birt's continuing Director Generalship.

Several other reporters, some of them household names, had been asked to sign the letter, but refused on the grounds that their reporting of the affair could not be seen as impartial if they did so. And John Birt was a stickler for impartiality.

With Bell's help, and some discreet lobbying from Howell James, Birt was starting to win the public relations battle, neatly deflecting the pressure in the direction of Hussey. The Chairman was something of a devotee of the political philosopher Niccolò Machiavelli, and was fond of quoting his advice that innovators, like himself, should expect 'fierce enemies and only lukewarm friends'. It was a pity he had not paid as much attention to Machiavelli's warning about freelance employees: 'in battle, arms belonging to mercenaries will fall from your back, and auxiliaries will weigh you down.'

Privately most of the Board of Management, and some of the Governors, were blaming Hussey for the crisis and saying he should go. The real villains of the piece were Hussey and Barnett, for the way they handled the transition from Checkland to Birt. The Governors had then handed the tax story to the press on a plate, keeping it going by refusing to comment or be decisive.

The hacks, including the BBC's own media correspondents hired as part of Birt's drive to recruit more specialists, were having a field day. Hussey's wife, Lady Susan, was observed in London society complaining about disloyalty from the BBC managers.

Hussey was handling the crisis badly, not realising the threat it posed to Birt and himself. He had not even bothered to call a Board meeting during the first ten days of the row, and had remained in Hong Kong, a guest of the British Governor, Chris Patten. Over the weekend some of the Governors began to consider moving against him.

Keith Oates, managing director of Marks and Spencer, and the Governor who sat on the BBC's salaries sub-committee, had not apparently been told about Birt's arrangements. He was ready to give Hussey a hard time. He had the support of Lord Nicholas Gordon Lennox, Bill Jordan and the national Governors for Scotland and Northern Ireland, Sir Graham Hills and Sir Kenneth Bloomfield.

Hussey arrived back in London furious that the Board of Management had failed to support him and that the revolt appeared to be spreading to his power base, the Board of Governors. He announced an emergency Board meeting for Tuesday night to call their bluff. Oates's revolt collapsed, crushed by the ranks of solid Hussey devotees like P. D. James. The Governors issued a statement supporting Birt but promised a more detailed assessment of the situation later in the week after a scheduled Board meeting.

The crisis was thus allowed to rumble on, helped by an

unhappy accident of timing. At the precise moment the Governors were concluding their deliberations at Television Centre, two miles away at the Royal Lancaster Hotel, Michael Checkland was addressing the Royal Television Society at a dinner organised months before to mark his retirement.

The former Director General introduced himself as 'Checkland, M. BBC staff number 113895'. This brought the house down. He then revealed how he had urged Birt to join the staff on becoming Director General. 'John Birt did not do so and this was a gross error of judgement which the press corrected in twenty-four hours,' Checkland said, before turning his fire on Hussey and Barnett. 'It was more wrong,' he said, 'that the Chairman and the Vice Chairman representing the wider public interest did not insist on that change in contractual arrangements.' He added a bitter observation on the way the long 'lame duck and Trappist monk' period had been handled: 'After all, they did have eighteen months to get it right.'

The attack was broadened out to the way Birt and Hussey had misunderstood what the BBC was all about. 'The BBC demands total personal commitment. Management involves moral leadership and the Director General must give it.' He said Birt should be put on twelve months' probation. Hussey should go by the autumn and Birt's performance could then be reviewed by a new Chairman.

Barnett, the man who had heaped so much humiliation on Checkland with his constant criticism of the way the BBC was run, was attacked for turning the Vice Chairmanship into a full-time executive job. 'I hope that in appointing a Vice Chairman we would revert to previous practice and make clear that this is very much a part-time job with no permanent office and support facilities at Broadcasting House,' he said.

After the Checkland speech the atmosphere of crisis was kept up when the BBC's general advisory council met the next day. Hussey was present. This normally mild-mannered group of worthies included Jane Asher, the actress and author of a best-selling book, *Party Cakes*, various MPs and Rodney Bickerstaffe, the union leader.

They asked Hussey and his colleagues to leave the room while they discussed the tax affair, forcing Hussey to sit in an anteroom with the catering staff. The Chairman was livid at being treated like one of the servants. He was then called back into the room and asked for his resignation. Acting more than ever like the hereditary owner of the Corporation, Hussey refused. He was not going to have some jumped-up advisory board telling him what to do.

After the Fuzzy Monsters episode Hussey had given an interview while opening new offices for the Wireless for Bedridden charity. 'Contrary to certain people's views I am really very lively,' he had said, adding: 'Nobody can sack me. Only the Queen or the Privy Council can remove me before my contract is up.' After this Hussey had gone around grumbling: 'I'm old. I know I'm old. Everyone says I'm a very old man. But so what?' Hussey told the advisory council that the affair was 'a media frenzy' that had to be ignored.

That evening the drama moved back to Broadcasting House, where Hussey was hosting a formal farewell dinner for Checkland. After the former Director General's demand for Hussey's resignation the previous night, the hacks were trailing the event as 'The Dinner from Hell', praying for an all-out slanging match between the two men.

The inevitable tension surrounding the dinner had been given another twist by the absence from the guest list of two of the most famous names in television: Paul Fox and John Tusa. Fox had decided to boycott the occasion because he thought it was hypocritical of Hussey to stage a dinner honouring the man he had treated so shabbily. Tusa had been missing from the list drawn up by Hussey, and was only invited at the last minute when Checkland insisted. He turned down the invitation, pleading a previous engagement.

The dinner got off to an awkward start. People arrived late to avoid as much of the embarrassing pre-prandial drinks session as possible. There were only a handful of people present when Checkland arrived, and he wandered around chatting to everyone except Hussey. As the crowd thickened people started wondering exactly how Checkland would extract his revenge.

The previous evening he had delivered a brilliant put-down by reading out his staff number. What would he do this time? There was a rumour that he would start off by tapping a wineglass to bring them to order; the gesture that had signalled the end of Milne. And what would he say about Birt, now that he had called for the new Director General to undergo a period of probation?

Birt arrived minutes before people were invited to sit down for dinner. He stood at the top of the room, sheepishly sipping his drink, cold-shouldered by everyone. Margaret Salmon, the BBC's Personnel Director, suggested to one of the guests it would be nice if he went up and talked to Birt. 'Nice for who?' came the reply. His agony was ended when dinner began with people seated on separate tables. Checkland, Hussey, and Birt sat at the top table and their wives, led by Lady Susan, seemed to break the ice. Soon they were chatting cordially.

Birt had survived the worst part of the crisis with the aid of Bell's emergency public relations campaign. Now it was time to go on the offensive, using the crisis to his own advantage and mopping up his enemies. 'On the face of it, it was a skirmish over John Birt's tax affairs,' Jonathan Miller wrote in a *Sunday Times* article entitled THE COUP THAT FAILED, 'but the real battle was being waged by the old guard as they attempted to regain their stranglehold on the BBC.'

At last the alleged coup plotters had been named: Alasdair Milne (who had not set foot in the BBC boardroom for five years); Sir Paul Fox (who was an admirer of Birt and who had done everything Birt and Hussey had wanted as Managing Director of Television), John Tusa (who had introduced a far-reaching internal market at the World Service, officially described as more effective than Birt's producer-choice idea);

and poor old Ian McIntyre, a former controller of Radio Three (who had never been on the Board of Management).

Now, at the 'Dinner from Hell', people were waiting to see if Checkland would deliver a knock-out punch. After dessert Hussey gave a two-minute speech praising Checkland as 'the man who saved the BBC' and who had started the Corporation on the path it was now following. John Birt, he said, would only be carrying on his work. Instead of the customary gold watch Checkland was to be presented with a more personal token of the Board's affection: a wooden bench. The joke circulated that it would come in handy. Checkland could sit in his garden ruminating on the fate of his Five-Year Plan and avoid having to watch Birtist television.

There was polite applause and Checkland stood up to give his reply. After the broadside delivered the previous evening, Checkland now towed the party line. The only slight *frisson* came when he said archly he 'hoped' he had left the BBC in safe hands.

The assembled great and good headed for their cars deeply relieved that there had not been a scene. Sir Graham Hills, the Scottish Governor, told the disappointed hacks: 'People were in a generous mood and a forgiving mood, but I think things will still have to be sorted out.' Checkland had been offered the opportunity to deliver a knock-out punch, but had chosen not to use it. Outside Broadcasting House, he told the hacks: 'It was a very nice evening. It was a very English occasion.'

# Postscript

The various traumas engulfing the BBC continued through the summer of 1993. The public ignored the Great Debate about the future of the BBC. Nobody really seriously expected them to take much interest. The real debate happened in every living room, every night, as it always had done. It boiled down to this:

> Question: 'What's on the telly tonight?'
> Answer: 'Not much.'

During the summer BBC 1's audience share nose-dived below 30 per cent. Shows like *Bruce Forsyth's Guest Night* and the politically correct *Rides* flopped with audiences well under six million. The repeated *House of Elliot* was down to just over two million.

By July BBC 1's audience share had slipped to 30 per cent. Sometimes overnight figures were as low as 27 per cent, and falling. This was the worst ratings position for eight years, and well below the figure the Corporation had always thought necessary to maintain public support for the licence fee. The last time ratings were this bad, the BBC 1 controller, the hapless Alan Hart, had been sacked and replaced by Michael Grade.

*EastEnders* was the only BBC-produced programme regularly watched by more than 10 million viewers. Ken Russell's critically panned version of *Lady Chatterley* got a 12-million rating; but everyone knew this was because it was basically a 'tit and bum show'. After all the Right On blather in *Extending Choice*, the endless repeats revived the social attitudes of the '60s and '70s and the BBC's channels were awash with the prejudices of yesteryear. Multi-racial humour included Corporal Jones's catchphrase 'Them fuzzy-wuzzies don't like it up 'em' in *Dad's Army*.

By mid-summer there were so many repeats, given the new Birtspeak title of 'classics' and 'revivals', on BBC1 that it became a standing joke. Privately BBC executives admitted that the Corporation could no longer afford to broadcast a real schedule all the year round. A cartoon appeared in the *Guardian* showing a viewer getting a visit from the television detector van squad and producing his licence for 1973.

Money had always been tight in the summer. But the BBC had responded with an invention called *The Great Summer of Sport*, with endless cheap material like golf and snooker. The budget crisis was eased by BBC2 declaring 'It's the sixties!' and showing a welter of Milne-era material, produced by the 'Old BBC' that had been purged by the Hussey-Birt régime. Most people saw through the wheeze. But it provided a welcome revival and burst of positive publicity for David Frost, Birt's old mentor from ITV. Frost was celebrated with a three-part profile, striking many people as gross overkill.

Meanwhile the forward march of Birtism at first seemed unstoppable. More and more money was being diverted into the black hole that Cotton, Wenham and others had feared would be created by the expansion of the news and current affairs directorate. An extraordinary advertisement appeared in the papers aimed at recruiting over a hundred new 'bi-media' journalists to be attached to local radio. This included no fewer than 13 new specialist regional health reporters, and 12 regional education correspondents.

As the Government and Rupert Murdoch might have hoped, things were so bad that there was renewed interest in satellite TV. A new 'multichannel package' was offered to

Sky subscribers. This consisted mainly of yet more repeats, hyped as 'cult' and 'Time Warp TV'. The Choice that was Extended mainly involved the launch of *UK Living*, a televisual version of a mid-market woman's magazine.

*UK Living* boldly promised at least two hours of original programmes every day ('more than on any other woman's channel in the UK!'). This was lashed together with Sky's Jewel in the Crown: live Premier League football, only available if people bought the whole Sky package, complete with a separate subscription, increased by 33 per cent to £95 a year for the new season, which was more than the whole BBC licence fee.

Bill Cotton, now working for Noel Gay Television, thought the BBC's problem was symbolised by the abrupt departure of Jim Moir, the long-serving head of light entertainment. It was, he said, 'a colossal mistake' for the BBC to abandon its role 'as the backbone of the entertainment industry in Britain. America has Hollywood and Britain has the BBC.'

In the crucial area of original TV drama there was nothing in the pipeline to compare with mid-80s' triumphs like *Edge of Darkness* or Dennis Potter's *Singing Detective*. After the savaging Grade had dished out in his MacTaggart lecture in 1992, Potter followed up with another attack that ran along similar lines.

Potter said Birt had plunged the BBC into a 'near fatal crisis,' adding: 'You can not make a pair of croak-voiced Daleks appear benevolent, even if you dress one of them in an Armani suit and call the other Marmaduke.' Potter said 'fear and loathing was swirling jugular high' in the corridors of the BBC. Birt replied by saying his mother would not agree with Potter's 'lyrical' description of his style. Birt then turned to Greg Dyke, the man who had inherited his LWT job and share option, and added a bitter postscript to the tax affair: 'Which would you prefer,' he rhetorically asked Dyke, '£7 million or national vilification?' There was yet more anguish when it emerged that the radio drama chief John

Tydeman was quitting because he could no longer face the more baroque aspects of Birtian management.

But if the Corporation claimed it was not retreating from quality drama and the mass television market, there were confusing signals coming from BBC Radio. The future of Radio One was under scrutiny. Dave Lee Travis, the 48-year-old 'Hairy Monster', announced live on air that he was quitting. In press interviews he said the BBC was 'falling apart'.

Although derided by metropolitan trendies, the fact remained that DLT provided a genuine and much appreciated service for five million people who wanted a bit of 'pop and chatter' in the background. 'I sat back for the last two years and watched a once great institution collapsing,' Travis said.

Alarmingly Travis related a conversation with Liz Forgan, who told him the BBC was no longer interested in the core 25–45 year old Radio One audience. Richard Branson's Virgin, in many ways the radio equivalent of Sky TV, had targeted this market, Forgan said. The BBC could not be seen to use the licence fee to compete with Branson. 'That knocked me off my feet,' Travis told the *Sun*, 'I couldn't believe what I was hearing and she told me not to be cheeky.'

The *Sun*, after plugging Travis's anti-Birt interview all week, took the opposite view in its leader column. Birt had 'brought proper business sense to an organisation that was in danger of dying under a mountain of paperwork,' the paper said. To those in the know this was a classic example of the *Sun*'s 'ferret up the bum' technique of turning criticism on its head. Even Liz Forgan had been heard to complain, in an unguarded moment: 'Christ! All that bloody paper.' The *Sun* rounded off its endorsement of Birt by saying 'In short, he is doing a damned hard job pretty well. He's on our side.'

Travis also complained about producer choice. 'Creative people are told to be accountants and ordered to keep crazy budgets.' This had resulted in confusion and exhaustion.

'Morale has never been lower, talented people are being pushed to the limit and they are hopelessly overworked.'

The BBC might have been able to write off these complaints from DLT as a man who was already past his sell-by date, or as an isolated dissident based in the most downmarket part of the Corporation. But his thoughts were shared by a man who worked at the opposite pole of the organisation: Mark Tully, the legendary India correspondent or 'Tully Sahib' as he is known to hundreds of millions in the subcontinent.

Tully had been prompted to speak out by remarks made by Polly Toynbee and Peter Jay. In their letter to *The Times* during the Armanigate crisis, they had accused Birt's critics of being too cowardly to speak out. For several weeks Tully had been thinking about what he would say. The result was a devastating indictment of Birt and Birtism delivered at the Radio Academy festival in Birmingham.

Tully's theme was essentially a reworking of Grade's Edinburgh criticism that alien forces were jeopardising the BBC's future by creating a repressive, Stalinist régime. Grade had not mentioned Birt by name. Tully was less bashful. The Director General was fingered as the guilty party and accused of starting a personality cult.

'I don't think he understands what the BBC was, or indeed, what it should become,' Tully said. 'So many managers parrot his name that staff feel there is some sort of Big Brother watching them.' Birt had turned the BBC into 'a secret monolith'; which was saying something after Tully's encounters with the Kafkaesque Indian civil service. Creativity was stifled while social engineering and revolutionary speak was imposed from above. Summing up, Tully said Birt had created 'a climate of fear'.

Tully's commentary on the desperate state of affairs at the BBC reverberated throughout the Corporation for days. A portrait of Tully hanging in the entrance of Broadcasting House was removed after an admirer drew a halo above the foreign correspondent's head. *Ariel*, the BBC's staff paper, nicknamed *Pravda* and known by the staff as 'the paper that always washes white', reported the incident rather differently. It said that Tully's picture had been taken down 'after being defaced and scratched'.

The Board of Governors had fallen out with Milne for the way he refused to take criticism seriously. Milne had kept a straight bat, in the best traditions of cricket. But Birt was more inclined to hit people over the head with it. The new Director General described Tully and other critics as 'ostriches' and 'old BBC soldiers sniping with their muskets'.

He insisted 'radical reform' was the only way. There could be no 'kinder, gentler way'. Unfortunately Birt's remarks were followed by publication of the findings of a BBC staff survey revealing that fear, mistrust and loathing of bureaucracy were rife in the organisation. The survey was commissioned at a reported cost of £80,000 and the 26-page questionnaire form sent to 6,000 staff came complete with its own special commemorative pencil.

*The Times*, instrumental since the mid-1980s in setting the agenda for the BBC, weighed in on Birt's side. A leading article blithely asserted that producer choice meant 'much less studio time is wasted now', ignoring the reality of spare capacity created at times of low demand. 'If critics of Birtism have a better map to ensure the BBC's survival, they have yet to reveal it,' the paper opined.

After surviving Armanigate Birt was ready for anything. Like Hussey he was invincible, fireproof. Amazingly he had been rewarded for joining the BBC's staff, and losing his freelance tax benefits, with a whacking pay increase. Birt's pay jumped by £50,000 to almost £200,000, around £35,000 more than Michael Checkland had been paid. At the same time the staff were told they could expect a 1.5 per cent pay rise.

Birt used at least part of the money to fête his wife Jane who had been forced to endure the stress of being the woman at the centre of the tax row. To celebrate her fiftieth birthday Birt organised an all-day 'magical mystery tour' celebration.

It started when selected friends including the *Sunday Tele-graph*'s Peregrine Worsthorne boarded a coach at 8.30 in the morning.

First stop was a South London go-karting arena, where Birt and friends zipped around for a while before setting off for lunch at McDonalds. Next stop was Cilla Black's mansion in Denham. The *Blind Date* star sang 'Happy Birthday' and lavished champagne on the trippers.

Then they were off to Jacob Rothschild's house for what was described as 'a birthday tea of indescribable glory'. From there it was on to Magdalen College, Oxford, for evensong performed by the full choir. This was followed by a drinks party at the President of Magdalen's lodgings. The day was rounded off with a banquet at St Catherine's, Birt's Oxford college. In terms of preplanned entertainment, victims of the Leatherhead 'joke test' six years earlier did not know how lucky they were.

Birt had been brimming with self-confidence at his first public appearance after Armanigate. The occasion was the Royal Television Society's annual Fleming memorial lecture. 'No one should doubt how much I regret exposing the organ-isation I am now privileged to lead to such unwarranted turmoil,' he said. Afterwards, most of the television VIPs present at the lecture headed for a drinks party at the Reform Club in Pall Mall.

Polly Toynbee, Birt's chief public cheerleader during Armanigate, enlivened an otherwise dull event by going around telling people that Birt was 'not venal', and that he did not do his BBC job for the money. But an attempt to soften hearts by stressing Birt's loyalty to Michael Henshaw, his accountant, another child of the sixties, came unstuck. 'All us creative people use him,' Toynbee said, 'Michael sorts it all out, and we just sign.' The idea that the Director General went around signing legally binding documents without reading them did not inspire much confidence.

*See For Yourself*, the BBC's annual television programme in which senior executives were grilled by viewers, had been quietly abandoned. As a result, the BBC's annual report now had to work much harder as a piece of propaganda.

Previous Director Generals had confined themselves to writing a short, signed introduction to the annual report. But Birt had insisted that forty-odd pages were devoted to the 'Director General's Review', embracing all areas of the BBC's activities. The revamped annual report was upgraded to an expensively produced coffee-table-style book with arty black and white photographs of individual licence-fee payers. These included Ian Witham of Enfield, a sad-looking person framed by flocked wallpaper and a well-stocked drinks shelf. His television was displaying a picture of the Cybermen. On top of the set was a pile of books including *Agony at Anzio*, which was where Marmaduke Hussey had his leg shot off.

The other model licence payers included an old-age pensioner slumped in front of the *Anne and Nick* show; a Belfast yuppie interested in the arts; the smug-looking Green family from Cornwall ('family life is important to us'); an Asian shop assistant from Coventry; and a hearty-looking primary school teacher from Edinburgh (gawping at a screen full of fish).

Instead of the mugshots of yesteryear, the Governors were pictured posing impressively in the boardroom. With all the talk about Stalinist methods, it was noted that Bill Jordan, the dissident Governor, did not appear. The Board of Management was photographed in a variety of heroic arm-flaying, finger-pointing 'we are the business' poses.

Birt's preface showed that he was very much in control of the organisation; even though the message was rendered in his familiar tortuous style. Birt began by saying 'I am conscious . . .' which was reassuring. Then, in the space of four paragraphs he invented a new verb form 'to have judged' and provided the mind-bending thought that the BBC must 'change in order to sustain its traditions'.

After throwing in the random observation that the BBC would 'insist on standards – in the use of language,' the Chairman changed his line on Armanigate. At the time he

said the tax row was just 'a media frenzy'. Now he said the
BBC had been 'riven by a public furore about the appoint-
ment of John Birt in 1987.' The problem had been caused by
Paul Fox and Michael Checkland, he said.

'Sir Paul Fox, then the Managing Director of Yorkshire
Television, recommended John Birt,' Hussey claimed. Checkland had told Hussey and Barnett that self-employment was
quite normal. 'The Director General assured us that the
practice already existed amongst the Board of Management
and elsewhere in the Corporation,' Hussey said. 'Accordingly,
we agreed the Director General's recommendations, and
accept responsibility for having done so.'

Endorsing producer choice, Hussey said: 'The Governors
insist that public money should be prudently used.' But
stories of waste and frustration resulting from producer
choice continued to emanate from Broadcasting House. The
papers reported how a new electronic system of financial
control had led to fourteen separate stages of authorisation
being needed to pay a simple invoice. Clerks were issued with
a special flow chart to make sense of it all.

The extra muscle given to financial managers was making
life ever more difficult for programme makers. Producers of
the Radio Four *Today* programme turned up for work to find
they had been left without telephones, the most basic tool of
their trade, because the system was being updated. After
furious complaints they were supplied with one mobile phone
that had to be shared by a dozen reporters. It was explained
that it was quite normal for business organisations to be
without phones for a day or two during changes like this.

Liz Forgan, contradicting Hussey, told a television conference the producer choice system was 'a shambles'. This
prompted Birt to reply defensively that it was a 'remarkably
efficient system'. Forgan's remarks were 'ludicrous', he said.
Unfortunately the latest group of consultants crawling over
the BBC's books agreed with the Director General: Birt was
so good at saving money by sacking people they promptly
suggested the government should use the savings to cut the

licence fee. The Board of Management was horrified and, after a brief tussle with the genial Heritage Minister Peter Brooke, managed to keep the fee linked to the rate of inflation until 1996. This narrow avoidance of total disaster was hailed as a 'licence fee victory'.

But at least the threat of all-out privatisation seemed to have disappeared until Ian Hargreaves, previously Birt's number two in news and current affairs, popped up to issue a think-tank tract on the subject.

Although Hargreaves' pamphlet received plaudits for its coherence, it hardly mattered because the politicians had lost their appetite for the scheme. This had a lot to do with disarray in the Conservative Party, where Mrs Thatcher stirred the pot by publishing her memoirs, backed by massive publicity from Murdoch's *Sunday Times* and the BBC itself. *The Downing Street Years* finally put on the record what everyone had always known about her attitude to broadcasting. The Prime Minister had pushed for phasing out the BBC licence fee and replacing it with advertising in the mid-1980s, but Douglas Hurd and Willie Whitelaw had stood in the way. Not much light was thrown on the extent of her involvement in Hussey's appointment, which will remain a mystery until secret cabinet papers are made available in the year 2016 AD. But she did reveal her admiration for the BBC regime she had helped create, as Ingham and Tebbit had done before her. Hussey and Birt, she said, 'represented an improvement in every respect' on the previous regime.

At the same time the Governors had been preoccupied with the latest embarrassing instalment in the long-running saga over 'rolling news' on radio. This was still a pet Birt project, but had been on the shelf ever since Hussey had buckled before the middle-class revolt aimed at keeping non-stop Birtism off long wave. This was just as well because it was later discovered that 17 per cent of listeners would have been left without Radio Four reception if the plan had gone ahead.

Undaunted, Forgan came up with the idea of hijacking Radio Five, the only BBC network that was increasing the size of its audience, and turning it into a strange mixture of continuous news and sport. The new style Radio Five was immediately derided as Radio Bloke (or Radio Jock-Strap by some) partly in tribute to Birt's mate David Mellor who had been installed as presenter of a football phone-in ('Where You The Fans get your chance to Have Your Say!'). Children's programmes were summarily dumped from Radio Five. But the market swiftly came to the rescue, continuing the tradition of *Bill and Ben* with *Beavis and Butt-head* on satellite TV. The moronic duo mixed casual sadism and pyromania with monosyllabic commentaries on pop videos. In the USA they had already been blamed for a spate of horrific cat murders and house fires. The normal moral panic gripped the newspapers for a couple of days, and *The Late Show* had a special item analyzing what it all meant for the future of western civilisation.

The Radio Five affair was Birt's first really serious U-turn since becoming director general. His ideal of an electronic version of a broadsheet newspaper like the *Financial Times* would now never come to pass. Instead it was reckoned that Radio Bloke would end up as an un-Birtist concoction, pitched in an ethereal locker room somewhere between the *Daily Express* and *Sporting Life*.

Birtism also appeared to be in retreat in its heartland of news and current affairs. Samir Shah was sidelined and there was a revival of 'story based journalism' at *Panorama*, including a remarkable exposé of corruption in the Metropolitan police that resulted in more than one bad apple facing charges. The Old Guard got back some of their self-respect, especially as the ill effects of the franchise auction began to be felt in ITV. Current affairs shows like Granada's *World in Action* became obsessed with the audience grabbing genre of 'camera in a bag' television. This had all the attractions of *Candid Camera* and *Beadle's About*, but could still claim to be dealing with serious issues. The BBC sniffily issued guidelines restricting the use of hidden microphones and cameras and also warned producers against over-reliance on populist techniques ranging from door-stepping (which, after his encounter with Chris Blackhurst, Birt knew all about) to the old trick of flaming up stories on the back of specially commissioned opinion polls. The guidelines, the latest of several instalments, followed a renewed debate about the role of the Nine O'Clock News on BBC1. Ron Neil's 'heart-warming' Queen Mum stories were by now a thing of distant memory and, of late, there had been more interest in the money spent on producing an electronically generated 'virtual reality' studio backdrop. This was dominated by an imposing BBC coat of arms which, in turn, reflected the Birtists' views of the value of the Corporation's 'brand name' (the Royal College of Arms had been engaged to restore the BBC's arms to medieval splendour as part of Birt's move into the future).

An anonymous file, entitled 'The Nine O'Clock News is Crap', appeared on the newsroom computer system, giving the remaining anti-Birtists an opportunity to record their complaints and score points. The file was particularly full on the day after the editor of the Nine O'Clock News decided to run the Queen's speech and the continuing talks in Northern Ireland above the story of the death of 13 schoolchildren in a mini-bus crash on the M40. The anti-Birtists called the decision 'a disgrace' and claimed it as proof positive that the people running BBC news and current affairs did not understand the feelings of the ordinary audience, had 'no humanity' and were still pandering to the politicians. The Birtists replied that they were 'contemporary historians': motorway accidents had no historical significance, but the Queen's Speech did, they explained.

Claims that the BBC was out of touch with the lives and priorities of ordinary people also surfaced at the parliamentary committee examining evidence contributed to the 'great debate' started by the Green Paper and Extending Choice. One MP accused Hussey of being 'a toff' who was heading a 'ludicrously unrepresentative' Board of Governors. Hussey replied he was glad to be thought of as a toff, but added: 'I may look like one, but I assure you I am not.' When Hussey said the Governors were a fair representation of the public, another MP piped up: 'But are there any unemployed single mothers?' Another MP said it was unfair to call the Governors middle class: 'You're upper class, white in the main, male dominated and London dominated.'

Back at Broadcasting House, Hussey and others might have reflected on the portraits of former Director Generals hanging on the walls of the Council Chamber. The roll of honour provided no shortage of Dead White Males, and included a good few toffs. Alasdair Milne, a Scot, had to suffer the indignity of having a portrait that was notably smaller than most of the others.

But at least Milne had done better than Michael Checkland. A year after his departure, Checkland's period in office was still marked by an empty space on the wall.

# *Chronology*

**1984**
Jan:   Public row over the screening of *The Thorn Birds*.
        Rupert Murdoch sets up forerunner of Sky TV.
        *Panorama* broadcasts *Maggie's Militant Tendency*.
Nov:   Michael Grade becomes Controller of BBC 1.

**1985**
Jan:   Series of anti-BBC editorials in *The Times*.
Feb:   BBC 1 ratings boosted by *EastEnders* and *Wogan*.
Mar:  Peacock Committee set up to investigate BBC finance.
Jun:   Michael Checkland becomes Deputy Director General.
Jul:   *Real Lives* crisis.

**1986**
Jan:   News International moves to Wapping.
Apr:   Peacock Report published.
Oct:   Marmaduke Hussey becomes Chairman of the BBC.
        *Maggie's Militant Tendency* libel settlement.

**1987**
Jan:   Alasdair Milne 'resigns' as Director General.
Feb:   Michael Checkland appointed as Director General.
Mar:  John Birt appointed Deputy Director General.
Jun:   General Election. Tories back with large majority.
Jul:   Leatherhead Conference merges news and current
        affairs.
Sep:   BBC Policy and Planning Unit established.
        Downing Street Seminar on Broadcasting Policy.

Nov:  Michael Grade leaves the BBC for Channel Four.
Dec:  *Newsnight* schedule row exposes splits in BBC management.

**1988**
Jan:  First annual *See For Yourself* programme.
Apr:  Paul Fox replaces Bill Cotton as Managing Director (TV).
Nov:  Broadcasting White Paper (more hostile to ITV than BBC).

**1989**
Jan:  *The Late Show* starts.
Feb:  Murdoch launches Sky TV.
Jul:  BBC pay dispute.
Aug:  Major Murdoch speech on future of TV at Edinburgh Festival.

**1990**
Jan:  BBC *Funding the Future* committee recommends big cuts.
Jun:  Strategy meeting to counter BBC 1 ratings slide.
Oct:  *Panorama* investigation of Conservative funds watered down.
Nov:  Margaret Thatcher resigns.
      BSB collapses and merges with Murdoch's Sky TV.

**1991**
Jan:  John Major praises BBC for coverage of Gulf War.
      *Panorama* about Iraqi 'supergun' pulled.
      Fifteen Charter Renewal taskforce committees established.
Feb:  Will Wyatt replaces Paul Fox as Managing Director (TV).
Apr:  Greg Dyke advises Governors to 'hack' at staff numbers.
      Kenneth Baker renews Hussey's contract as BBC Chairman.
May:  ITV franchise auction.
Jul:  Birt made Director General (designate) due to take office in March 1993.

Nov:   Birt resources committee announces producer choice.
Dec:   Checkland knighted.

## 1992

Mar:   *Sliding into Slump* edition of *Panorama* pulled.
Apr:   General Election. Tories back with working majority.
       Joint BBC-Sky deal over Premier League football.
       BBC annual accounts reveal 'missing millions'.
Jul:   First episode of *Eldorado*.
       Checkland announces 24-hour rolling news service plan.
Aug:   Michael Grade attacks 'pseudo-Leninist' management of
       BBC during Edinburgh TV festival.
Oct:   Checkland makes 'Fuzzy Monsters' attack on Hussey.
Nov:   Government publishes Green Paper on future of BBC.
       BBC publishes *Extending Choice*, its case for Charter
       renewal.
       Checkland announces he is standing down as Director
       General in December.

## 1993

Jan:   John Birt takes over as Director General.
Feb:   *Independent on Sunday* reveals John Birt's freelance
       status.
Mar:   *Eldorado* scrapped.
Apr:   Producer choice officially starts.
Jul:   Mark Tully says the BBC is gripped by a 'climate of
       fear'.

# Bibliography

BBC. *Annual Report and Accounts* (series; 1982–1992), BBC Information Services.

BBC. *Extending Choice*, BBC Corporate Affairs, 1992.

Belfield, R., Hird, C. and Kelly, S. *Murdoch*, Macdonald, 1992.

Bolton, R. *Death on the Rock (and other stories)*, W. H. Allen, 1990.

Bose, M. *Michael Grade: Screening the Image*, Virgin, 1992.

Bracken, W. and Fowler, S. *What Price Public Service?* Adam Smith Institute, 1993.

Briggs, A. *The BBC: The First Fifty Years*, Oxford University Press, 1985.

Brittan, S. *The Case for the Consumer Market*, Institute of Economic Affairs, 1989.

Cain, J. *The BBC: Seventy Years of Broadcasting*, BBC Information Services, 1992.

Chippindale, P. and Horrie, C. *Stick It Up Your Punter*, Heinemann, 1990.

Chippindale, P. and Franks, S. *Dished!*, Simon and Schuster, 1991.

Clarke, N. and Riddell, E. *The Sky Barons*, Methuen, 1992.

Collins, R. *Satellite Television in Western Europe*, J. Libbey, 1990.

Davidson, A. *Under the Hammer*, Heinemann, 1992.

Department of Trade and Industry. *Competition and Choice; Telecommunications Policy for the 1990s*, HMSO, 1990.

Docherty, D. *Running the Show – 21 Years of London Weekend Television*, Boxtree, 1990.

Dunkley, C. *Television Today and Tomorrow*, Harmondsworth, 1985.

Dunnett, P. *The World Television Industry: An Economic Analysis*, Routledge, 1990.

Ehrenberg, A.S.C. *The Funding of BBC Television*, London Business School, 1984.

Ehrenberg, A.S.C. *Viewers' Willingness to Pay*, International Thompsen Business, 1990.

Federation of Engineering Unions. *Backing the BBC*, BECTU (etc), 1992.

*Financial Times* Special Reports. *The New Face of British Television, Financial Times*, 1990.

Goodwin, A. *Understanding Television*, Routledge, 1990.

Green, D. *A Better BBC: Public Service Broadcasting*, Centre for Policy Studies, 1990.

Green, D. *Freedom of the Airwaves: The Broadcasting Bill in Perspective*, Conservative Political Centre, 1990.

Harris, R. *Good and Faithful Servant*, Faber, 1991.

Hollins, T. *Beyond Broadcasting: Into the Cable Age*, BFI/Broadcasting Research Unit, 1984.

Hopson, C. *Reforming the BBC: Public Service Broadcasting in the New Market*, European Policy Forum, 1992.

Horrie, C. *Sick as a Parrot*, Virgin, 1992.

Ingham, B. *Kill the Messenger*, Fontana, 1991.

Isaacs, J. *Storm over Four: A Personal Account*, Weidenfeld, 1989.

Kingsley, H. and Tibballs, G. *Box of Delights: The Golden Years of Television*, Macmillan, 1989.

Leapman, M. *Barefaced Cheek: Rupert Murdoch*, Coronet, 1983.

Leapman, M. *The Last Days of the Beeb*, Allen and Unwin, 1986.

MacDonald, B. *Broadcasting in the United Kingdom: A Guide to Information Sources*, Mansell, 1988.

Milligan, S. *What shall we do about the BBC?* Tory Reform Group, 1991.

Milne, A. *DG: The Memoirs of a British Broadcaster*, Hodder and Stoughton, 1988.

Moss, N. *The Network Television Story*, BBC, 1991.

Murdoch, R. *Freedom in Broadcasting: Text of the MacTaggart*

*Lecture delivered at the 1989 Edinburgh International Television Festival*, News International, 1989.

Peak, S. *The Media Guide*, Guardian Books, 1993.

Peacock, A. *The Politics of Investigating Broadcasting Finance*, The David Hume Institute; Heriot-Watt University, 1987.

Price Waterhouse. *Television Licence Fee: A Study for the Home Office*, HMSO, 1990.

Shawcross, W. *Murdoch*, Chatto and Windus, 1992.

Taylor, P. *War and the Media: Propaganda and Persuasion*, Manchester University Press, 1992.

Tebbit, N. *Upwardly Mobile*, Futura, 1989.

Trethowan, I. *The Next Age of Broadcasting*, Conservative Political Centre, 1984.

Trethowan, I. *Split Screen*, Hamish Hamilton, 1984.

Tuccille, J. *Murdoch*, Piatkus, 1989.

Tunstall, J. and Palmer, M. *Media Moguls*, Routledge, 1991.

Tusa, J. *Conversations with the World*, BBC Books, 1990.

Veljanovski, C. and Bishop, W. *Choice by Cable: the Economics of a New Era in Television*, Institute of Economic Affairs, 1989.

Veljanovski, C. (ed) *Freedom in Broadcasting*, Institute of Economic Affairs, 1989.

Veljanovski, C. *The Media in Britain Today: The Facts, The Figures*, News International, 1990.

Young, H. *One of Us*, Pan Books, 1990.

# Index